This is a rich mine of a book. A 25-year compendium of advertising money-makers; rock-solid case material; wisdom distilled from some of the world's most successful marketing campaigns; and creative inspiration. Marketing directors will read it anyway; but so should their CEOs and financial directors.

Sir Martin Sorrell, CEO, WPP

The more that creative and media opportunities proliferate, the more important it is to be guided by a sense of effective campaign best practice. The cases in this book may be from the industry's recent past, but nonetheless provide critical clues for the future.

Alan Rutherford, Global Media Director,
Unilever

The IPA Effectiveness Awards are the gold standard internationally. Government departments and the COI are always delighted when campaigns are selected for an award. In a broader context, these Awards add credibility to the contribution that advertising can make to business success.

Peter Buchanan, Deputy Chief Executive,
Central Office of Information

In bringing together the best of the best, the IPA renews the high standards it promotes for UK advertising. You will not, you should not, agree with everything in the essays that accompany the Grand Prix winners but they should force you to reconsider your own search for effective ads. Buy it.

Tim Ambler, London Business School

In the current business climate our members need, more than ever, to show marcomms expenditure as a measurable investment rather than an unaccountable cost. The IPA Effectiveness Awards is a key benchmark for effectiveness, and the quality of the work undertaken by the advertisers and agencies who take part shines through. ... I therefore commend this thoughtful book to anyone who wants to understand more about the role of advertising and marcomms in building successful brands.

Malcolm Earnshaw, Director General,
Incorporated Society of British Advertisers

In a world of low inflation and limited pricing power, cost cutting has overtaken revenue growth as the key driver of bottom-line performance. This is why advertising has to work harder than ever to justify itself as an investment rather than a cost, and why advertising needs to create great brands that generate immense intangible value. Investment, by definition, requires a return that is precisely measurable.

Lorna Tilbian, Director,
Head of Media Research, Numis Securities

When junior planners ask me why they should waste hours of their life toiling away on an IPA Effectiveness paper I have one very simple answer – show me one great planner who has never won one.

George Bryant, Head of Planning,
Abbott Mead Vickers.BBDO

Advertising Works and How

Winning communications strategies for business

Edited by Laurence Green

First published 2005 by the World Advertising Research Center
Farm Road, Henley-on-Thames, Oxfordshire RG9 1EJ, United Kingdom
Telephone: 01491 411000
Fax: 01491 418600
E-mail: enquiries@warc.com
www.warc.com

A CIP catalogue record for this book is available from the British Library

ISBN 1 84116 173 X

Typeset by Godiva Publishing Services Ltd, Coventry
Jacket design by Glen Tarr
Printed and bound in Great Britain
by Cromwell Press, Trowbridge

Contents

Preface

It is particularly appropriate that ITV should support this publication for two reasons.

The first consideration is that we have been supporters of the IPA Effectiveness Awards for most of their 25-year history. The second reason is that 2005 marks another significant anniversary: it is 50 years since our corporate ancestors launched, enabling advertisers to embrace television as a communication medium for the first time.

Since 1955, our medium has helped the development of many of today's most famous brands. The PG Tips case study is a notable example of how a communications strategy with television advertising at its heart has delivered long-term market position and price premium benefits. These benefits can be attributed to the fact that PG Tips established a fame above and beyond the functional properties of the brand.

There is no monopoly on generating research that can be both insightful and practical, and ITV is committed to contributing to the debate about advertising effectiveness. We see this as particularly important given the advance of the procurement function, which carries with it the danger of boiling everything down to measurable short-term effects.

We are particularly interested in answering three questions:

- How can we support the marketing community, as its members seek to demonstrate the value to their businesses of building brands through advertising?
- Can we get under the skin of brand fame, understand the constituent parts of fame and demonstrate the link with business success?
- What return on investment can be attributed to television advertising, and how does this compare to other marketing channels?

Looking back at the winning papers from the first 25 years of the IPA Effectiveness Awards, we are naturally pleased that television has been at the heart of the communication mix for the vast majority of winners. But life moves on, and we shouldn't be complacent that this will always be the case.

Having said that, we are confident that television should continue to feature prominently. Not least because digital technology opens up new creative and commercial opportunities, as well as solutions which can provide richer data for advertisers.

The winners of the 2004 IPA Effectiveness Awards suggest this confidence isn't misplaced. Integrated campaigns, exemplified by the likes of O_2 and 118 118, have demonstrated how television advertising remains a very effective springboard towards brand fame, amplifying the effects of other communication channels along the way.

Congratulations to the IPA for pulling together the articles in this book, which shine a light on the latest in best practice thinking. Having been able to read most of the contributions in this book before writing this piece, I've learned a few new things, and I hope you do too.

JUSTIN SAMPSON
Director of CRM, ITV Sales

It all began
with an ad ...

Foreword

In the spring of 1980 the IPA ran an advertisement: 'Advertising Works. And we're going to prove it'. A very straightforward ad, a bit dull even, but, appropriately, the ad worked. It called for entries for a new awards scheme. Thirty agencies responded, entering a total of 80 case studies. The IPA Advertising Effectiveness Awards were born. This book marks and celebrates the 25 years that have passed since then.

All the Grand Prix winners are brought together here for the first time, but this book is much more than that. Accompanying these winners is a series of essays, from some of the very best of the communication industry's current practitioners, illustrating just how much progress has been made and how much has been learned since the Awards began. And, more than anything else, these Awards have been about learning.

Those of us who can remember the days before the Awards would find it hard to argue with the word 'primitive' to describe our approach then to the business of advertising evaluation. There was an all too ready acceptance that we couldn't really measure advertising effectiveness, so why try. Yes, as the man said, maybe half our advertising was wasted, and we didn't know which half either!

No longer. Thankfully. And in very large part due to the IPA Awards and the culture that has progressively grown around them.

We are learning all the time now about just how much we can and should measure. We have learned more and more over the years, as the Awards have evolved. And they certainly have evolved. We have gone beyond just the immediate sales effect, beyond the short term, beyond influencing only end consumers, beyond advertising alone and, indeed, recently we've gone beyond just UK case studies.

In 25 years we have gone from an activity deemed by many to be impossible to measure, and thus questionably effective, to something that increasingly demonstrates the depth and breadth of its potency as a vital business tool. To something more potent than we ever thought perhaps. Are we still underestimating it?

Many myths, about how communications work and how to measure them, have been demolished along the way. Not least the myth that a choice has to be made between the effective and the creative (always defined in this choice as creative award winning). It is a false choice: you can have both. Not only have many of the same agencies featured prominently in both kinds of awards but so, very often, have the same campaigns. More myths to demolish in the next 25 years? For sure.

So where we now are, 25 years on, is with an awards scheme that has not only stood the test of time but has evolved; with a whole host of learnings as a result; with an easily accessible databank of case studies more comprehensive than anywhere else in the world; with a model for effectiveness awards that is widely admired and that has been adopted by a number of countries; and with something that continually drives our professional standards higher.

In short, this book celebrates something we should be very proud of. How many other industries work so hard to demonstrate their value?

Back in 1980 a new age began – the effectiveness age. History will show this to have been a real watershed year. The industry, after years of perpetual adolescence, decided to grow up. And there's still more growing to do.

The communications industry should never stop thanking Simon Broadbent and the other founding fathers. Through them an industry challenged itself to stand up and be counted. This book demonstrates just how well that challenge has been met.

How right and proper that it all began with an ad.

JOHN BARTLE
Founder, Bartle Bogle Hegarty

Introduction

The IPA Advertising Effectiveness Awards were launched in 1980 to encourage what was then an occasional and indeed controversial pursuit: to prove beyond reasonable doubt that advertising paid back – against hard business measures, that is, not soft creative ones. Since then the Awards have morphed, reflecting and often leading changes in marketing and advertising campaign practice and theology. But they have never wavered from that critical central premise: did the work work?

Twenty-five years from launch the Awards' legacy is obvious: it is generally accepted that the UK boasts not just the most credible proofs that advertising works but also the richest understanding of how it works.

A treasure trove of best practice

This one-off compilation of the 13 Grand Prix winners to date (the best of the best, if you like) was conceived to celebrate the learning accumulated by the Awards over the years. Although the primary purpose of the papers submitted has always been to demonstrate return on investment, it stands to reason that the most effective campaigns are not only examples of best practice in evaluation but also in some or all of strategy, creative and media. The Grand Prix winners of yesteryear are therefore potentially inspiring source material for anyone seeking to launch, grow or defend a brand or market. They are examples of effective campaigning in practice, rather than in theory.

The Grand Prix winners are of course the tip of the Awards iceberg. Beneath that tip sit the 1000 or so papers submitted to the IPA over the period. This broader collection of papers – now readily available to data miners in the guise of the IPA dataBANK[1] and at WARC.com – is the biggest single database of effectiveness learning in the marketing world.

---

1. *The IPA dataBANK has been developed from author-completed questionnaires for as many of the awards as possible. The primary aim of the dataBANK is to act as a new reference tool for both agency and academic research in the future.*

In the spirit of creating a practical guide as well as an easily navigated read, we have arranged the papers according to six core issues for marketers and their agencies – from the basics of launching and revitalising brands, through the core of 'adding value', to the more audacious tasks of organisational engineering and market manipulation.

It's an unscientific clustering exercise, since some of our cases straddle more than one category, but one that we hope makes the collection more purposeful. Thanks go to our six summarisers for aggressively editing what were already well-structured papers and well-honed arguments, and for commentaries that draw from the source material but extrapolate beyond. Each offers up a sense of tomorrow's best practice rooted in an understanding of yesterday's.

Malcolm White encourages those launching into established categories to pay as much attention to what they are launching into as to what they are launching. Richard Warren fires a warning shot across the bows of any advertiser inclined to revitalise its brand on a purely superficial basis. Richard Storey and Neil Dawson underscore the enduring power of emotion to decommoditise and add value to brands. David Golding offers a CEO-friendly take on how advertising-led branding can direct an organisation rather than just engage consumers. Guy Murphy, finally, posits a future where returns might best be achieved through collaborative (or at least common) rather than competitive communications efforts as we seek to build 'Market Brands'.

A rear-view mirror and a road map

So the silver anniversary of the Awards encourages us to package the winners, to sift through the campaign data and propose best practice for the modern marketer. But it is also a point at which to draw breath and take stock. Tim Broadbent – author of two of the Grands Prix that follow – offers us a timely and thought-provoking perspective on the value of advertising agencies. Paul Feldwick reminds us of a few less scientific truths about the business of adding value through branding and advertising. Will Collin challenges the primacy of the idea as we enter a new era of communications.

In such capable hands as our contributors', the history of the Awards is not just a useful rear-view mirror, but also a map for the journey ahead. We can think of no other industry that demonstrates its ability to create value as regularly and systematically as the advertising community does, and thank authors and clients (past, present and future) for their contribution both to the body of learning and the momentum of the industry.

A word about a word: advertising

The past ten years or so have seen much hand-wringing over the word 'advertising'. Ad agencies that felt it was a limiting descriptor of their services began to call themselves ideas agencies. Most famously, perhaps, Saatchi & Saatchi Advertising rebadged itself as plain old Saatchi & Saatchi. The IPA Awards have not been untouched by the debate.

Until 2002 they were known as the Advertising Effectiveness Awards, to demonstrate specifically that above-the-line advertising delivered a return on investment. It was a title, however, that arguably betrayed an isolationist mentality and compounded a tendency for authors to discredit other marketing disciplines as a way of proving that advertising – and advertising alone – was responsible for a brand's good fortune.

Clients, of course, and the best agencies, were busy marching in the opposite direction, treating the marketing mix as an inseparable whole: generating positionings, strategies and ideas that impacted on PR, DM, design and web communication in equal measure. Hence the Saatchi-like tweak in 2002 from the Advertising Effectiveness Awards to the IPA Effectiveness Awards. The spirit of and motive for the change lives on: the IPA Effectiveness Awards now look to reward business-building creative ideas from any source or discipline.

Since this book boasts contributions from across the decades, however, you will at times find the word 'advertising' used to specifically denote above-the-line activity and at other times as shorthand for the broader swathe of communications. As ever, context is all.

LAURENCE GREEN
Planning Partner, Fallon

Case studies referred to, but not featured, can be accessed via the IPA dataBANK or www.WARC.com.

Roll of honour

Grand Prix winners
1980–2004

1980
Krona
Davidson Pearce
Stephen Benson

1982
John Smith's Bitter
Boase Massimi Pollitt Partnership
James Best, Tim Broadbent

1984
ICI Dulux Natural Whites
Foote Cone & Belding
Kevin Green, Richard Dodson

1986
TSB School Leavers
J Walter Thompson
Jeremy Elliott

1988
Winalot Prime
Ogilvy & Mather
Lee Taylor, Gerard Smith

1990
PG Tips
BMP DDB Needham
Clive Cooper, Louise Cook, Nigel Jones

1992
Milkman
BMP DDB Needham
John Grant

1994
BMW
WCRS
Tim Broadbent

1996
BT
Abbott Mead Vickers.BBDO
Max Burt

1998
HEA Drugs Education
Duckworth Finn Grubb Waters
Lori Gould, Rachel Walker

2000
Tesco
Lowe Lintas
Ashleye Sharpe, Joanna Bamford

2002
Barnardo's
Bartle Bogle Hegarty
Dan Goldstein, Mary Daniels

2004
O$_2$
VCCP
Sophie Maunder, Alex Harris, Joanna Bamford,
Louise Cook, Andrew Cox

The margarine that raised questions in an Australian parliament.

In Sydney, Australia, several years ago, an extraordinary rumour started amongst housewives.

It grew to such proportions that the New South Wales Government became involved. And it all began over something as simple as a margarine.

So successful did this margarine become, that housewives were even buying it by the caseful. People were taking it off lorries when it was delivered at supermarkets, to be certain of buying some.

All this activity led to the Minister of Agriculture being asked questions about the product in parliament.

For the rumour was that it wasn't margarine at all. Its taste was that good.

The counterpart of this Australian margarine is on sale in Britain.

It's called Krona.

1980 **Krona**

1982 **John Smith's Bitter**

1984 **ICI Dulux Natural Whites**

1986 **TSB School Leavers**

1988 **Winalot Prime**

1990 **PG Tips**

1992 **Milkman**

1994 **BMW**

1996 **BT**

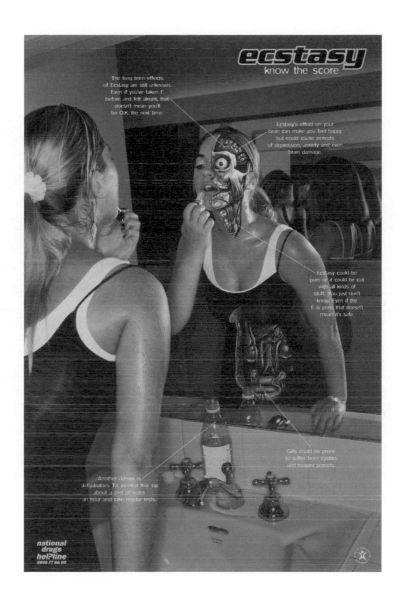

1998 HEA Drugs Education

2000 **Tesco**

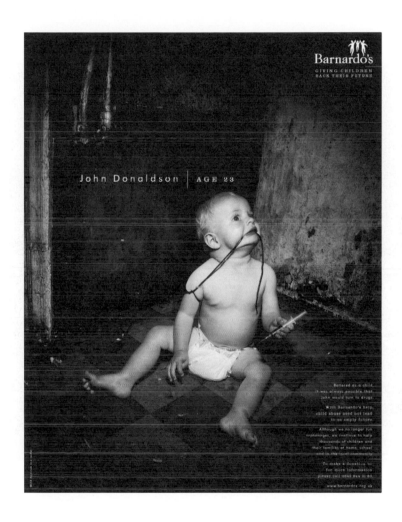

2002 **Barnardo's**

2004 **O₂**

PART ONE

Essays on effectiveness

The client view

Chapter 1
Niall FitzGerald, KBE
Chairman, Reuters

Imagine, if you will, you are enjoying a day out at the races. The horses are lined up in the starting-gates; the jockeys are full of nervous excitement, keen to start the race and eager to take on their rivals. The race begins and the odds-on favourite to win bursts into the lead, striding ahead of the field. This horse displays all the best qualities possible; he is talented and in an advantageous position due to the investment of time, money and care his owner and trainer placed in him from the outset, and is well deserving of his lead position on the rails.

After a few furlongs the leading jockey looks over his shoulder to see the other horses so far behind him that he decides he can relax and enjoy his position as race leader. But having done so, it's not long before his competitors make up the ground. Encouraged, enraged even, by the apparent complacency and arrogance of the front-runner, the other jockeys are galvanised into action and whip their mounts into top gear. The gap soon closes and 20 lengths' lead suddenly becomes a short head, and then the original leader is pipped at the post.

Backers of the odds-on favourite tear up their betting slips in disgust, while holders of stakes on the winning outsider celebrate their ability to pick a rising star.

The same can so very often be true of brands. A common reason for a brand's decline is complacency. The story is a familiar one. A company or brand builds a good reputation, sits back and rests on that reputation, only to wake up one day to discover that faster, hungrier, more innovative competitors have passed it by. IBM is a good example, not least because it's a company that, since feeling the pain, has successfully reinvented itself.

The sequence of events goes like this. To begin with, you are, for example, a very technologically advanced company – and deservedly very successful. As the market becomes more and more competitive, you realise that you need both product performance and brand character to stay ahead. Brilliantly, you build a great image for the brand, so that users not only respect the company but feel loyal to it as well. You become even more successful.

Then comes the critical stage. You become such an enthusiast for the notion of brand personality – and become so fixated with your own – that you come to believe that competitive product performance is no longer your highest priority. So you neglect to innovate, you neglect to invest in R&D, you stop listening intently for those faint murmurs of discontent – and for a month or two, or even a year or two, your success continues and your profits mount. You may even be tempted to believe that you have discovered the secret of perpetual motion.

Then, with savage suddenness, your once healthy brand becomes an invalid, losing share and reputation with precipitate speed. What has happened? Your market has discovered what you have done, and suddenly realised a once-loved brand has taken its users for granted. The response of said users is brutally unforgiving. What happened to a computer company has happened to car manufacturers, to retailers, to banks and to fmcg companies.

A company's decision not to maintain its financial investment in its products, whether it be in innovation, R&D or marketing and communications, usually results in poor performance and a fall from grace while the fresher, more astute companies that continue to invest in their brands flourish. By not keeping the levels of investment on a par with or ahead of market share, what had once been a truly successful brand surrenders its prime position and falls into a downward spiral, resulting in customer dissatisfaction and the erosion of the loyalty of those once devoted to the brand. This show of contempt for the competition – and it is true for every sector, be it fmcg, automotive, retail or financial – is one of the simplest ways to lose customers and kill off a brand.

So what can be done to guarantee brand strength and the continuing attraction, retention and development of the customer base? In short, marketers must make constant efforts to reach out to their customers. Differentiating a brand from other challengers within the market is best achieved through a company constantly being in touch with its buyer base, forging a two-way dialogue and understanding what the customer wants and expects of the product.

Always remember the purchaser is a person, not simply a statistic, and is worthy therefore of being treated as a human being in this mutually beneficial relationship. Understanding the likes, dislikes, attitudes and behaviour of the customer is key to the growth of brand value: a sensational yet ill-targeted product can be outsold by merchandise of lesser value, simply because it is backed by a strategic marketing plan. The message that is sold is just as valuable as the product itself.

The 2004 IPA Effectiveness Awards winning paper for Lynx demonstrates a comprehensive understanding of its target audience of young men, but it didn't only sell them the functional benefits of a deodorant, it established and elaborated, in a truly creative way, the idea that they could be the guy who gets the girl. A brand should always try to strike a deep chord like this with its customer base and, if it achieves this, it can profit enormously from that identified common ground.

Complacency and over-reliance on presentation over substance is one of the easiest ways to bring a brand to its knees and cause it, like the odds-on favourite, to lose the race to a more determined challenger.

The IPA Effectiveness Awards celebrate a range of marketing achievements, from the odds-on favourite that hasn't grown complacent to the determined challengers, and back. I'm delighted to have won some and chaired one.

Twenty-five years of Advertising Works

Chapter 2

Laurence Green

Planning Partner, Fallon

Despite the vast sums of money staked on marketing by 'UK plc', rigorous campaign evaluation is a relatively recent phenomenon. Beliefs in the power of advertising, especially, have tended to oscillate wildly, its reputation enjoying something of a rollercoaster ride over the decades, from strong force to weak force and back again.

The IPA Effectiveness Awards are now a familiar fixture in the marketing and advertising awards calendar. At launch in 1980, however, they were an audacious counterpoint to the accepted wisdom: that advertising effects, although presumed to be powerful, could not satisfactorily be measured. The Awards changed everything. As Charles Channon, the 1986 Convenor of Judges, concluded:

> It seemed at one time as if the 1970s were likely to develop a folklore of the ineffectiveness of advertising to offset or destroy the folklore of its effectiveness. Now the industry can point to an accumulating body of evidence which is an antidote to cynicism outside the industry and a prophylactic against complacency within it.

Since then, the 'accumulating body of evidence' has reached critical mass and more. Yet the prophylactic is just as useful today: for clients defending their budgets in the boardroom, and for agencies defending their fees.

That was then, this is now

By definition this compilation celebrates the most provenly successful advertising campaigns of the past three decades. By implication it charts an industry's evolution. The core qualities of the campaigns submitted to the Awards over time are consistent: they are ideas that create business results. The environment in which those ideas play out, however, is much changed.

In 1980, the Awards' year zero, the UK boasted one commercial TV station. Few could have predicted the extraordinary mix of media we consume today – the launch of CNN, and of Hewlett Packard's first PC, the only tangible pointers that year to the future. Media planning, perhaps predictably, was in its infancy.

Back then, grocery was the staple diet of Britain's ad agencies. Manufacturer brands ruled the roost, the power of today's retailers an unimaginable prospect. The stock market was something for brokers to worry about.

Despite this apparently benign environment the IPA Awards sailed at launch against the prevailing wind: an accepted wisdom that 'it is a delusion that the results of advertising can be isolated and assessed'. Early contributors and convenors railed against this complacency, employing a winning logic in favour of more vigorous evaluations:

> *Advertising earns its keep when without it, or with less of it, the firm would be worse off. Without evidence of this connection, the defenders of the advertising budget come unarmed to the budget meeting.*
>
> Simon Broadbent (1982)

That such basic arguments needed to be made reminds us how underdeveloped the effectiveness ethic was, in agencies and marketing departments alike. Advertising was an article of faith rather than a proven, measurable business tool. As opaque and unknowable a cost of doing business as Lord Leverhulme had declared it to be a century or so previously.

The fluidity of markets – the ongoing shifts in a brand's relative price, distribution and saliency – was typically invoked to excuse this state of affairs. How might we credibly pick out ad effects from this complex web of influences? Before the advent of the IPA Awards, the brainchild of Simon Broadbent, then Media Director of Leo Burnett, too many were daunted and too few inspired by this challenge. A self-defeating reticence, as would later be explained:

> *A finance director might conclude that if advertising effects are so thoroughly swamped by other activities as to be 'immeasurable', they can only be small effects at best.*
>
> Tim Broadbent (2000)

An industry evolves

Since the early 1980s, of course, we have lived through an era of explosive growth in the sheer volume of communication, in media channels and choices. We have seen the balance of power shift emphatically towards retailers, and the balance of adspend tilt from products to services. The consumer has become more elusive and more literate than ever. And as the market has morphed, so too has the business of evaluation.

Over the past three decades, the IPA Awards, by their nature, have closely tracked and occasionally predicted the evolution of marketing. The first Grand Prix winner, Krona, was an fmcg launch deploying TV as lead medium and boasting short-term sales effects. The latest Grand Prix winner, O_2, describes by contrast the contribution of integrated marketing communications to the growth, value and orientation of a service brand.

The 1980 Awards featured no financial services winners and concluded: 'Advertising is arguably more peripheral to these sorts of companies than to the mainstream consumer goods manufacturers.' By the end of the decade, the deregulation of financial services had prompted a tidal wave of financial communication, a category comprising one-third of all IPA submissions by 1988.

In other ways, the Awards have been remarkably prescient. Ambient media was acknowledged as early as 1982, with a paper dedicated to Kellogg's Cornflakes' use of advertising on milk bottles; and 1986 ushered in a shift to measures of profit, rather than sales, as the stock market and the ad industry's understanding of the City matured:

> *The increased pace of the stock market in recent years has dramatised, as nothing else can, the accountability of marketing not to sales as such, but to profits.*
>
> Charles Channon (1986)

As early as 1990, payment by results was being proposed as the future bedrock for agency remuneration: 'It may be that, in the future, techniques of evaluation are used to win not just awards, but rewards, for advertising agencies.'

Multi-market advertising arrived in 1992: the Levi's case study the first to 'prove it can be done'. The benefits of integration are mentioned as early as 1994. Media neutrality, profit orientation, payment by results, globalisation and integration: the IPA Awards predate the very essence of today's marketing agenda.

Three turning points and their legacy

Looking back, three step-changes in the Awards' emphasis over the years testify especially powerfully to the determination of their convenors to encourage new learning and to inform and shape the ROI debate.

Year	Step-change
1990	Reporting and understanding of longer and broader effects is encouraged.
1998	Reporting and understanding of manifold effects (e.g. staff effects, share price effects) is encouraged.
2002	Reporting and understanding of integration (advertising in collaboration rather than competition with other disciplines) is encouraged.

The first of these changes demands particular scrutiny: it literally changed the rules. Judged against short-term sales response, most advertising will not pay back. This is not to say that it does not pay back, but rather that it does so in a less direct but often more powerful way. (Apart from anything else, the many advertisers in mature markets cannot all grow their sales through advertising; advertising may instead influence relative shares or a brand's staying power.)

Most advertising pays back by building or sustaining a brand, which in turn generates more profitable returns over time than would otherwise have been the case. Writing at the end of the 1980s, Paul Feldwick critiqued the winners to date thus:

> *The papers conform to the Awards logo: a dramatically upward sales graph. And yet much advertising does not fit this pattern and is no less effective for all that. Many of the major spending brands year after year are examples of this. The benefits they realise from advertising:*
>
> *– a relatively static sales trend in the face of competitive threat*
> *– maintenance of margins in the face of competitive discounting*
> *– overall, security and predictability of their business.*
>
> *For such brands it is absurd to evaluate advertising in terms of its incremental effect on sales. The evaluation of advertising needs to move beyond the simple model of spending a pound this year, getting two pounds back next year.*

The commercial power of brands sustained by advertising seized centre stage from the 'direct response' model.

The identification of manifold effects – or 'holistic return' as it was described at the time – moved the debate on again. In the words of Nick Kendall, the 1988 Convenor:

> *Many cases demonstrate a kind of multiple effectiveness where the investment is paid back not only in sales but also in employee buy-in, and then in City understanding, belief and so on and so on. Advertising investment achieves an accumulator return and so becomes efficient not only in a sales per pound sense but in a wider, holistic sense also. Such an ability argues strongly for a CEO's (re)involvement in the creation and sign-off of such advertising.*

Although the CEO has yet to re-engage in advertising, many now appreciate the power of 'the brand' to orientate their business, to enthuse and direct employees, to influence intermediaries and other stakeholders. As Tim Broadbent later commented, 'These additional sources of return are invisible to consumer research, but are real nonetheless.'

The Awards' transformation was complete once emphasis was placed on the cumulative effects of integrated communication and the collaborative effects of agencies.

Ideas, channels, brands and profits have come to replace the old vocabulary of ads and sales. Each of these editorial turning-points has helped in its own way to cement the new advertising orthodoxy:

- That investment in advertising typically pays back over time, rather than immediately.
- That advertising may pay back even if sales do not rise as a consequence.
- That the most potent returns are achieved when the marketing mix is deployed in concert, when ideas stretch beyond the silos.

The best marketers not only understand these truths but behave accordingly. They market marketing in the boardroom, so that short-term pragmatism does not damage a brand's long-term fortunes. They arrange their agencies to collaborate more often than they compete. They aspire to ideas that are bigger than any one channel.

Potatoes and diamonds: new tasks for new times

The tasks on which clients and agencies embark are another barometer of changing times. The objectives described in the Awards' earliest papers are winningly simple: launch, relaunch, reposition. These are themes that played out over time across an extraordinary spectrum of products and categories – from potatoes on the one hand to diamonds (quite literally) on the other.

As our understanding grew of what advertising could do (and as the commercial requirement for it to work harder intensified), so too did the scope and ambition of our objectives. The most recent Grand Prix winners (HEA, Tesco, Barnardo's and O_2) all deployed communications profoundly – to inform all elements of service and brand delivery, rather than just as the surface dialogue with consumers. We've come a long way from 1984 and Dulux's somewhat more mundane objective to 'reawaken consumer interest in white paint'. Advertising is increasingly used not just to position companies rather than simply their products, but also to steer them.

A task-centric description of the Awards cheers more than just the commercial lobby. Alongside the tales of increased sales, margins and profits, we are reminded of the extraordinary range of civic and public health causes advertising has been called on to address over the past few decades – to prevent domestic abuse, encourage road safety, advance children's literacy, defeat AIDS, discourage smoking and dent drugs culture – and of how effectively communication can be seen to tackle these causes.

Public service communication certainly commands an unfair share of IPA Awards. Is it more potent because there is no commercial agenda? Because agencies do their best work when inspired by a human cause rather than a commercial one? Are authors more inclined to play effectiveness detective when the cause is 'good', or judges atypically generous? Whichever, there is no doubting the contribution that these case studies make to the industry's general understanding of what communications can do and how. This year's Central London Congestion Charge paper, for example, offers up a new role for communication, which we might expect to be mimicked over time: that of 'briefing the consumer'.

Creativity: the ally, not the enemy, of effectiveness

The traditional caricature of the agency–client relationship or contract is this: the agency guys prize 'the creative'; the clients care only for effectiveness. Agendas are opposed rather than coincide; the campaign that emerges is a kind of negotiated settlement between warring camps. Over time that caricature has become less resonant, less truthful.

Agencies no longer exhibit a glib 'it's the idea, luv' mentality; the most commercially minded companies do not disdain creativity as a lever of success. (Indeed, some of the most powerful brands and successful companies of our times are themselves a creative idea: Google, eBay, Amazon all spring to mind.) Today we see a broad consensus that creativity, properly directed and responsibly deployed, can improve business fortunes.

The IPA Awards have made a uniquely powerful contribution to the alignment of the 'creative' and 'effective' camps. Even in the early days of the competition, where its emphasis on short-term sales results might have been expected to favour the bluntly effective, the Awards have consistently demonstrated the critical contribution of winning creative content rather than just media muscle.

Area tests featured in the Awards at the beginning of the 1980s were among the first evidence of the claim the creative community had been making all along:

> *Beecham's experiments suggest that sales effects are more responsive to differential creative than to differential weight ... the old polarity between 'creative' and 'effective' is beginning to be seen for the false opposition that it is.*
>
> Charles Channon (1984)

A further bridge between the camps was established in the early 1990s as the Awards featured proofs that likeability of communication frequently lay at the core of effectiveness. More generally, even a cursory glance at the winners over the years suggests that the creative and effectiveness agendas are complementary more often than they are competitive.

The IPA Awards' roll call is a veritable 'Who's Who?' of campaigns feted either in the creative community, the real world beyond, or both. Think PG, John Smith's, BMW, Wonderbra, Häagen-Dazs, Volkswagen, Oxo, Andrex,

Boddington's, Walkers, Barclaycard, Tesco, Orange, *The Economist*, Levi's and Stella (winners all). It seems that popularity in the living room is a must-have not a nice-to-have, after all.

Even this underestimates the contribution of creativity to effectiveness, focused as it is on the traditional understanding of creativity as the responsibility and contribution of copywriters and art directors alone. As the Awards and the industry have matured, so too has our understanding of creativity. It is now a commonplace that creativity in strategy and in media thinking can make a powerful contribution to outcomes.

Over the decades, media especially has moved up the communications supply chain. Once media was charged with buying the right space to show off the creatives' wares; now creatives are charged with filling the space that media has planned and bought. In an era of channel fragmentation and innovation, of media independents and a quest for neutrality, it is perhaps no surprise to find that media now lives at the beginning of the communications process, not at the end.

The potency of consistency

If there is one over-arching message for marketers and agencies, perhaps it is this: the most effective brands are those that are the most consistently communicated. A winning virtue that has two components: consistent *presence* and consistent *presentation*.

First of all, consistent investors in communication appear to perform better than inconsistent investors. An argument supported not just by the apparent correlation of ongoing investors and IPA winners, but by the PIMS database and its conclusion that sustaining marketing spend is 'a strategic imperative'.

Second, brands that boast a consistent voice also appear to return more cash to their paymasters. The strongest brands boast such a consistent voice that the consumer encounters the same brand and sense of brand in every channel: from retail to web, from advertising to packaging, and so on. At any point in time, and over time.

At their most basic, brands remain 'trustmarks' for consumers. Brands that behave or present themselves inconsistently invite doubt rather than inspire confidence, and we turn to more trustworthy competitors. Our fascination as an industry with the new, the next campaign, step-changes and a break with the past often blinds us to this enduring truth. Advertising and marketing people are not just idea generators but brand guardians, and we forget the latter responsibility at our peril. As a brand's voice is heard in more media than ever before, consistent presentation is non-negotiable. Integration is part of this but so is the now unfashionable pursuit of a campaign idea that will last for years or even decades.

Three of the most recent Grand Prix winners testify to the power of this consistency: O_2, Barnardo's and Tesco all work the same brand idea through the mix and adhere to it over time. Their activity is integrated; their brands consistently presented; their results spectacular.

Where next?

So indivisible are the Awards from their environment that, as we imagine where they go next, we are actually imagining where marketing goes next, post-PVR.

The 2004 IPA vintage tells many stories – most broadly, that branding drives business and that creativity drives brands. The former is best evidenced by O_2's reinvention and Virgin Mobile's 'badging' of T-Mobile's network, the latter by Honda's recent fortunes. More specifically, it features campaigns that already draw inspiration from the era of engagement (the consumer willingly participating in branded content) rather than the era of interruption (the brand owner renting media space to push communication at the consumer). Despite the lack of precedent, and the lack of an obvious evaluative framework, these efforts can already be seen to pay back for their sponsors.

When Bartle Bogle Hegarty introduced Lynx 'Pulse', it launched a hit single as assiduously and purposefully as it launched the fragrance itself (Figure 1). Fallon, meanwhile, flipped BMW's traditional TV media investment into the production of eight web-based mini-movies. That both activities not only fired the imagination of the consumer and marketing community but already demonstrate a credible ROI may signal the genuine arrival of branded content as an effective, and not just fashionable, marketing tool.

Both campaigns set new questions for marketers and those charged with evaluation alike. How can we cost, predict and justify new 'engagement-era' activities? (A TV spot may require a more sophisticated media plan than it used to, but its delivery in terms of frequency and reach remains largely predictable.) How much of a budget should we deploy against engagement activity versus interruption activity? (Both the Lynx and BMW cases used advertising alongside their content initiatives: Lynx with a famously popular commercial, BMW to trail the movies.)

Figure 1: The Lynx Pulse TV commercial

Both campaigns also potentially usher in a dramatically new marketing model: one where traditionally punitive media costs are traded for an investment in content. And one where – at an extreme – marketing might even create its own revenue stream beyond its contribution to ongoing brand health and margins. Some 40,000 people have ordered the BMW Films DVD. Might the paid-for marketing of the future sometimes be paid for by consumers rather than clients?

The evaluation efforts of the future are obliged to keep pace with this executional proliferation and these new marketing models. Beyond this it is hoped that they will occasionally lead the dance: that a step-change in evaluation might itself nurture a new creative or media orthodoxy, rather than vice versa.

Future contributors to the Awards are encouraged to draw inspiration from the papers that follow, and to look beyond the current tramlines of effectiveness thinking. The ongoing good health of the IPA Awards depends as much on a spirit of adventure and leaps of invention as the business it reports on.

The value of advertising agencies

Chapter 3
Tim Broadbent
BrandCon

One of the first things the history of advertising teaches is how little things change. For instance, a challenge clients and agencies face today is dealing with a plethora of new, niche media channels. They feel attractive enough, but how to plan, integrate and evaluate them? It turns out there's nothing new about this problem.

The sheer volume of advertising in the Victorian era would amaze us. The conventional media were full to bursting: *The Times* of 12 May 1855 contained 2575 ads in its 16 pages.

Advertisers turned to new, ambient channels as well, just as we have done. Ads were placed on the tops of mountains, on risers of steps at railway stations, in public houses and dining rooms. Ads were placed on matchboxes, horses and airships. Ads were carried in the streets by sandwich-men, sandwich-dogs and, something I'd pay to see, sandwich-elephants. Some Victorian media channels seem remarkably advanced. We may think SMS text (mobile phone) advertising is a new medium. But in 1875 five thousand homes received telegrams at the same time – at 'the fashionable dinner hour, when families would be assembled' – telling them of a load of bedsteads ready at the advertiser's store. So text ads are nothing new. Or again, you may remember the fuss a few years ago when an advertiser projected the image of a young woman's bottom onto the Houses of Parliament. There's nothing new in projected ads either. Victorian agencies used to project ads onto Nelson's Column in Trafalgar Square.

But the similarities between the present and the past go deeper than that. I had always thought, rather lazily, that advertising agencies were an American invention. Not so. The first ad agency was founded in Britain by King James I on 5 March 1610, more than two centuries before Volney Palmer's curiously named Real Estate And Coal Office became the first American ad agency in 1841.

King James made Sir Arthur Gorges and Sir Walter Cope advertising agents for the kingdom. The problem facing them was money: how much should they be paid? A condition of their grant was that *clients would not be charged more than pleased them.* Gorges & Cope went out of business within a year.

Much the same problem is with us today. Advertising has always been a high-risk business – as Nigel Bogle of Bartle Bogle Hegarty has said, all agencies are three phone calls away from disaster. But it used to be a high-risk/high-reward business. Now it seems to be a high-risk/low-reward business. That's not a great combination.

A recent study by David Haigh of Brand Finance for the IPA showed that agencies' profit margins have become wafer-thin. Haigh found agencies only make profits by drastic cost-cutting. As the biggest cost by far is staff, wages are falling compared to other professions. Most alarmingly for the future, new recruits are offered less than they would get in other jobs – not just in accountancy and the law but less than they would get in client marketing departments.

It raises the question why the great strategists of the next generation would want to work in ad agencies any more. Agencies don't just pay less, they have less influence on marketing and communication decisions than they used to. But if agencies no longer attract the best strategic brains, if they merely execute marketing plans developed by clients, they will become vendors of technical services and nothing more. It could get even worse. Clients have more to worry about than the relationship between their brands and their customers. Brands themselves may weaken if ad agencies decline. How did we get into this predicament?

In the past, agencies were paid by the media, not by clients. George Rowell, who did as much as anyone to establish the media commission system, described his first deal in his book *Forty Years An Advertising Agent, 1865–1905*. His idea was to buy columns of space in New England country papers at a wholesale price. If he charged clients half the standard retail price per line, and sold half the lines, he would get $13,000 for space that had cost him $7500. To a young newspaperman earning $18 a week, this was real money. Rowell's discovery made him, and his agency, so rich he took four months holiday a year for the rest of his working life. Once the splendid man took seven years off.

Agencies started competing for media commissions by offering added-value services. Strategic services came first. The first known research survey was carried out by the NW Ayer agency for a pitch in 1879, as it happened against George Rowell's agency. The client was impressed and tried to buy the findings. The agency said the survey results were not for sale, but were free if they got the account. Ayer won the pitch, and the practice of giving away strategic advice to win media business had begun.

Next came creative services. The first agency copywriter was hired in 1892. Before then, copywriting was anyone's business – sometimes clients wrote the ads, sometimes they hired freelancers, and there were even handbooks containing slogans for all occasions. Producing ads, rather than just placing them, was also a loss leader for agencies; it was another way of attracting media commissions. However, in-house strategists and creatives changed agencies' focus. The new breed of agency copywriters saw the results of their work every day. Many ads were direct response, and it was easy to measure the effectiveness of mail-order ads: one simply counted how many boxes were sold per ad. Creatives became the aristocracy of the advertising business because they knew how to extract more sales from a given media space.

John Caples put the copywriter's case in his book *Tested Advertising Methods*. He wrote:

> *I have seen one mail order advertisement actually sell, not twice as much, not three times as much, but 19½ times as much merchandise as another ad for the same product. Both advertisements occupied the same space. Both had photographic illustrations. Both had carefully written copy. The difference was that one used the right appeal and the other used the wrong appeal.*

Nineteen and a half times higher sales for the same media spend ... No wonder agencies came to believe their real value to clients was devising 'the right appeal'. But they were still paid by how much space they bought until 1985, when Saatchi & Saatchi ended full service by separating Zenith as a media-only agency. It seemed like a progressive move at the time. Zenith could buy space cheaper than any single ad agency, and that had to be a good thing for clients. But the law of unintended consequences bit back.

In the past, ad agencies made marketing *cheaper*: they offered media space at a lower price than clients could buy it themselves. Agencies' strategic and creative services came free with the media buying. But now agencies have to charge for these services separately. Signing cheques to agencies seems to *add* to a client's marketing budget. Ad agencies seem to have moved to the dark side of the balance sheet – from being a saving, to being an expense.

Today's ad agencies are therefore in a different business from the industry I joined nearly 30 years ago. At the annual account review, the Media Director would explain how much money the agency had saved the client: 'This is what the space you bought would have cost on the open market,' he would say, 'and this is how much less you spent by using us.' An objective measure of agencies' value was how much money they saved. But agencies are no longer in that business. In the circumstances, it is not surprising client procurement departments are asking awkward questions about agency fees. When you get down to it, they have a good point: what value do agencies add? How *should* agencies' strategic and creative services be priced?

I'm not sure the industry has good answers yet. In fact, I suspect we don't. Jeremy Bullmore has written that with the de-coupling of media, among other factors, 'advertising agencies have no self-evident future function' (Bullmore, 2003). As poor old Gorges & Cope discovered all those years ago, if clients pay what pleases them, rather than pay for an agreed function, agencies may go out of business.

However, the IPA Effectiveness Awards may offer a solution. They have re-established the link between getting 'the right appeal' and sales. This link, created by mail-order advertisements, lasted until the 1960s, when new recruits who applied to work as copywriters at Masius, for instance, were told to spend six months behind a counter at Selfridges first, 'to learn selling'. But it was broken by the 1970s, when many came to believe advertising's effects on sales were unknowable and immeasurable. This foolish idea has been largely discredited. After 25 years of the Effectiveness Awards, and with hundreds of case histories in the IPA dataBANK, it seems clear adspend *can* be accountable. It *is* possible to find out what advertising contributed to a client's business, if the will to do an evaluation exists. The huge variety of cases in this book – cars and charities, retailers and telecoms – shows the commercial value of advertising can be isolated and quantified in almost all product categories.

As Simon Broadbent wrote in his Introduction to the first volume of *Advertising Works*, the cases show that:

> It [advertising] is a serious commercial tool. It can be a contributor to profit, handsomely repaying investment in it. It is not a cost, irrelevant to sales volume and drawing directly on the profit at the bottom of the balance sheet, as accountants [and we would add today, procurement departments] sometimes treat it.

It was competition for media commissions that got advertising agencies into the strategic and creative markets in the first place. I believe competition in evaluation will help establish their future profitability, and perhaps even survival. It's a Darwinian struggle out there. Analysts are the longer teeth and sharper claws that will give some agencies an edge in proving their worth.

Ad agencies differ from other marketing consultants because agencies execute the strategy too. Other consultants may know the way, but can't drive the car. Only agencies translate an understanding of the brand and market into executions that grow the client's business. It is precisely because what agencies do is unique that pricing is such a difficult problem. The current fee-based arrangement was borrowed from a system that may work for consultants or lawyers or merchant banks, but it does not seem to capture the essential difference in what advertising agencies do for clients.

In future, perhaps every campaign will be evaluated for its effects in the market and that will determine how much the agency earns. My impression is that UK agencies, spurred on by the Effectiveness Awards, are closer to creating 'effectiveness cultures' than agencies in other countries. I would not say we are there yet, and agencies will need more analysts to deliver on the promise, but the UK already has an army of planners with experience of doing evaluations to the highest and most rigorous standards in the world.

Agencies would also be demonstrating *marketing*'s worth. The Effectiveness Awards resonate within client companies too, proving the marketing budget has been well spent. Peter Drucker argued companies have only one sensible business purpose: to create customers (Drucker, 2003). It follows from this that companies have two, and only two, basic functions: marketing and innovation. By proving the value of investment in marketing to the boards and shareholders that pay for it, the Effectiveness Awards have created 'a serious commercial tool' for our clients' futures too.

For more than a century, ad agencies grew as the media grew. But now they need to develop new payment systems that reflect their unique contribution to a client's business: consultants that provide solutions. The Effectiveness Awards may offer answers to the cost-cutters in procurement, and the learning and evaluative techniques they contain may be essential for the industry's future prosperity.

References

Bullmore, J. (2003) *More Bullmore*. WARC, Henley-on-Thames.
Drucker, P. (2003) *The Essential Drucker*. HarperCollins, London.
Haigh, D. (2004) *Rewarding the Advertising Profession*. IPA, London.

A true story

Chapter 4

Paul Feldwick

Worldwide Brand Planning Director, DDB London

Some 14 years ago, the agency I worked at – it laboured then under the unwieldy name of BMP DDB Needham Worldwide – was invited to pitch for the Barclaycard account. Barclaycard was one of the two leading credit card brands in the UK. It had a history of famous advertising, which for the previous nine years had featured the television presenter Alan Whicker. One of the questions posed to agencies in the pitch was whether to keep Whicker, who was strongly associated with the brand, or move on to something new.

Barclaycard was facing a challenging business environment. Shifts in interest rates and growing levels of fraud had reduced profitability. Meanwhile, many new credit cards were marketing themselves aggressively with interest-free offers. Despite this competition, Barclaycard management proposed the bold step of adding extra services such as purchase insurance to their product, investing in improved customer service, and – to pay for all this – introducing for the first time an annual fee for card users.

The Barclaycard clients were delightful to work with. They gave us a brief of exemplary detail, and were never too busy to see us during the run-up to the pitch. By the time of the presentation, we felt we understood them and their business very well; and they must have thought so too, as they awarded us the business.

As we got to know the company it became clear that no one there really wanted to retain Whicker, and we agreed. Not only had the campaign run out of steam, but Whicker himself was getting older and his much parodied blazer and moustache were looking increasingly old-fashioned. So at the pitch we presented a new creative idea that everyone found very exciting. We told them they no longer needed a celebrity. Instead, we had a big blockbusting relaunch commercial, something on the scale of British Airways' 'Manhattan'.

We would see a great city of skyscrapers from the air. As we zoomed in, we would see people everywhere running up stairs and spilling out onto the rooftops. Music would build excitement. We would cut to the pavements, where bits of something, like tickertape, were floating down from the sky. As one fell into a cup of coffee at a café table, people would look up to see what was happening. Eventually we would all see that the people on the tops of the buildings were joyfully cutting up all their old credit cards and throwing them away. As the music swelled to a climax the final words on screen would read 'Barclaycard. We think it's all the credit cards you'll ever need.'

We began to work together with great enthusiasm. Then we hit a few snags. The new campaign was pre-tested by a well-known qualitative research company. Although the results were – to put it mildly – disappointing, the researchers were keen to show the agency that they could be constructive. They assured us and the client that with a few tweaks, the idea could be made to work.

Meanwhile the first production estimates were coming in. No one had ever pretended that this film would be cheap. But the costs that were now becoming apparent, involving helicopters and casts of thousands, were threatening to use up most of the media budget. At the same time the TV companies' statutory copy clearance people were looking at the campaign. We could not, they told us, show competitors' cards being cut up. And throwing things off buildings raised a number of problems: danger to others, encouraging litter, etc.

So the original idea was modified and scaled down. Out went the helicopter shots, and we would see only crowds of people running up stairs. A voice-over explained more product benefits. We took out the shot of the card falling into the coffee.

The second round of research was even less encouraging than the first. Still, the research company insisted that it was just a matter of getting the detail right – while of course we at the agency were equally keen to save our great, pitch-winning idea. And the copy clearance people were still unsatisfied.

When we came to the third test animatic, the crowds of people had been reduced to one man in a macintosh. He was standing on a fire escape cutting up an anonymous credit card and putting the pieces in a paper bag. At this stage, the initial lukewarm response in the groups turned to total mystification.

It was now at last reluctantly agreed that the original idea was dead. A new campaign was proposed. This would dramatise the benefits of the new card by showing what could go wrong if you didn't have one. For instance, to demonstrate that Barclaycard now offered medical assistance we had a commercial that opened on a totally deserted beach. We heard gloomy music as a sinister wind stirred magazines on empty sunloungers. A doomladen voice announced 'Every year, 40,000 people have to cut short their holidays due to illness …'.

It was now nearly six months since our appointment. Our clients had been endlessly patient and understanding, but even they were now beginning to drop hints that the relaunch date was very close, the airtime was booked, and they would really appreciate being able to approve something soon.

Research was booked in a hurry. The research company who had worked with us so far was unable to meet the tight deadline, so I ended up doing the groups myself. At the last minute someone suggested that it might be a good idea to hedge our bets – just in case the new idea wasn't right. One of the creative teams, we heard, had an idea involving Rowan Atkinson.

Hurriedly the Rowan Atkinson animatics were prepared. These bore no relation whatever to the final campaign. The first one began with a joke competition to find the replacement for Alan Whicker. A variety of unlikely people were doing very poor Whicker impersonations, culminating in Atkinson tearing off his false moustache and deciding to be himself. In the following scripts we saw Atkinson in a Whickerish reporter role, but getting it all wrong.

The empty beach campaign was among the most disliked ideas I have ever shown to consumers. Miserable, gloomy, doomladen, and also extremely boring, were some of the kinder things said about it. I was glad I had an alternative in my art bag. Sadly, the Atkinson campaign didn't fare much better. The Whicker impersonation was embarrassingly unfunny. The scenes that followed met with a fairly stony response too. There was nothing for it at the debrief but to tell the truth. I explained that the first idea was a total dog. I admitted that the Atkinson scripts weren't right. There was only one shred of hope, which I had to make the most of. When I asked the groups rather desperately at the end what they thought we should do, everyone agreed that 'you should use Rowan Atkinson, because he's funny whatever he does'.

It is enormously to the credit of our clients at Barclaycard that they accepted this recommendation, such as it was, with equanimity. We began negotiations with Rowan Atkinson. Luckily for all of us he was open to the idea of doing TV commercials. However, he didn't want to appear as himself. In fact, he had a very good idea of who he wanted to appear as – a new character he was already thinking about called Richard Latham, a sort of bumbling secret agent, Blackadder meets James Bond.

Far from causing us a problem, the Latham character offered a providential answer to the one remaining detail of the campaign: the lack of any actual scripts or ideas. So our creative teams were briefed to write scripts about Latham. Rowan Atkinson and his producer John Lloyd were closely involved at all stages, often rewriting the scripts themselves during the actual shoot. They were of course complete professionals, and – perhaps because they had no need to prove their 'creativity' – always understood that they were creating advertising, not pure entertainment.

The airdate was now so close that there was no time for another round of animatic testing. We and Barclaycard had to trust Atkinson, Lloyd and our own judgment, and so three films were shot and put on air. At the same time, the finished films were Link-tested by Millward Brown – not, we agreed, as a go/no-go decision, but as the first stage of our diagnostic learning about the ads. This approach was continued throughout the campaign, and the findings used to upweight or downweight different treatments and to carry out minor improvements. None of the commercials was ever researched as an animatic. The rest is published history, and the campaign's success in defending the brand, transforming its image and its profitability, is described in *Advertising Works 9* – the paper won a Gold in 1996.

I've told this story as honestly and accurately as I can from my own memories. Others who were involved may be able to correct some details, but I am confident that it's fairly close to the actual events. And the reason I've told it is because it's the sort of story that you never usually hear. As Jeremy Bullmore has pointed out in one of his essays,[1] advertising case histories are written like scientific papers – the actual process, which is generally a story of confusion, mistakes, luck and happy intuitions, is carefully rewritten to appear as a logical series of steps, thus reinforcing a conventional myth of how such things should be done.

Looking back over 30 years in the agency business, I don't think this story is especially unusual; at least, it represents the generality as well as the typical post-rationalised case history does. For example, it's really quite rare for the creative work that wins the pitch to become the campaign that succeeds in the marketplace. Everyone in advertising knows this, and yet clients continue

1. *Bullmore quotes the Nobel scientist, Sir Peter Medawar: ' "Scientific papers in the form in which they are communicated to learned journals are notorious for misrepresenting the processes of thought that led to whatever discoveries they describe". That was magic. That was marketing case histories. That was truth.' (Jeremy Bullmore, Archimedes and the efficacy of prayer, in* Behind the Scenes in Advertising, *WARC 1998).*

to assume that creative beauty parades are an effective way of finding successful campaigns. Between the initial idea that gets everyone excited and the final outcome lie a number of minefields – the politics of copy clearance, the practicalities of production, the judgements of research and the reality of consumers. And the opinions of many, many people who each think they alone know best.

This story might have turned out differently in so many ways. Our clients might have approved the original idea without research and spent millions on something that, probably, wouldn't have worked. Or, they might very easily have rejected our slightly vague proposal to 'use Rowan Atkinson because he's funny' and required a new set of scripts (quite possibly a new agency too). They might have insisted on agreeing every word in the Latham scripts by committee and subjecting them to animatic testing – which might have done little harm but by my guess would probably have hamstrung the apparently effortless craft that Rowan Atkinson and John Lloyd were allowed to bring to the end result. And so on.

The campaign was allowed to emerge as it eventually did because everyone involved was prepared to trust one another and to work together as a team. Anyone who had used their power to assert control over the process would quite likely have killed it – whether it was the client insisting on approving every word of the scripts, or a creative director refusing to work within Atkinson's idea, or a planner or researcher demanding some impossible standard of 'proof' before making any decisions. It takes only one person to kill a great campaign. It takes many people to allow it to happen. And sometimes the most important thing you need to do is also the most difficult: just get your ego out of the way.

The IPA Awards show, to the best of our ability, the kind of campaigns that actually work in the marketplace – not just those that fit some narrow theory of how advertising ought to work. These papers show us what success really looks like. They will tell you a great deal about strategic thinking, and learning from research. They will tell you about business results, about consumer responses, about the logic and rigour of proof. But I suspect they do not usually reflect the amount of muddle, error, guesswork and pure luck that actually led to each of these successful campaigns.

So perhaps when reading these cases as a guide to best practice, we should remind ourselves that in the real world of business there are no additional prizes for elegance, logic or neatness – only for ending up with something that works.

Back to our roots

Chapter 5
Will Collin
Director, Naked Communications

I was fortunate enough to attend a dinner hosted by the Newspaper Marketing Agency at which Jeremy Bullmore gave the after-dinner speech. His entertaining monologue, which culminated in a celebration of the increasingly forgotten art of copywriting, began with a glimpse back into the history of the advertising agency. For a relative greenhorn such as myself, who had long assumed that year zero in advertising began with the now much-venerated full-service agency, it was a surprise to learn that my historical horizons were too short: the advertising business began with media agencies.

What I learned was that in the late 1800s in America, the original advertising agencies were specialists in what was even then a busy marketplace of newspapers and other publications. These agencies were essential intermediaries who gathered disparate market information (such as readership research and ad rates) and then brokered the deals between advertiser and publication, charging a commission.

What happened next was that some of these proto-media independents sought to add extra services to compete better with their rivals. Specifically, they offered not only to procure the ad space but also to write the copy to fill it. That was the inauguration of 'full service', and to my surprise its origin lies in the media part of the business.

The reason I was surprised is that the largest part of the subsequent history of the advertising business, running well into the 1980s, is really the history of the creative product and its producers, and it is this history that I absorbed during my formative years in the business. From Vance Packard's *Hidden Persuaders* and Rosser Reeves's 'unique selling proposition', through the many wisdoms of Bill Bernbach to Stanley Pollitt's 'relevant distinctive', my advertising education was rooted in the quest for better advertising. If history is written by the victors then it seems that the media side of the business had been thoroughly subordinated: the nineteenth-century space brokers had been airbrushed out of the team photo.

1980: the end of advertising history?

Writing in 1989 as communism collapsed across eastern Europe, Francis Fukuyama made the bold claim in his book *The End of History and the Last Man* that history itself was coming to an end. According to Fukuyama, the essence of history is the ongoing struggle between competing ideologies. The ultimate victory of liberal democracy over alternatives such as hereditary monarchy, fascism and communism signals the end-point of humankind's ideological evolution, and hence the end of history itself. Western democratic capitalism was finally established as the enduring model for human civilisation. All subsequent events would merely be variations on this established theme.

However, Fukuyama's view was soon to be challenged by an unforeseen discontinuity: the rise of a competing ideology – religious fundamentalism – most spectacularly seen in the events of 9/11. Fukuyama seems to have called time on history too soon.

It could be said that the inauguration of the IPA Effectiveness Awards in 1980 was the ad industry's equivalent of the fall of the Berlin Wall. Until then, Lord Leverhulme's pronouncement (that he knew that half of his advertising budget was wasted, but not which half) had cast a shadow over the industry. Cynics could, and did, argue that advertising was more art than science and that its commercial benefits fell short of its cost. The brand-led approach to business was far from being the universally accepted model.

The body of evidence in the IPA Awards provided a convincing rebuttal to the lack of accountability implied by Leverhulme's dictum. Successful advertising does indeed pay back more than it costs. Creativity applied to commerce does generate profits. This could have been seen as the end of history for advertising: the argument had been won. All subsequent progress would be just refinements of the established model. Successive 'waves' of agencies would go on to launch with various innovations in their working methods, but in reality they were all offering variations on the accepted theme: coming up with the best advertising ideas. Better ideas mean more effective advertising, which leads to greater return on investment.

But just as Fukuyama did not foresee the impact of Al-Qaeda on western democratic capitalism, so the ad industry had not anticipated the impact of media fragmentation on the presumption that crafting better advertising ideas is the goal we must all strive towards. History hadn't ended after all.

Media fragmentation challenges the consensus

Sky TV launched in February 1989, nine months before the fall of the Berlin Wall. While several years were to pass before multi-channel TV gained significant penetration, the trend was nevertheless one way. Niche channels gained at the expense of mass channels, eating into their large audiences. The effect on this is obvious when one looks at the long-term trend in audience share for the terrestrial channels versus 'others', the aggregate of all the multi-channel TV stations (see Figure 1).

Of course, choice has also multiplied in other media as well as television. There are over twice as many radio stations, more than twice as many pieces of direct mail being sent out, a third more consumer magazines and almost twice as many cinema screens. That's not to mention the arrival of a wealth of new digital media, from the internet (52% of homes having access in 2004 according to National Statistics) and SMS (2.1 billion messages sent in September 2004 according to the Mobile Data Association) to DVD players (58% of households have one, says NRS January–June 2004). MP3 players, personal video recorders and DAB radios are rapidly building penetration. Finally the growth in the use of ambient media means that advertising has popped up in unexpected places, from moustachioed runners wearing branded vests to Minis attached to building walls.

This proliferation of media channels has had the effect of bombarding the consumer with more brand messages than ever before. This adds up to a blizzard of branding within which any individual message is a diminishing

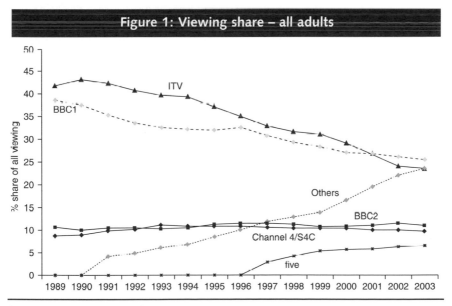

Figure 1: Viewing share – all adults

Source: BARB

fraction of the whole. This unstoppable fragmentation of consumers' media consumption is challenging the consensus that had become established in the ad industry in the mid-1980s: that the key to effective communication is the development of the best advertising idea.

It is clear that the willingness of the consumer to pay attention for long enough to engage with the idea is now a defining factor. In his May 2002 *Admap* article, Julian Saunders quotes CIA Medialab research, claiming that only 45% of message takeout is attributable to its content, while its context (i.e. the medium) accounts for the majority of the rest. Whether or not one believes this particular statistic, it's clear that the 'best idea wins' principle no longer holds true in every case. A great idea served up to the consumer at the wrong time when he or she isn't willing to take notice will be less successful than a weaker idea that is presented at an opportune and relevant moment. Of course the ideal combination is the best idea at the right moment, but the genie is nonetheless out of the bottle. The unchallenged primacy of the idea in advertising is under threat.

Looking at the 2004 crop of IPA Effectiveness Awards winners, two of the top papers seem to demonstrate this. First, the Gold award-winning paper describing the launch of the Central London Congestion Charge makes it clear that there was precious little need for an idea at all in that campaign. Rather it was a public information campaign where effectiveness came from delivering a simple message to London drivers at specific moments and locations, whether that be roadside posters or drivetime radio, or any of the many other channels used. What was important was the effective delivery of the message rather than imagination in its content.

The Grand Prix-winning case study for O_2 places great emphasis on the importance of integration within its campaign, such that all its activity – whether brand-led or promotion-led – has a positive contribution to long-term sales. The critical factor here seems to be a ruthlessly consistent visual style that, when delivered across a range of relevant media contacts (from retail stores to TV ads and billboards to offer-based press ads and *Big Brother* sponsorship), adds up to a highly memorable campaign.

Arguably the two main planks of success in O_2's campaign were the distinctive brand identity and the relevant ways in which this has been served up to consumers – not the advertising idea itself. These two campaigns have been judged the most commercially effective out of a selection of the very best the industry has to offer, and yet I would argue that neither is reliant on breakthrough creativity in terms of the advertising idea. Is this just a coincidence or have things really changed?

Looking back over the entire set of IPA Effectiveness Grand Prix winners, it seems that there are only three other papers where the effect is attributed in significant part to the communications strategy as opposed to just the strength of the idea:

1. Barnardo's in 2002 took the idea 'giving children back their future' and brought it to life across a range of touchpoints, from internal roadshows and lobbying MPs, to advertising, PR, DM, telemarketing, corporate relations and face-to-face recruitment.
2. Tesco's 'Every Little Helps' in 2000 was a mantra not just for advertising but also for customer service (e.g. One In Front checkout-opening policy), product development (e.g. Value range) and CRM (i.e. the Clubcard).
3. In 1998 the Health Education Authority's anti-drugs campaign succeeded in 'infiltrating the fortress of youth culture' through the use of relevant media channels such as style magazines and dance radio stations. Being present in those media was the key to getting the message assimilated into the audience's world.

Prior to these three papers, none of the Grand Prix-winning cases placed any great importance on the way the message was delivered: the arguments focused solely on originating the most motivating idea. From the launch of Krona, which referenced the product's runaway success in Australia, through BMW and its product-based claim to be the Ultimate Driving Machine, right up to BT in 1996, which sought to change our attitude to calling via a cuddly conscience figure, the key to success was in finding the right idea.

If we take the IPA Awards to be a measure of what makes for successful campaigns, then on this evidence we would conclude that in recent years media strategy has become an increasingly essential component of commercial success. Getting the right advertising idea is only one ingredient: finding meaningful ways to engage with the target audience is now just as important.

Consumers in control

The change I have focused on up to this point has been the effect of fragmentation in consumers' media consumption. Increasing fragmentation is the effect of ever-increasing media choice. But alongside increased choice, consumers are also being given – and are exercising – greater control.

In part this is as simple as the increased likelihood of flicking between channels during the ad breaks within multi-channel homes. But in this digital age it also means the selective visiting of websites that are interesting or relevant, while ignoring the billions of others (and the banners that point towards them). It means the occasional, genuinely funny email attachment that gets virally circulated (unlike the hundreds of would-be virals that fail). It means the blogs and message boards where consumers discuss and critique their favourite brands to a level of detail that would amaze the jaded marketer. It means the increasing adoption of personal video-recorder technology like Sky+, where research shows that users watch more recorded TV than they do live broadcasts.

What will be the effect of this consumer empowerment on advertising? One parallel comes from the world of news which, like advertising, seeks to disseminate information to mass audiences using the media. One of the biggest issues facing news organisations today is how to adapt in a world where stories are often 'broken' by individuals posting stories on weblogs, rather than coming from conventional news providers in the mainstream media. This happened during the 2004 US Presidential election campaign when a CBS news item about George W. Bush's military service in the Texas Air National Guard was revealed to be false by bloggers who spotted the inaccuracies in CBS's report.

The effect is to undermine the assumed authority of official media channels: their right to determine what is news, and their interpretation of that news. In his book *We the Media: Grassroots Journalism by the People for the People*, Dan Gillmor describes the shift in the balance of power between news organisation and consumer in ways that sound remarkably familiar to us in the advertising industry:

> *Big media ... treated the news as a lecture. We told you what the news was. You bought it, or you didn't. You might write us a letter; we might print it ... it was a world that bred complacency and arrogance on our part. It was a gravy train while it lasted, but it was unsustainable.*
>
> *Tomorrow's news reporting and production will be more of a conversation or a seminar. The lines will blur between producers*

and consumers, changing the role of both in ways we're only
beginning to grasp. The communication network itself will be a
medium for everyone's voice, not just the few who can afford to
buy multimillion-dollar printing presses, launch satellites, or win
the government's permission to squat on the public airways.

The same trends are affecting branded communication. Whereas once a big brand would promote a desirable image via mass advertising delivered through mainstream media, now the power balance has shifted in the consumer's favour. The scarce resource now is no longer the ability to craft highly polished commercials, but the consumer's attention span. While highly polished commercials can still be the means to capture that attention, so can a cheekily placed ambient ad, a street marketing team surprising people on the way to work, or an imaginatively produced microsite.

It's long been said that consumers 'use' advertising rather than just receive it, meaning that it's their involvement in decoding and interpreting advertising that is the source of its influence. Now as people have an increasing control over the media they consume, successful communication will be that which gives the consumer an opportunity to take part in the process rather than presenting them with a perfect, shiny campaign in which they have no role other than as passive receivers.

Another of the 2004 IPA Effectiveness Gold award winners, 118 118, provides an example of this. While the campaign certainly used mass media such as TV and radio in large amounts, the simultaneous deployment of hundreds of pairs of '118 runners' in towns and cities right across the country gave people the opportunity to interact for real with 'the blokes off the telly'. Together with the distribution of 118 running vests, which people willingly adopted as the fancy dress code of 2003, this activity made the campaign feel like common property and this was a large part of how 118 118 was taken to heart so much more than competitor brands spending similar amounts.

In conclusion

I learned from Jeremy Bullmore that the origins of the advertising industry are to be found on the media side of the business. That was a surprise to me because the subsequent history of the industry has been the rise and rise of the creative idea as the primary determinant of campaign success.

However, media fragmentation has changed the landscape, so that we can no longer take consumers' attention for granted. Finding relevant occasions where consumers are willing to engage with the message is now equally important in determining campaign success – as evidenced by the more recent IPA Effectiveness Awards winners.

In the future, the balance of power will shift still further in the consumer's direction. It remains to be seen how that will affect the advertising industry, but it's clear that the role of media and communications strategy will be central.

References

Saunders, J. (2002) Back to the Future (With a Difference). *Admap*, May 2002.

PART TWO

A guide to profitable communications investment

Launching into an established market

Chapter 6

Malcolm White

Executive Planning Director, Euro RSCG London

Brands get launched into all types of markets all the time. Markets that are at different stages in their life cycle: new markets, developing markets and – the subject of this chapter – established markets.

The IPA Effectiveness dataBANK identifies 144 prize-winning papers that deal with success in established markets,[1] from 1980 until 2002. Because only 19 of these 144 papers are brand launches (rather than relaunches or repositionings) we might conclude that launching a new brand into an established market is especially difficult and that the endeavour is more likely to end in failure than success. It is interesting, also, that the majority of even these 19 papers are concerned with launches pre-1994. We might conclude from this that it is increasingly difficult to launch into established markets.

Market life cycle also exerts an influence on the type of strategy that brand owners and their agencies can end up going for. Like gravity, it is an invisible force but exerts a considerable pull.

Consider the characteristics of a market in the established stage of its life cycle. Product innovation has probably dried up to not much more than a drip. All the obvious positioning bases are likely to be occupied. The market is probably sufficiently large that even small percentage share gains can generate a good return. Why struggle for a different answer when something pretty much the same as the competition will probably do, and probably be successful? It is no wonder that 'a bit better', rather than different, is a common solution in these markets.

It is no surprise therefore that, according to the dataBANK, only a minority of prize-winning papers in established markets have strived for and succeeded in doing something different from the market norm. Only 59 out of those 144 papers consider that the intermediate effects they achieved were to do with 'differentiation ... setting the brand apart'.[2] In other words, market life cycle can have a deadening effect in established markets. Certainly, it is the context into which any launch must fit.

---

1. *'Prize-winning' means that a paper must have at least won a commendation. I have used question 13 from the authors' dataBANK questionnaire to identify these established market papers: 'At what stage in the product life cycle is the category ...?' Brands that tick the 'mature' box against this question are included in my total of 144.*
2. *These data are derived from question 26 in the IPA Effectiveness dataBANK questionnaire.*

It is strange then that, in my experience, we spend a disproportionate amount of the time available to us when devising a launch strategy in thinking about *what* we are launching, and very little time thinking about what we are launching *into*.

Content is king

Two IPA Effectiveness Awards Grand Prix winners from the 1980s, namely Krona (1980) and Winalot Prime (1988), show how time spent thinking about context is actually time very well spent. They both illustrate how what might be called 'context analysis' can inspire strategic and creative innovation, like rich soil promoting strong plant growth.

We learn from both papers that their particular markets are huge and relatively static. Critically, we are told that price is the generally accepted success factor in their markets:

> *Movements in relative price are quite clearly the dominant influence on sector shares of the yellow fats market.*
>
> Krona

> *Quality is directly associated with price ...*
>
> Winalot Prime

Both these prize winners also saw the prevailing communication context as an opportunity – an opportunity that could be grasped by departing from the prevailing communication context in each market:

> *There exists a legacy of distrust of claims of butter parity deriving from Stork. In addition, Stork has pre-empted a number of possible advertising routes to the extent that they are closed to Krona.*
>
> Krona

> *Chum advertising, particularly Pedigree, has remained with a formula which has varied little over the last 20 years.*
>
> Winalot Prime

In fact, the 'context analysis' in both papers created a clear and vivid definition of the problem both brands faced in their launch into their respective established markets. This was important because, in the words of John Dewey, 'a problem well-defined is half-solved'.

Go further than the USP

However, context analysis only got both brands to 'first base'. How and what to do about it? Interestingly, both stories start with product innovation. In the Krona paper we are introduced to the improbably named margarine, 'Fairy', launched by a Unilever company in Australia. We are told that when that product was tested in the UK by Van den Bergh, '40% of tasters thought Fairy was butter, compared with only 7% for Stork' (Krona, 1980).

Similarly, Winalot Prime was

> *based on a new way of presenting the raw materials of canned dog food so that they looked like pieces of meat rather than a solid cylinder of a product.*
>
> Winalot Prime

Product difference was a clear and unique selling proposition (USP) for both brands, and less ambitious marketers may well have ended up 'sticking' with this and putting it at the heart of their advertising strategy. Why did those responsible for Krona and Winalot Prime go further? I believe it is because they saw a bigger, more profitable prize in speaking to the hearts of consumers, not just to their heads.

Krona did this by understanding, a good 20 years before it became fashionable, the power of discovery and self-completion.

> *The tone was telling not selling. It left choice to the consumer; it treated her like an adult.*
>
> Krona

To do this it created a documentary style of advertising featuring René Cutforth, a long-established and well-respected reporter. He told the story of what happened in Australia with the Fairy brand and how that brand was now on sale in the UK, called Krona. By communicating in this way Krona leapfrogged the quaintly named 'Margarine Regulations' (which prohibited margarine making a comparison with butter). Equally importantly, it significantly enhanced its chances of being believed.

Winalot Prime's version of going beyond the USP was to go for the emotional high ground:

> *The Winalot Prime advertising ... unashamedly pandered to the*
> *audience's love of dogs. Rather than concentrating on the*
> *product, the commercial tugged at the heart strings.*
>
> Winalot Prime

This resulted in the 'Long March' advertising epic, about the adventures of a large number of dogs on their journey to find Winalot Prime.

A lesson from both these papers is that anyone who is launching into an established market needs to develop a strong and compelling 'it' (where 'it' = a product USP), but that they need to say 'it' with feeling.

Think of advertising as a strategic weapon, not just a delivery mechanism

Getting your target audience to identify deeply with the advertising so that the advertising is a real source of competitive advantage is something we think of as a twenty-first century communications phenomenon – one that we today attribute to so-called sexy categories and brands such as Honda, Lynx and 118 118. Yet this is surely what Krona and Winalot Prime did 20 years ago. Certainly, it is the way they explained their success. In the Krona paper, it is stressed that 'the advertising had been identified by consumers as the primary influence on their initial purchase'. The authors of the Winalot Prime case see things in a similar way:

> *Perhaps the most surprising and encouraging aspect of the case*
> *is the ability of advertising to make a difference in a market*
> *which, like many others, is dominated by a highly professional,*
> *immensely powerful company [Pedigree] which seems to have all*
> *the avenues of attack well-defended.*
>
> Winalot Prime

Be radical and professional

As you can probably tell, I am deeply impressed by the radicalism of both these prize-winning stories. But of equal importance, I think, especially when launching into a large established market, are virtues that seem to be the opposite of being radical: thoroughness and learning via doing, for example. This is demonstrated in both papers. Both radical solutions were achieved not by a leap into the dark but by careful, and carefully evaluated, preliminary steps. The Krona paper is actually about a TV test in Westward and Harlech. In the case of Winalot Prime the award-winning 'Long March' advertising was developed as a result of the relative failure of two previous commercials, from which the agency and client learnt important lessons.

Food for thought

There are four things that I believe will increase the chances of a successful new brand launch into an established market:

1. Explore the context and identify the context-breaking opportunities.
2. Say whatever you have to say with feeling. Don't just 'stick' at the rational unique selling proposition.
3. In established markets, where it appears that all avenues of attack and all new means of competitive advantage have already been tried, advertising in a new and different way can actually be the 'silver bullet'.
4. Trial and error, learning by doing, appears to be a sensible way to proceed. This is because while the gains to be made in an established market are significant, so are the potential losses.

Overall, the evidence of these two Grand Prix winning cases and learning from the IPA Effectiveness dataBANK is that difference always beats sameness, and that difference is better than just being better.

Krona
How advertising helped make Krona a brand leader

Grand Prix winner 1980

This case history analyses the launch of Krona margarine, a new product from Van den Bergh, into the Harlech and Westward TV areas.

Krona was launched to exploit the widening gap in price between butter and margarine and to attract butter users who were trading down. The brand succeeded beyond all expectations and by the end of the first year was established as brand leader in the launch areas with a national equivalent turnover of £32m at RSP.

Following this successful test market Krona has been extended to other areas. In all but one of these Krona is now brand leader or number two brand.

Business background

The yellow fats market
Krona operates within the yellow fats market, which comprises butter, margarine and low-fat spreads. This is a huge market, worth £600m at RSP in 1979, but it is not showing many signs of real growth. Indeed, it has declined by about 1% since 1975.

Within this total picture there have been major shifts in the consumption of butter and margarine. By the end of 1979, butter and margarine shared the market equally. The trend to margarine has continued strongly in 1980.

Abridged version of the original case study written in 1980 by Stephen Benson (Davidson Pearce) for Van den Berghs.

Movements in relative price are quite clearly the dominant influence on sector shares of the yellow fats market.

Market opportunity

The motivation and mechanism of the move to margarine from butter can vary. But the inescapable common element is the fact that butter users are moving – indeed, until Krona, are forced to move – to very different products, which match neither the physical characteristics, the taste, nor the texture of butter. This does leave unsatisfied that large potential group of consumers who find the increasing price of butter a problem but are unwilling to sacrifice what they see as the unique qualities of butter. So as the price gap widened, a major opportunity was seen to exist for a margarine that duplicated the characteristics of butter but at a significantly lower price.

However, there existed both a technical problem in making an acceptable product and a considerable credibility problem in persuading consumers that such a product could exist.

The background to Krona

A few years ago a Unilever company in Australia, EOI, had considerable success with a margarine called Fairy. This was a hard block margarine that bore a remarkable likeness to butter. Samples of the product were tested by Van den Bergh in the UK. In a blind product test 40% of the tasters thought Fairy was butter, compared with only 7% for Stork. A lengthy development process then ensued to match Fairy using UK production facilities and in due course this was more than achieved. Launch date was then finally determined by a judgement on the optimum price gap between butter and margarine. The brand was launched as Krona margarine in 1978 with TV advertising breaking in October 1978. It was a block margarine in a foil wrapper, initially selling at around 20p for $\frac{1}{2}$ lb, compared with the average butter price of 30p.

Marketing and advertising objectives

The marketing objective was to increase the company's market share in the premium sector by securing for Krona a share of at least 5%.

The advertising objective was to encourage trial of new Krona margarine by establishing that it is the first margarine with a taste and texture indistinguishable from butter.

Creative strategy and execution

The prime target group was housewives currently spreading salted butter, who are being forced to trade down because of the increasing price of butter, but who do not wish to sacrifice the taste and texture of butter.

The campaign was designed to communicate the basic consumer benefit that Krona margarine has a taste and texture indistinguishable from butter.

Supporting evidence
When the counterpart of Krona was on sale in New South Wales, housewives could not believe it was margarine and a rumour that in fact it was New Zealand butter rewrapped as margarine spread round the state. The result was that the brand became brand leader within weeks.

A brief word of explanation is needed, both about the strategy and the execution. Any brand with a claim and a position such as Krona faces two substantial problems in putting these across:

1. The Margarine Regulations, which are government regulations prohibiting any presentation of a margarine that either implicitly or explicitly compares it to, likens it to, or refers to butter. Thus there is no legal way in which Krona's benefit can be directly expressed to the consumer.
2. There exists a legacy of distrust of claims of butter parity deriving from Stork. In addition, Stork has pre-empted a number of possible advertising routes to the extent that they are closed to Krona.

Out of a number of possible creative routes identified, a campaign was therefore developed in which a long-established and well-respected reporter – René Cutforth – talked about the astonishing success of the Fairy brand in Australia: how a rumour spread that it was not margarine at all and how it became an almost overnight brand leader. The counterpart of this Australian product was now on sale in the UK and called Krona margarine. No direct claim was made for Krona itself. The implication was, however, that a similar success might occur in the UK. Three commercials were produced for the launch campaign, each explaining different aspects of the 'Fairy Story'.

Media strategy and plan

Budget
The national equivalent launch budget was set at £1.5m. This figure was based on an assessment of what the brand could afford in year 2, assuming targets were met, upweighted by 20% for the launch year. Company experience on necessary weights for launching premium brands was also influential.

Area choice
Westward and Harlech were selected for the launch of Krona for two main reasons:

1. Approximately 10% of the UK would be covered – a sample judged to be large enough to assist in network forecasting, yet small enough to minimise capital investment.
2. The area was strong for butter and relatively poor for all margarine. If Krona achieved target, then it was likely to be successful elsewhere.

Media group selection
Television was the most appropriate medium for announcing Krona. Its various advantages, in combination, were judged to outweigh the disadvantages associated with its sole use.

Campaign evaluation

Brand performance
Performance was affected by two industrial disputes: the lorry drivers' strike (2 January to 5 February 1979) and a dispute at Van den Bergh's Bromborough factory. The former sharply reduced deliveries in cycles 1 and 2 of 1979 while the latter meant that there were no deliveries of Krona (or of other Van den Bergh brands) between the beginning of April and the beginning of May 1979.

Distribution
Figures are available only for sterling weighted distribution in the two areas combined, in multiples and co-ops only (Table 1).

Very strong distribution was thus achieved within two or three months, and growth in distribution cannot fully explain the growth in deliveries.

Within three TCA periods, Krona had achieved a 10% share, making it the second brand in the market (Table 2).

Table 1: Krona sterling distribution, Harlech and Westward	
	%
October/November 1978	78
December 1978/January 1979	95
February/March	95
April/May	89
June/July	95
August/September	86
October/November	93

Source: Stats MR

Table 2: Krona volume brand share	
	%
1978	
14th October	–
11th November	5
9th December	10
1979	
6th January	9
3rd February	5
3rd March	8
31st March	12
28th April	5
26th May	3
23rd June	14
21st July	15
18th August	18
15th September	16

Source: TCA

This was a time of rapid sampling. Cumulative penetration had reached 24% by November (Table 4).

There was a temporary setback as a result of the lorry drivers' strike but share recovered strongly by March, only to be hit again by the Van den Bergh strike.

The consumer

If we look at sales of Krona with regard to the consumer, there are four scenarios to be considered: awareness, trial, repeat purchase and product positioning.

Beginning with awareness, the first post-check showed that after only five weeks of advertising, awareness had already reached a high level and this was then maintained in subsequent months despite the interruptions in supply caused by strikes early in 1979 (Table 3).

Table 3: Krona awareness (%)			
	Nov. 1978	Feb. 1979	July/Aug. 1979
Spontaneous	20	22	25
Prompted	79	86	80

Source: Quick Read

As regards trial, to be tried by one-quarter of all housewives within little more than a month was obviously an exceptional achievement and the brand continued to gain trial in the succeeding months (Table 4).

Table 4: Krona trial (% bought in last six months)		
Nov. 1978	Feb. 1979	July/Aug. 1979
24%	38%	43%

Source: Quick Read

Obviously, the advertising cannot take sole credit for initial trial. A door-to-door coupon was dropped during October and there were a number of in-store demonstrations. By the end of 1978, distribution in multiples and co-ops exceeded 90% sterling. However, there is good evidence that advertising played a major role; Table 5 shows the findings of the November Quick Read survey.

Moving on to repeat purchase, the Quick Read monitors show a steady increase in the number of housewives intending to purchase Krona next time (17% of respondents by July/August). By July/August, more than two-thirds of buyers had bought more than one pack.

Table 5: Influences on first purchase of Krona	
Coupon received or not	
No. of respondents aware of Krona	248
Yes (%)	47
No (%)	50
Don't know, etc. (%)	3
Whether coupon first encouraged trial	
No. of respondents	44
Yes (%)	34
No (%)	66
Don't know, etc.	–
Awareness of Krona TV advertising	
No. of respondents aware of Krona	248
Yes (%)	91
No (%)	7
Don't know, etc. (%)	2

Source: Quick Read

Finally, there was the issue of product positioning. The aim of Krona advertising was to present the brand as a high-quality spreading margarine, indistinguishable from butter. Was this being borne out in practice in the marketplace?

The November 1978 Buyers' Survey indicated that even in the earliest stage of the brand's life, when sampling was at its peak, around half of current Krona buyers felt they had stopped buying other brands or cut down on them. In each case the largest single source of Krona business was butter.

How the advertising works

Communication
The problem, as we discussed earlier, is to overcome the hurdles provided by restrictive regulation and credibility. It is clear from the evidence that the communication was understood:

> It's as good as butter.

> Closer to butter than other margarines.

Tastes more like butter.

Alternative to butter.

Implying it was as good as butter.

Source: various qualitative studies

The March Taylor Nelson Study showed that over half of acceptors and 42% of rejectors expected either a new brand of butter or something similar.

Persuasion

In terms of persuasion, we have the evidence of image statements from the various Quick Read studies. These show that:

- Despite the legacy of incredibility and the current status of packet margarines, communication and persuasion that Krona was a high-quality margarine with a butter-like taste were well achieved.
- Levels of agreement were high, even in November 1978 when a substantial majority had only the evidence of the advertising to go on.

Style and tone

The novel 'documentary' style of the commercials was liked because:

- It was different from other, particularly margarine, advertisements.
- The tone was 'telling not selling'; it left the choice to the consumer – it treated her as an adult and did not talk down to her; the personality of René Cutforth was important here.
- The tone was serious and gave stature to the product.

All combined strongly to enhance credibility.

Trial and repeat purchase

Finally, the evidence suggested that the campaign was trial *and* repeat purchase orientated. While for some people it clearly on its own could not overcome rooted scepticism about margarine claims, for the majority it provided a strong inducement to try. Once people had tried and accepted the product, the advertising was seen as a confirmation of their experience. They too had made this discovery. They too could not believe it was a margarine. What had happened in Australia was only to be expected. In addition, the intelligent tone of the commercials complimented them as consumers and confirmed the good sense of their choice of Krona. It is quite reasonable on the evidence, then, to claim that the Krona advertising, far from simply conveying a highly desirable message, has by its distinctive character become an essential part of the brand's character and therefore a crucial element in the success of this very major grocery brand.

Conclusion

That Krona represented a major marketing success in Harlech and Westward over the period under review is amply demonstrated by the facts. Nor was it a temporary phenomenon. Krona is achieving similar results in other areas as it is extended and has more than maintained its dominance in its original test areas.

We say 'marketing success' because advertising was only one, albeit significant, factor in Krona's success. The other factors are listed below.

Timing
The increasing price premium of butter over margarine provided the opportunity for a brand aimed at people forced to trade down.

Product quality
Krona was the first margarine to successfully simulate butter. It exceeds expectations and arouses almost a religious fervour among converts.

Naming and packaging
The presentation of the brand communicates the required positioning and reinforces the belief of users that Krona is closer to butter than margarine.

Pricing
While Krona is clearly a premium-priced margarine, it is sufficiently cheaper than butter to make the incentive to switch as strong as possible.

Marketing investment
Van den Bergh recognised the potential of the brand and was prepared to spend heavily behind it, above and below the line, in its first year. Significantly, the bulk of this money was spent on the consumer in order to encourage the critically important first purchase and not to reduce price at point of sale.

The march of Winalot Prime

Grand Prix winner 1988

Winalot Prime was launched by Spillers Foods in January 1985. Up to 1988 there were two advertising campaigns. The first ran from March 1985 to April 1986. This paper focuses particularly on the effect of the second campaign, featuring the 'Long March' execution, which was first aired in January 1987.

The paper not only demonstrates how the 'Long March' advertising has helped to build Winalot Prime, but also illustrates two principles:

1. That advertising, imaginatively conceived and boldly executed, can give a brand a competitive advantage against the strongest, most determined and most entrenched opposition.
2. That commercially effective advertising can be synonymous with a campaign that the public like and that the advertising industry has applauded.

Background

The market for canned dog food in the UK is large, growing and lucrative. Worth £206m at RSP in 1981, it had increased to £350m by 1987. The canned dog food market can be divided into premium brands and others. Premium brands are higher priced and regarded by the housewife as better-quality products.

Abridged version of the original case study written in 1988 by Lee Taylor and Gerard Smith (Ogilvy & Mather) for Spillers Foods.

The marketing opportunity for Spillers

In the 1960s Spillers was the dominant manufacturer of canned dog food. Towards the end of that decade it lost leadership to Pedigree Petfoods, which, successively with Pal and then Pedigree Chum, redefined the product standards in the market from chunks in gravy towards more solid cylinders of meat and jelly.

The main marketing task for Spillers in the canned dog food market throughout the 1970s and 1980s has been to find an effective competitor to Pedigree Chum and Pal.

The new product
Winalot Prime was launched after five years of development. It was based on a new way of presenting the raw materials of canned dog food so that they looked like pieces of meat rather than a solid cylinder of a product.

The launch advertising
The role of the launch advertising was to position Winalot Prime as a superior premium brand and thereby to encourage trial. Two commercials were screened. Both 'Hall' and 'Garden Party' were based on a parody of the recent television version of *Brideshead Revisited*.

Evaluation of the launch

Sales of Winalot Prime in the period of the first campaign, January 1985 to December 1986, show that the brand was immediately successful in gaining share. However, while sales of Prime continued to increase throughout 1986, by the middle of that year Spillers was beginning to feel that the brand was not performing to its full potential.

The new (Long March) advertising strategy: August 1986

The advertising objective remained unchanged: to build the positioning of Winalot Prime as a canned dog food superior to Pedigree Chum, and to encourage trial and repeat purchase among buyers of premium brands.

The role of advertising was defined in much sharper terms than at the launch stage and contained two key elements:

1. Advertising had to communicate that the era of dominance by Pedigree Chum was coming to a close – to produce a genuinely 'mould-breaking' campaign for this category that would change the way in which consumers thought about canned dog food.
2. To substantiate the 'mould-breaking'claims of product superiority by means of a benefit other than (but in addition to) the meaty appearance of the brand.

The target audience for the new campaign remained housewives who were buyers of premium brands – Pedigree Chum, Pal and Mr Dog – though concentrating on purchasers of Pedigree Chum as the most likely source of business. To this group were added the small but growing number of buyers of Winalot Prime, whose brand choice the advertising would seek to confirm.

The proposition for the advertising was derived from the physically superior meat protein content of Winalot Prime.

> *Winalot Prime is the best canned dog food you can buy because it contains over 50% more meat than Pedigree Chum.*

The advertising O&M produced was a 60-second commercial called 'Long March'. It featured the adventures of a large number of dogs, all different breeds, on their journey to find Winalot Prime.

The difference between the new Winalot Prime advertising and the launch campaign was that it unashamedly pandered to the audience's love of dogs. Rather than concentrating on the product, the commercial tugged at the heart strings. The product 'sell' came at the end of the commercial as a climax and a coda.

Media plan

The media plan for 1987 was based on four closely spaced bursts of advertising. The January–February burst was designed to achieve parity of exposure with Pedigree Chum in terms of the number of propositions made, but using 60-second commercials only. The 30-second executions were introduced in March in equal rotation with 60-second films, moving to 1:2 in favour of the 30-second executions in August–September. In November and December 1987, 30-second executions only were run.

Ten-second films were introduced in January 1988 and run in rotation 2:1 in favour of 30-second executions.

What happened?

By December 1986, immediately prior to Long March, Winalot Prime's market share was 5.9%. By February 1987, after Long March advertising was first exposed, it was 6.9%, and by April 1988 had grown to 8.2%.

Allowing for what might reasonably have been achieved, principally through gains in distribution, the net share gain was an annualised 1.5 share points. In value terms, share grew from 6.7% (December 1986) to 9.0% (April 1988), again giving a net annualised gain of 1.5 share points, and this in a market where (in 1987) each extra share point was worth £3.5 million at retail prices.

Evaluation

The focus of this paper is the Long March advertising and its effect on Prime's sales. However, this needs to be seen in the context of the entire sales history, starting in January 1985.

The variation in Prime's market share up to December 1986 could be almost entirely explained in terms of variables such as market share and overall distribution. However, from January 1987 share increased far in excess of the prediction (see Figure 1). Our explanation for the difference is of course that it is due to the Long March advertising. To prove this, we shall seek to demonstrate a statistical connection between the increase in share and the advertising. This involves adding an expression of advertising to an economic model. We have four variables: overall distribution, the distribution of Giant size, price relative to Chum, and advertising.

Including adstock in our model improves the fit dramatically (and significantly, in the statistical sense), to the extent that we are quite confident of the advertising contribution to share growth (Figure 2).

How did the advertising work?

The evidence suggests that Long March worked as we intended it to, and in two main ways:

1. It captured the imagination of its audience. Dog owners are more interested in looking at dogs than dog food, and Long March give them a chance to enjoy lots of dogs in natural surroundings. The

advertising idea achieved the objective of getting some Pedigree buyers to 'suspend their disbelief' about the claims of Winalot Prime.

2. It communicated the product benefit of superior meatiness.

Continuous campaign tracking (Millward Brown)

The Long March campaign has been evaluated since December 1986 using a conventional Millward Brown tracking study among matched samples of dog

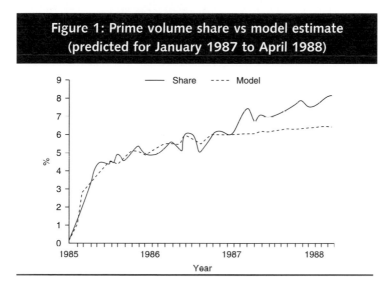

Figure 1: Prime volume share vs model estimate (predicted for January 1987 to April 1988)

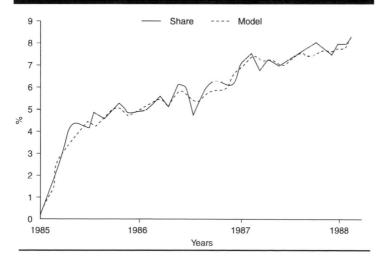

Figure 2: Prime volume share vs model estimate including 'Long March' advertising

owners. Table 1 shows some of the key figures from the study, with comparative data for Chum over the same period. These exaggerate the effect of Long March because the December figures relate to a time when Prime had not received advertising support for eight months; however, it is the relationship between the measures for Prime and Chum that is significant.

The success of Long March in setting up an alternative and more attractive brand style to the Pedigree advertising is evident from the scores relating to viewing enjoyment, but is perhaps best illustrated by the percentages claiming to be fed up with seeing the commercials. For Prime this moved from 2% to 3% over the period, for Chum 10% to 20%.

The communication of meatiness is also evident from the scores on 'the meatiest dog food you can buy'.

Qualitative research
Since the campaign was first aired, Spillers has conducted a number of qualitative research studies into Winalot Prime and its advertising. Without

Table 1: Millward Brown tracking study (December 1986–April 1988)

| | 4 Weeks to 4 January 1997 | | 8 Weeks to 10 April 1988 | |
	Winalot Prime	Pedigree Chum	Winalot Prime	Pedigree Chum
Base	600	600	622	622
Total spontaneous brand awareness (%)	24	84	38	87
Spontaneous TV advertising recall (%)	17	64	38	63

Prompted comments from those aware of the relevant TV advertising (% agreeing)

Base	102	360	236	367
Advertising				
I enjoyed watching it	20	29	62	31
It made me interested in the product	8	13	15	8
It was a distinctive advert	15	23	29	17
I'm getting fed up with seeing it	2	10	3	20
Product				
The meatiest dog food you can buy	16	20	14	11
Keeps dogs fit and active	32	31	54	30

fail these studies produce quotations from housewives who eulogise about the advertising. For example:

> *It's a lovely advert that Prime one, it brings tears to your eyes.*

> *You look out for your dog, you just have to watch it.*

They also provide evidence that the product message is communicated.

> *Fifty per cent more meat than the best-selling brand. They mean Chum.*
> Liz Hauck Research, September 1987

AGB TCA panel data
Gains/loss analyses conducted by AGB, comparing the 40 weeks ending December 1986 with the 40 weeks ending September 1987, show that of volume gained from buyers of other brands, 88% came from buyers of Pedigree Chum and Pal, the core target audience for the advertising.

Additional publicity
The campaign attracted the attention of the media, giving the brand significant additional publicity. The *Daily Mirror* ran a double-page spread about the advertising, and the campaign was discussed on BBC's *Fax* programme and on ITV's *Central News*, altogether providing the brand with an estimated 14 minutes' free television exposure.

Awards
The campaign also won a Creative Circle Gold award in March 1987 for the 'most encouraging change of advertising direction', and a Clio award in June 1987.

Conclusion

Perhaps the most surprising and encouraging aspect of the case is the ability of advertising to make a difference in a market that, like many others, is dominated by a highly professional, immensely powerful company that seems to have all avenues of attack well defended.

Spillers identified advertising as an area in which there was an opportunity to outperform the competition, was prepared to back its judgement that Long March was able to do so, and has reaped the commercial reward.

Revitalising your brand

Chapter 7

Richard Warren

Director of Strategy, Delaney Lund Knox Warren

Revitalising brands is big news. The world is currently watching to see whether the likes of Sainsbury's, Marks & Spencer, WHSmith and Boots can revitalise their businesses. Much current venture capital and private equity activity involves the purchase and attempted revitalisation of underperforming brands. Burger King, Debenhams, Weetabix, Typhoo, BHS, Topshop and Homebase are all examples not just of strategies for more cost-efficient operations but for brand revitalisation.

Revitalisations are big business because, if successful, they can generate far faster and greater returns than the launch of new brands. Existing brands have existing customer franchises, distribution and consumer goodwill. Revitalising equities can pay back fast.

The term 'brand revitalisation' covers a multitude of sins, however. Some use it to denote a change of ad campaign or imagery, some to describe more profound product or service surgery. More recently, 'root-and-branch' rebranding has also come to fit the description. This is arguably a response to the industry's growing suspicion that – in today's world of communications literacy and multiple consumer touchpoints – surface revitalisation is not enough, except in the most image-led, ad-led of categories,

Types of revitalisation

The IPA Grand Prix winners that are best described as brand revitalisations straddle three decades and fit neatly into this schematic:

John Smith's Bitter, 1982	Image only
TSB, 1986	Image plus substance
O$_2$, 2004	Complete reinvention

'Image only' brand revitalisations
The John Smith's Bitter case is an excellent example of how to revitalise your brand purely through a change of image. The case describes how John Smith's had fallen behind Tetley's in its Yorkshire heartland as a result of Tetley's positive associations with 'hand-pumped' and therefore 'cask-conditioned, real ale', and John Smith's brand imagery becoming static, older, more traditional and taken for granted.

John Smith's had a choice: to invest in installing cask-conditioning capacity (i.e. brand revitalisation via image and substance) or just to change brand imagery. This case demonstrates how pursuing the latter was a profitable route to restoring share.

The reason that John Smith's was able to achieve a successful revitalisation of the brand via 'image only' was, as the authors note:

> *because of the significance of brand imagery in brand choice ... beer drinking is essentially social and group pressures can be strong. The public selection of a brand of beer reflects the buyer's self-image in the same way as choice of cigarettes, clothes or car. Buyers want to feel that they are making ... a choice that reflects well upon them as knowledgeable beer drinkers.*

The other successful ingredient of the John Smith's brand revitalisation was the 'leveraging of existing equity'. John Smith's didn't ignore its Yorkshire heritage, or the generics of the bitter-drinking market; rather it made them relevant and contemporary. As the authors note:

> *The communication, most importantly, should be that while John Smith's remained proud of its Yorkshire heritage, it was nonetheless as successful, popular and right today as it had ever been.*

The 'Big John' idea blended brand and drinker to synthesise John Smith's as a 'big' pint, flavourful and strong, and the drinker as a popular character, an aspirational real drinking man. This was executed with 'the modern elements of "the Big Bad John" music, humour and special effects'.

The 2002 Marmite case also demonstrates how a brand revitalisation can occur through 'image alone'. In addition, it illustrates the need for focus when attempting brand revitalisation. By focusing only on 'lapsed adult users' and even more specifically 'lapsed pre-family adult users', Marmite was able to turn a brand that 'is taken for granted by its users (in the store cupboard but not top of mind) into a national icon via a groundbreakingly honest description of its taste – "you either hate it or you love it".' Marmite's sales uplift of £47m was the direct result of an investment of £12m behind a completely different, and very brave, way of depicting the brand image of Marmite.

Brand revitalisation through 'image alone' is particularly feasible where image is the primary consumer brand decision-making criterion (e.g. beer, fashion, cigarettes). It is also feasible where the brand is a 'low-risk/

'expenditure' purchase (e.g. most packaged goods: see the 1998 Colgate case). The 2000 Lurpak case is of interest because it describes a brand revitalisation achieved by combining a change of 'brand image' (the more 'sophisticated' butter) with the launch of a more modern, relevant variant (Lurpak spreadable). Which takes us neatly on to ...

'Image and substance' brand revitalisations

The TSB case is a classic 'image and substance' revitalisation. It is nigh on impossible to achieve a successful revitalisation of a service company or a retailer without a change in both substance and image. M&S, Sainsbury's, WHSmith and Boots' current travails couldn't be fixed just by a change in brand image; it has to be accompanied by a change in brand 'experience' too.

The TSB case shows how it was able to revitalise its brand among the school-leaver market and treble its share of the youth market. Crucial to this brand revitalisation though, was the substance behind it. Not only was the youth school-leaver's image of TSB changed but the advertising was actually promising concrete benefits – most notably, free banking and music discounts.

The same need for substance in brand revitalisations is writ large in the 2000 Tesco case. As described more fully in Chapter 10, the 'Every Little Helps' campaign was built around initiatives – baby-changing facilities, one-in-front checkout-opening system, the Clubcard, the Value range, and so on. Key to revitalising the brand was the revitalising of the service, product and value offer. The brand image 'Every Little Helps' articulated these initiatives into a coherent customer-focused brand strategy.

Equally, the 2002 Halifax case describes how financial services advertising, in particular, is guilty of trying to revitalise brands through 'image alone'. Halifax's 'Staff as Stars' campaign demonstrates its commitment to 'Always giving you extra' not just by making its staff seem 'friendly, approachable and trustworthy' but also by having them extol the merits of products that offer outstanding value versus the competition.

The need for brand revitalisations to be built in substance, as mentioned earlier, is also important for brands that are 'high-risk' purchases, such as cars. The 2002 Skoda case perfectly demonstrates the powerful alchemy of substance and image in revitalising Skoda. Not for one moment did VW, Skoda's new owner, think that a brand revitalisation could take place without a step-change in the quality of cars being produced. And, indeed, the Felicia, Octavia and Fabia were all testament to this, garnering numerous awards and praise from the motoring press. But as the case demonstrates, it wasn't until an attendant change in the broader consumer image of the brand took place – as famously achieved by the 'It's a Skoda. Honest' campaign – that a full revitalisation of the brand occurred.

Complete brand reinvention

The 2004 O_2 case is unique in that it demonstrates that the most effective way to revitalise the BT Cellnet brand was, in fact, to create an entirely new brand. On the demerger of mmO_2 plc from BT it was decided that Cellnet had fallen too far behind, particularly Orange and Vodafone, and was too mired in its 'technology'-ridden culture and behaviour to make conventional 'brand revitalisation' even possible. As the authors note:

> *Although well known, [BT Cellnet] lacked a clear identity and had little sense of forward momentum ... it had been unable to make its market-leading technology count with the consumer ... morale was flagging ... it was struggling on all the key metrics – new connections, total subscriber base, non-voice transactions, ARPU and revenue.*

The only solution was a brand rebirth.

The O_2 brand was built on two key foundations: 'custom building a brand for the times' and 'full integration'. Both are lessons in how to fast-track brand revitalisation.

A brand for the times

'Custom building a brand for the times' allowed O_2 to take advantage of the fact that the historically most appealing brand in the sector, Orange, had failed to move on from its mid-1990s heyday. Equally, both Vodafone and new entrant T-Mobile, were constrained by their pan-European brand legacies and operating models. To O_2's core market (British 16 to 34 year olds) mobile phones are what lager brands were to the 1980s and 1990s – part of how you define yourself, a badge you wear and, indeed, carry with you and hold in your hand at all times. Orange had had this badge appeal but was losing it. In a market where consumer decision-making is a function of a unique mix of technology, looks and fashion, there was a surprising window of opportunity to build a brand specifically for the new millennium. This O_2 did with a modern and relevant insight into how people were using their phones.

Rather than pontificate about the fact that no one could possibly have predicted the astonishing growth in texting, O_2 embraced the fact that – to its target market – texting was a bigger deal than calling. O_2 was a brand built for the text generation. Note the fact that all of its sponsorships have texting at their heart – *Big Brother* voting, Arsenal's man of the match, etc. When picture messaging arrived, O_2 didn't mention 2.5G. It stimulated and suggested social behaviour but, ultimately, viewed itself as an 'enabler' not a 'prescriber'. Better than any other brand today, it understands the significance of mobile phones to its target, and how they use them.

Total integration: a fast track to brand revitalisation

The second lesson we can learn from the O_2 case study is the merit of 'total integration'. O_2 understood that to build a new brand from scratch, fast, would require not just fast-track awareness and image but actually getting existing customers to use their phones more, persuading people to switch networks and getting others to want to switch networks. All of this had to be done together, at the same time. Not sequentially or in parallel.

O_2 recognised that its target was more visually literate than conceptually literate, and that a fresh, modern look and feel used everywhere would build brand awareness and image faster than any other type of communication. The 'bubble' iconography is instant, branded aspiration. Further, it acknowledged that communications had to drive behaviour, not just awareness and image. Eighty per cent of its communication spend is behind price, product or offer, and every attempt is made to make these offers proprietorial or branded as opposed to generic.

Food for thought

- Start with what are the key decision-making drivers in your category. Are they image, salience, value, service, performance, taste?
- If image/salience are the sole drivers, then a successful brand image campaign alone can achieve brand revitalisation. This is likely to be true of image-based categories and low-risk purchases.
- If substance is a driver – most retail, service companies, high-risk purchases – brand revitalisation cannot occur by changing brand image alone.
- If the brand is well and truly broken, only a new brand might do.

John Smith's Bitter
The 'Big John' campaign: advertising in the beer market

Grand Prix winner 1982

Introduction

This paper attempts to show how the 'Big John' advertising campaign boosted John Smith's Bitter's brand share among Yorkshire beers and helped to increase sales at a time of market decline.

As the £6bn beer market has fallen into decline under the effects of the recession, the fight for brand share has intensified and the brewers have increased their advertising expenditure. In 1981 they spent well over £40m on television alone, of which more than £12m went to promote bitters such as John Smith's, an increase over 1980 of some 60%. While this expenditure does not appear to expand the market, it is clearly believed to influence drinkers' brand choice. To determine whether it can do so is the aim of this paper.

With John Smith's Bitter we were fortunate. The number of variables was smaller than usual. Courage and John Smith's have good data from a wide variety of sources over several years, so we were able to measure sales (and consumer response) before the advertising and after, and in the advertised area against non-advertised areas. Thus we were able to estimate the incremental sales stimulated by advertising.

Abridged version of the original case study written in 1982 by Tim Broadbent and James Best (BMP) for Courage.

The study is chiefly concerned with brand sales through John Smith's 'tied' public houses. This is for three reasons: retail (pub) sales account for the bulk of brand volume at a secure margin; the brand's problems were most evident in this sector; and better data are available to us for the tied trade than for the 'free' (club) trade.

Background

The brewery
John Smith's brewery was founded in 1758 and taken over by Courage in 1970. It still produces all its own beers at Tadcaster, Yorkshire. John Smith's 1500 pubs are widespread across the north of England, and account for 15% of all pubs in the heartland of Yorkshire. Tied houses account for some 60% of total sales; the remainder goes through the free trade (mainly clubs). These proportions are roughly in line with those of other major brewers.

The brand
John Smith's Bitter accounts for about half of the company's total sales and is sold in every John Smith's pub. It is a well-established Yorkshire beer, whose formulation was last altered in the mid-1970s. It is a medium-strength, session bitter with an original gravity of 1036°.

The competition
John Smith's chief rivals among the major brewers, who account for some 80% of the Yorkshire market, comprise: Tetley (Allied), with 14% of Yorkshire pubs and a massive free trade presence; Stones (Bass), 16%; Whitbread, 11%; and Webster (Grand Metropolitan), 7%. Competition is fierce: draught bitters accounted for some 30% of all Yorkshire TV beer advertising, against some 20% in England and Wales (1981).

The problem

John Smith's Bitter's volume sales started to fall in 1979, even though the Bitter I market was static. The decline was due to lost pub sales. Sales in the so-called free trade (the largely finance-dependent clubs) continued to grow, reflecting distribution increases (Table 1).

The pub share decline in 1979 represented a loss of 5.7 million pints (worth some £1.9m at 1979 retail prices).

Table 1: John Smith's Bitter trade performance 1976–1980 (1976 = 100)				
	12 months to December			6 months to June
	1977	**1978**	**1979**	**1980**
John Smith's volume share of:				
Pubs (%)	100.7	100.7	95.4	95.4
Free trade (%)	99.5	107.4	113.8	127.4

Base: major brewers, north-east
Source: BMS

The BMS north-east region includes Yorkshire and Tyne-Tees. Company sales figures, collected on a regional basis from 1979, show that the 1980 sales decline was in Yorkshire. Non-Yorkshire sales were growing, reflecting pub acquisitions (Table 2).

Table 2: John Smith's Bitter volume sales (pubs) by region, 1979–1980	
12 months to October 1979 (fiscal year)	**Percentage change 1980 vs 1979**
Yorkshire (75%)	-4
Non-Yorkshire (25%)	+7

Source: Courage

We turned to consumer research to understand what appeared to be a consumer problem with the brand.

Understanding the consumer problem

We conducted ten group discussions in June 1980 when reappointed to the brand. The sample comprised regular drinkers of both John Smith's and competitive bitters, in five Yorkshire towns covering strong and weak John Smith's trading areas.

Findings were consistent across locations. Essentially, John Smith's Bitter lacked character. Although acceptable to most drinkers, it did not arouse enthusiasm among its users. It was known to be local and long-established (both positive attributes), but so were its competitors. It was regarded merely as 'one of' Yorkshire's bitters, while Tetley's was the paradigm, especially

Table 3: Claimed 'most often' drunk brand of bitter (18–24 year olds in brackets)			
	1974	1978	1980
Base: total sample	449	314	264
Percentage of total sample			
John Smith's	10 (13)	9 (10)	6 (5)
Tetley's	19 (19)	27 (34)	29 (32)
Trophy	–	9 (9)	11 (9)
Stones	–	9 (6)	12 (14)

Base: all male bitter drinkers weekly or more often
Source: Marplan, Yorks

among young drinkers, who saw John Smith's as an 'old boy's drink'. Younger drinkers in particular spoke highly of hand-pumped Tetley's (the consumer symbol for cask-conditioned, traditional 'real ale'). We deal with this important point in more detail later.

Survey data corroborated these findings (Table 3). The measures reflected but exaggerated the sales loss among drinkers in general, and young drinkers in particular.

The 'most often' drinkers appeared to decline much more than sales. This, we believe, is because the 'most often' claim measures both behaviour and consumer preference – a greater propensity to think of the brand as 'my brand' when asked a market research question like this. Thus the loss of 'most often' drinkers reflected the loss of commitment to the brand among its users, evident in the group discussions.

In particular, we seemed to have a problem with young drinkers in Yorkshire. The importance of the younger drinkers is threefold: they tend to consume more bitter than older people; they go to more pubs and are more willing to try different drinks; and they represent the market's future and will retain, in later years, the tastes they now develop.

Reasons for loss of young drinkers
There seemed to be two factors affecting the decline in young drinkers. First, there was a change in the market. This period saw the northern revival of hand-pumped, cask-conditioned 'real ales' from major brewers, of whom Tetley's was at the forefront. Hand-pumped bitter showed significant share growth: +3% year on year.

The demand for hand-pumped ales is most prevalent among young drinkers. However, John Smith's Bitter was not available in hand-pumped form; John Smith's brewery produces only 'bright' (keg) beers, so the brand could not profit from the new trend among young drinkers.

The second factor was a decline in John Smith's Bitter's share of advertising voice. Moreover, its advertisements had stressed the brand's 'Yorkshire heritage' during the 1970s, and similar claims had been adopted by other bitters, so that confusion existed in consumer recall of particular brands' campaigns.

In conclusion, we believed that sales were down because the brand had declined in appeal, particularly to young drinkers, who had lost interest. It lacked hand-pumps, and the advertising had failed to offer something new in the face of heavy competition from similar bitter campaigns and more exciting lager commercials.

The case for advertising

The marketing objective was to increase volume sales. Various options were assessed. Installing cask-conditioned capacity at the brewery and hand-pump facilities in the pubs was judged not to be financially justifiable.

The 18–24s appeared to be the most volatile group in terms of brand imagery and choice, and produced the greatest volume return for a given proportional change. If brand advertising could regain the loyalty of only a small proportion of these drinkers, share would be regained, and with that would follow benefits for total pub revenue.

The advertising

The task was to create a more relevant brand image for John Smith's Bitter (without any changes to the product or its presentation at point of sale), which would give the brand greater appeal in the face of increasingly aggressive competition.

Objectives
The main objective was to restore the commitment of John Smith's Bitter drinkers to the brand, thus increasing their frequency of purchase.

The secondary objective was to attract lapsed drinkers, both those who had switched to other pubs and those who had adopted other brands in the free trade.

The role of advertising

These objectives were realistic because of the significance of brand imagery in brand choice, particularly among younger drinkers. Beer drinking is essentially social and group pressures can be strong. The public selection of a brand of beer reflects the buyer's self-image in the same way as choice of cigarettes, clothes or car. Buyers want to feel that they are making a sensible, defensible choice that reflects well upon them as knowledgeable beer drinkers. This can override actual taste preference; the brewery adage that 'people drink with their eyes' has been repeatedly confirmed by blind and branded product tests, where the brand names can reverse the preferences expressed 'blind'.

The under-30s tend not to be beer experts: they are too young. Their drinking is more influenced by what is popular and fashionable among their peer group. With them, the problem was to find a brand personality for John Smith's Bitter that could match the appeal of hand-pumped rivals, be talked about in the pubs, and revive their confidence in the brand.

Target market

The primary target market was defined as young bitter drinkers (18–30, C1C2D). They were the most frequent buyers, the future market, the least enthusiastic about John Smith's Bitter and the most interested in advertising.

The brief

As a mainstream brand in the biggest sector of the beer market, John Smith's Bitter had, to some extent, to be all things to all men: its advertising had to express the essential qualities of a major Yorkshire bitter, and attach them unmistakably to John Smith's.

The execution, therefore, needed to be masculine, sociable, working-class and pub-based; drinkers in the commercials must really want the beer and be seen to enjoy it.

The tone should be assertive and the style contemporary, so that it could rival lager advertising in its appeal to young drinkers.

The communication, most importantly, should be that while John Smith's remained proud of its Yorkshire heritage, it was nonetheless as successful, popular and right today as it had ever been. Drinkers of the brand, we wanted consumers to believe, were not the 'old boys' of current criticism, but admirable drinking men who knew their beer.

The campaign

The creative solution was the 'Big John' idea. This stemmed from the fact that drinkers often ask for 'a pint of John's' at the bar. The advertising aimed to create the impression of John Smith's Bitter as a 'big' pint – popular, widespread, drunk by everyone. 'Big' also implied a flavourful and strong pint.

The ingenuity of the campaign came from the blend of brand and drinker: 'Big John' was also a character, a real drinking man.

Classic values were expressed through the pubs and their signs, the traditional occupations of the characters, and the role of the beer as reward and refreshment after labour. 'Yorkshireness' was not overt – a reversal of earlier campaigns and a distinction from most competitors.

The modern elements of the 'Big Bad John' music, humour and special effects, gave the idea its freshness and strong branding. The music track was faithful to the original country-and-western song, well-known by drinkers when tested.

Media

Television was chosen as the sole medium. John Smith's Bitter needed to establish a major advertising presence. Also, the chosen strategy involved a change to the brand's perceived character, which only television was felt able to achieve quickly.

Four bursts ran in Yorkshire. Timing was related to market seasonality and to cost-efficient time periods. Weight was determined by the media budget available (£250,000) and deemed sufficient at over 1500 male TVRs during 1981.

With the launch of the new campaign, John Smith's Bitter's weight and share of advertising expenditure in Yorkshire rose substantially, returning to historic levels.

Response to the advertising

Three stages of qualitative research were carried out by BMP to confirm the relevance and appeal of the strategy, and to develop the executions. Post-campaign qualitative research revealed that the desired communications were being achieved (as they were during pre-testing). The following verbatim quotations from the group discussions illustrate the consumer response to 'Big John'.

The beer:

> *It's a big pint, it's good value with a good taste.* (Leeds, 18–30)
>
> *It goes down big and it sells a lot.* (Doncaster, 25–40)
>
> *It says the beer's strong, a man's drink.* (York, 18–24)

The drinker:

> *It's drunk by big and manly chaps.* (Leeds, 30–45)
>
> *It's a masculine ad, all macho.* (York, 25–40)
>
> *They're aimed at a big lad who's been knocking down a tree and wants to get down to tap room.* (Leeds, 18–30)

The brewer:

> *It shows that John Smith's are still in business, still as good as ever was, as traditional as ever was.* (Leeds, 30–45)
>
> *It's big John Smith.* (Leeds, 18–30)

Source: BMP Qualitative

The post-campaign research also indicated positive improvements in the brand's status. A year earlier, John Smith's was simply overlooked, and placed among the crowd of lesser brands, behind Tetley's. But now its drinkers displayed considerable enthusiasm for the brand, and even most Tetley's drinkers acknowledged it as an acceptable choice. Nor was it seen particularly as an 'old boy's drink' – it was for everyone, young and old.

The 'Big John' campaign seemed to have affected this attitudinal shift more than any other factor. Drinkers vastly enjoyed the advertising and saw the advertiser (John Smith's) in a new light:

They're new and something different, not run of the mill adverts like the others. (Leeds, 18–30)

The Woodman one was brilliant. They're trendy and they're always bringing them up to date. (York, 18–24)

Source: BMP Qualitative

The effects of advertising: sales

The campaign appeared to work in terms of increased sales, and also the intermediate measures we would expect.

The brand's volume sales in its Yorkshire pubs rose in 1981 by 4.8%, even though the Bitter I market there declined by 7.7%. Market share thus increased to its highest ever level, from 97.2 in 1980 to 105.5 in 1981 (1976 = 100). Year on year, the share improvement continued throughout 1981, although the greatest growth was seen in the first quarter, when the heaviest advertising took place.

The difference between the 1979 and 1981 shares represented additional sales of 10.3 million pints, worth some £5.1m at 1981 retail prices.

The additional effect of the campaign on free trade sales is hard to measure as distribution increased, but the brand's share rose from 100 in 1980, to 114 in 1981.

Comparing sales in the advertised area with those in John Smith's other trading regions, the turnaround in Yorkshire looked all the more remarkable, as sales growth slowed elsewhere (Table 4).

We examined other possible explanations for the rise in sales, as follows:

Table 4: John Smith's Bitter volume sales (pubs) by region, 1980–1981		
	% change year on year	
12 months to Oct. 1980 (fiscal year)	**1980**	**1981**
Yorkshire (75%)	-4	+5
Non-Yorkshire (25%)	+7	+3

Source: Courage

Table 5: Claimed 'most often' drunk brand of bitter (18–24s in brackets)				
	Yorkshire		Non-Yorkshire	
	1980	1982	1980	1982
Base: total sample	264	412	540	797
Percentage of total sample				
John Smith's	6 (5)	19 (19)	3 (3)	4 (3)
Tetley's	29 (32)	30 (32)	11 (12)	13 (8)
Trophy	11 (9)	9 (10)	5 (6)	4 (4)
Stones	12 (14)	10 (11)	4 (3)	7 (6)

Note: non-Yorks = North-West/Lancs plus Tyne-Tees
Source: Marplan

- Distribution: static in Yorkshire; volume improvements were attributable to increased consumer offtake.
- Pub standards: investment in the estate and improvements in licensee selection continued, and both are probably more significant than advertising in the long term; however, Yorkshire pubs did not receive proportionately more attention than non-Yorkshire ones.
- Price: in line with competition.

Consumer research helped us identify a causal link between the advertising and increased sales (see Table 5).

As with the decline, the rise in claimed 'most often' brand share reflects the Yorkshire sales increase but exaggerates it, suggesting an increase in preference as well as actual consumption. Such a large increase may seem incredible, but our confidence that the measures reflect a real change in our drinkers' loyalty to John Smith's was confirmed by the stability of the non-Yorkshire John Smith's and the competitive brand figures.

In claimed behaviour, it seemed that the advertising had more effect on the younger drinker. The proportion of loyal drinkers who were aged 18–24 came back into line with other brands (see Table 6).

Summary

In a market where advertising can seldom be confidently shown to have an effect on volume, this campaign seems to have succeeded in restoring sales growth to John Smith's Bitter cost-efficiently. Whereas in 1980, drinkers

Table 6: 18–24s as proportion of 'most often' plus 'regular' drinkers		
	1980 (%)	1982 (%)
John Smith's Yorkshire	14	21
Non-Yorkshire	22	20
Tetley's	23	23
Trophy	23	23
Stones	24	21

Source: Marplan

appeared to be losing their confidence in the brand and transferring their loyalty to competitors, sales and their claimed behaviour in 1982 indicated renewed commitment to John Smith's Bitter. This turnaround was reflected in drinkers' improved attitudes to the brand on scales relevant to the advertising content.

These improvements in sales, claimed drinking and brand imagery were largely confined to Yorkshire, the only area to receive substantial media support throughout 1981. Competitive brands did not enjoy similar improvements, and indeed the bitter market as a whole declined in the area, in contrast to John Smith's growth.

Qualitative and quantitative consumer research studies underline the role of advertising in stimulating the brand's success. The absence of any identifiable changes in the marketing mix or retail environment, apart from advertising investment and content, help to confirm this role. A total investment of some £300,000 in television advertising thus contributed to a revenue increase for John Smith's draught bitter of some £5m in the pub trade alone, while free trade growth continued, all in a declining market. The profitability of such a return on investment in the tied trade alone is assured.

We believe that, by rejuvenating the brand's imagery among younger bitter drinkers in particular, so that they could confidently claim it as their pint in a sales environment where social pressures predominate, the 'Big John' campaign played a significant part in this improved performance.

TSB's school-leaver campaign 1984–1985

Grand Prix winner 1986

Background

The TSB has its origins in the Industrial Revolution and in the development of independent trustee savings banks operating as small savings institutions.

Today's TSB offers the full range of services of a major banking and financial group, and competes on equal terms with other major high-street banks.

This case history deals with one particular marketing operation out of the many that the TSB conducts: the recruitment of new customers among school-leavers.

Recruitment strategy

The TSB Group handles more than 13 million accounts on behalf of some 6 million customers. The profile of this customer base is less middle-class than the other high-street banks, understandable given the origins of the TSB and its reputation as the 'people's bank'. Less understandable – and a source of concern – is the fact that the customer profile is also older.

The high-street banks compete intensely for share of new accounts opened. Since the main opportunity to recruit new customers is to catch them when

Abridged version of the original case study written by Jeremy Elliott (J Walter Thompson) for TSB.

they first need banking services, this competition is directed chiefly at the youth market. Half the new cheque accounts opened each year are owned by people under the age of 25.

To redress the imbalance in its age profile, the TSB needed to gain an above-average share of new youth accounts. But there was a severe problem. The other banks had traditionally directed most of their activity towards the student market. These young people, it was judged, would become valued customers in the future. But TSB's share of the student market was weak, largely because of a lack of accessible on-campus branches.

In 1983, the TSB decided that the investment needed to raise its share of the student market could not be justified. Instead, it decided to focus attention on the remaining three in four school-leavers who were not going on to higher education and were available for full-time employment. Members of this group might not present as good a potential source of profitable business in the future as the students, but in quantity they amply made up for any shortfall in quality. Moreover, much less marketing activity from the banks as a whole had been addressed specifically to school-leavers. They presented a relatively untapped opportunity.

The marketing strategy for youth recruitment in 1984/85 was defined as follows:

- *Target audience*, namely 15- to 19-year-old school-leavers:
  - going into full-time employment (primary target)
  - going on to higher education (secondary target).
- *Objectives*:
  - increase the number of new cheque accounts opened by school-leavers with the TSB (progress in 1984 led to a more specific target of 79,000 new accounts in 1985)
  - increase total awareness and, in particular, the salience (unprompted awareness) of TSB among the target audience
  - enhance the TSB's image as efficient, warm, friendly and welcoming to school-leavers.

Communications strategy

School-leavers are tugged in different directions. On the one hand, they need to demonstrate their new independence (from school and parental 'authority') by publicly rejecting the mores of the previous generations. On the other hand, having money of one's own, and being able to handle it sensibly, are also outward symbols of being adult and independent. Banks are regarded with a mixture of respect (they are experts) and fear (they appear forbidding and difficult to approach).

We therefore needed a communications strategy that would dissipate the fear without damaging the respect. We had one advantage. The TSB image was less firmly fixed in the traditional bank mould than its competitors. It was already less unapproachable. We could capitalise on this if we could find a language that struck a chord.

The solution adopted was a carefully tailored mix of a promotional package, conventional media advertising and a new and unconventional medium.

Promotional package

A package of incentives when you first open a cheque account is usual in this market. Aimed primarily at students, such incentives have typically included free railcards and temporary overdraft facilities at special rates of interest. For school-leavers a different package was devised.

In 1984 this consisted of three years' free banking plus discounts on top albums, hi-fi equipment and keyboards. For 1985 the package was further expanded to include a discount card for use in Virgin music stores, a mail-order programme offering savings on records, cassettes and videos, and discounts on Yamaha and other musical instruments.

TS Beat

Continuing the music theme, *TS Beat* was devised as a free magazine for specific and carefully targeted circulation. *TS Beat* was also made available at rock concerts and dispensed, in large quantities, through TSB branches. The magazine runs to three editions a year, and is now in its third year of publication. Total distribution has been 2.3 million in 1984 and again in 1985.

Primarily devoted to chart music matters, *TS Beat* also carries articles on financial matters for the school-leaver. And it carries advertisements for TSB banking services and promotional offers.

Conventional media advertising

The primary medium in 1984 and 1985 was television, with a commercial in the style of the overall 'The bank that likes to say Yes' campaign, but recognisably addressed to the youth market. It emphasised the free banking offer, the availability of cheque guarantee and Speedbank cash dispenser cards, and the music and Virgin discount card offers.

Magazine and radio advertisements were written in the language of teenage culture, whereas for the TV and cinema media, with their wider audiences, the commercials were in TSB's usual brisk, modern and youthful (but not teenage) style.

Results: accounts opened

Results exceeded expectations. From a total of 33,000 new youth accounts opened in 1983, when no advertising was specifically addressed to school-leavers, the number doubled in the first year of the campaign to 66,000. The target then set for 1985 (79,000) was handsomely exceeded, with 126,000 new accounts. Figure 1 graphs the monthly results. The largest increases in both years coincided precisely with the start of television advertising.

There is one complicating factor in the data. A new monthly reporting system for youth market accounts was introduced at the start of 1985, and there is evidence that this improved the correct classification of new accounts at

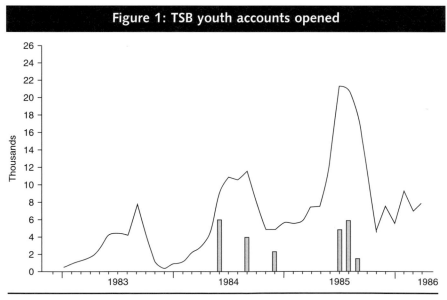

Figure 1: TSB youth accounts opened

Base: 15 to 19 year olds, England and Wales
Source: TSB

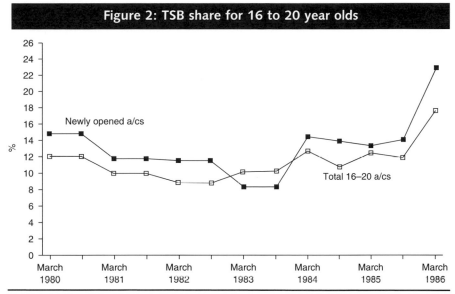

Figure 2: TSB share for 16 to 20 year olds

Source: NOP Financial Survey

branch level. But by no stretch of the imagination could this account for more than part of the recorded rise. Even if 1983/84 were somewhat under-recorded, this does not detract from the 1985 performance. In a year when 783,000 youngsters left school, of whom perhaps half would open a bank account, a recruitment score of 126,000 represents a very large share.

Consumer research confirms this. Between 1983 and 1985, TSB's share of accounts opened by 16 to 20 year olds has trebled to reach 22% (Figure 2), which has raised the bank's overall share of a market sector that has itself been growing.

Analysis of internal statistics shows that at the time of account opening:

- some 18% were still at school
- a total of 50% were in full-time employment
- some 10% were in full-time further education
- some 15% were neither studying nor in employment.

This is confirmed by market research data (Table 1). TSB's share of the student market remained weak at 5%. But share among those who had gone into employment was no less than 32%, nearly twice as high as the next best bank.

Table 1: Banks' share of school-leavers' accounts, 1985		
	In first year of full-time employment (%)	In first year of further education (%)
Have current account with:		
TSB	32	5
Bank A	18	27
Bank B	14	18
Bank C	13	34
Bank D	12	23

Source: Millward Brown School Leavers' Study; RSL Student Banking Survey

How did it work?

Awareness

Consumer awareness and knowledge of TSB has not kept up with its remarkable metamorphosis over the last two decades into a major full-service bank. Spontaneous awareness of TSB, for instance, has lagged behind the other high-street banks.

Among school-leavers, however, there have been marked changes during 1984–85. Spontaneous awareness of the bank is catching up (Figure 3).

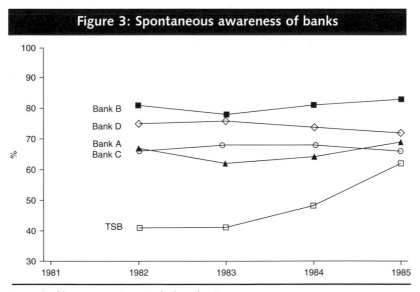

Base: school-leavers not going on to further education
Source: Millward Brown

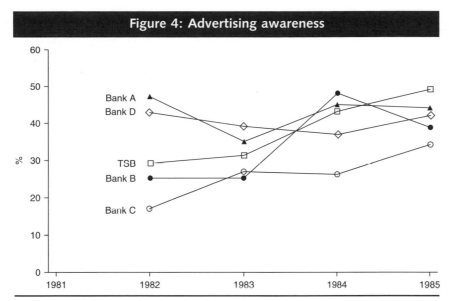

Figure 4: Advertising awareness

Base: school-leavers not going on to further education
Source: Millward Brown

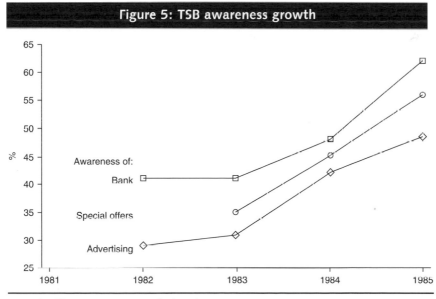

Figure 5: TSB awareness growth

Base: school-leavers not going on to further education
Source: Millward Brown

Table 2: Awareness of special schemes for school-leavers			
	1983 (%)	1984 (%)	1985 (%)
Aware of schemes offered by:			
TSB	35	45	56
Bank A	20	22	28
Bank B	22	46	46
Bank C	10	16	21
Bank D	16	21	21

Base: school-leavers not going on to higher education
Source: Millward Brown

Awareness of TSB advertising has overhauled the field (Figure 4). And awareness of TSB's promotional schemes for school-leavers has risen higher than any of the competitors (Table 2).

Comparing all three indices (Figure 5) shows the close correlation between the rise in spontaneous awareness of TSB and the rises in awareness of its advertising and promotional activity. Correlation, of course, does not prove causation, but it is difficult to see how awareness of the bank could have risen except as a result of its advertising and promotions, which are its public face. Few 'unbanked' school-leavers ever go into bank premises.

Why school-leavers chose TSB
While successfully retaining the loyalty of most of the teenagers whose parents banked with the TSB, we also succeeded in breaking down, to a markedly greater extent than any other bank, the second-generation loyalty of those whose parents banked with competitors (Table 3).

Table 3: Second-generation banking					
Parents bank with:	TSB (%)	Bank A (%)	Bank B (%)	Bank C (%)	Bank D (%)
School-leavers bank with:					
TSB	68	24	24	26	19
Bank A	7	47	20	15	21
Bank B	4	9	28	20	9
Bank C	7	6	11	31	7
Bank D	6	6	7	8	34

Base: school-leavers in full-time employment, with current account, 1985
Source: Millward Brown

Table 4: Main reasons for choosing bank					
	Total mentions				
	TSB (%)	Bank A (%)	Bank B (%)	Bank C (%)	Bank D (%)
Contact/recommendation	87	114	111	119	98
Help young people	70	33	33	32	14
Offered free banking	45	61	22	27	16
Convenience	43	55	69	55	68
Saw/heard advertising	23	22	8	11	5

Base: school-leavers in full-time employment, 1985
Source: Millward Brown

Recommendation by parents or friends is probably the single most important factor affecting choice of bank. It is also a relatively weak point for TSB because of the older customer base. Research (Table 4) showed that we had overcome this weakness, by:

- appearing more helpful and approachable than any other bank, and offering appropriate and desirable incentives
- registering the free banking offer clearly
- communicating these facts and impressions through the advertising more effectively than most other banks.

Teenagers chose TSB because they noticed the communications, they liked what the bank was offering them and they felt more at ease about approaching the TSB than other banks.

For recent school-leavers who had not yet opened a bank account, the TSB was at least the equal of any other bank (Table 5), and markedly superior on friendliness, being interested in people even if they did not have much money, and being a good bank to save with.

This image appears to have been built up by all elements of the marketing programme working together as a whole. Awareness was high for *TS Beat* and for the discounts, as well as free banking and money-handling advice for school leavers (Table 6). All demonstrated the bank's understanding of teenagers' interests and needs.

Table 5: Images of banks					
	TSB (%)	Bank A (%)	Bank B (%)	Bank C (%)	Bank D (%)
Up to date	51	38	54	28	36
Interested in helping school-leavers	46	18	45	16	17
A good bank to save with	46	17	31	15	15
Understands the needs of school-leavers	44	16	41	13	15
A very friendly bank	38	31	29	12	14
Sort of bank I'd be happy to join	38	19	38	15	19
Treats young people like responsible adults	36	19	35	12	16
Interested in people even without much money	33	20	24	18	13
Good at explaining things	32	21	34	15	15
Sympathetic to customers' problems	29	15	24	10	13

Base: school-leavers without a bank account, not going on to higher education, 1985
Source: Millward Brown

TS Beat had been seen by no less than 38% of school-leavers. Comparison of those who had seen the magazine, and those who had not, showed that it contributed significantly to raising awareness of the bank, its advertising and, in particular, its special offers, and to encouraging the choice of TSB for opening an account.

All these elements combined to build a more rounded and attractive image for TSB than for any other bank. On its own, none is likely to have been as

Table 6: Awareness of special offers					
	TSB (%)	Bank A (%)	Bank B (%)	Bank C (%)	Bank D (%)
Special magazine for young people	43	10	20	6	8
Discounts on records and tapes	42	4	7	3	1
Booklet with practical help for school-leavers	35	15	30	7	11
Free banking	31	25	27	8	12
Free banking for two years	17	12	17	6	8
Cash dispenser card	23	23	35	17	22
Cheque card if employed	21	13	29	14	16
Starting work kit	13	7	17	4	5
Cheaper insurance on personal goods	9	2	6	4	5

Base: school-leavers without a bank account, not going on to higher education, 1985
Source: Millward Brown

effective. Collectively, they worked extremely well. Could we in some way disentangle and separate out their respective contributions?

What each element of the marketing programme contributed

To investigate this we turned to econometric modelling. The model finally chosen was the one we judged to make the best *marketing* sense. The model fits the data very closely (R^2 = 0.930, and see Figure 6).

Given the simultaneity of all the media advertising (as well as the difficulty of expressing the *exposure* of other media schedules with anything like the accuracy of TV ratings data) we were unable to disentangle the effects of cinema, teenage press or radio from those of television. The TV variable in the model almost certainly represents the effect of the total media mix.

The 1984 music-based incentive package was similar in effect to previous years' offers. The expanded 1985 package pulled much more strongly. But because the 1985 offer started at the same time as the new reporting system for youth accounts, it is not possible to separate the gains achieved by the incentive package from the effects of improved classification.

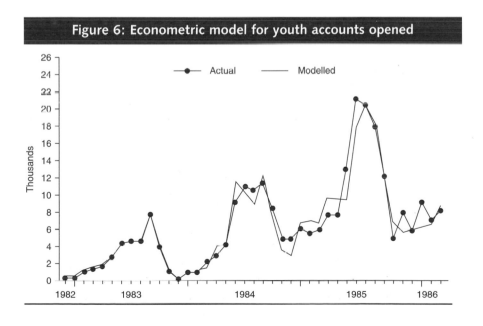

Figure 6: Econometric model for youth accounts opened

Table 7: Contributions of the elements of the campaign	
	Accounts per year
Base level (including effect of 1983/84 offers)	33,000
TS Beat (1984/85)	10,000
Advertising (TV and other media)	
■ 1984	23,000
■ 1985	27,000
The following three factors are inseparable:	
■ 1985 incentive package	
■ New account reporting system (1985)	56,000
■ Long-term cumulative advertising effect	

There are indications of a cumulative advertising effect, which the model fails to capture, but which is visible in Figure 6. In June 1984, when TV began, the actual number of accounts opened fell short of the model's predicted figure. In July 1985, however, the start of television produced an excess over prediction, implying that advertising's contribution to the mix had further increased in effectiveness.

The relative contributions of the various elements of the school-leaver campaign can be estimated as shown in Table 7.

Conclusions

We concluded that the expanded incentive package in 1985 had been a considerable success and the prime cause of the huge growth in new accounts. But it would not have worked anything like as effectively had the contents of the offer not been widely and attractively communicated to the target market.

Without advertising, the special offers would not have been widely known about. Without all the communication elements, the bank's image and salience would not have seemed so approachable and sympathetic to the school-leaver.

The campaign fulfilled all its objectives and surpassed its targets. It gave TSB the leading share of new accounts opened by school-leavers. And it won share even from households who had no previous contact with the TSB.

Total expenditure on TSB youth marketing (advertising, brochures and *TS Beat*) was £1.7m in 1985. This worked out at rather less than £14 per new account. The profitability of a new account is not usually measurable before some years have passed, but in this case it seems certain that, when the final assessment of this campaign's profitability is made, the bank will say 'Yes'.

O_2
It only works if it all works: how troubled BT Cellnet transformed into thriving O_2

Grand Prix winner 2004

O_2 is the story of a corporate transformation.

In April 2002, BT Cellnet was a troubled business, losing ground consistently to competitors. A month later it was reborn as O_2: a vibrant, modern brand that has generated a turnaround that would have been inconceivable only weeks before.

Of course, O_2 has made ongoing improvements to various structural facets of its business, but the most significant change has been the re-engineering of the brand. This case is emblematic of how brand engineering can transform not just the metrics of a business, but the morale of its staff, the esteem of its public, its ability to sustain competitive advantage and its potential to deliver future earnings.

The role of communications in this transformation is substantial. O_2's investment in communications will pay for itself more than 60 times over, generating at least £4799m incremental margin over the long term.

Over 80% of O_2's marketing funds have supported sales-driving initiatives. Yet because of its brand-centric approach to communicating these initiatives,

Abridged version of the original case study written in 2004 by Sophie Maunder and Alex Harris (VCCP), Joanna Bamford (Consultant), Louise Cook (Holmes & Cook) and Andrew Cox (O_2) for O_2.

they have been unusually effective in securing long-term sales, akin to what might typically be expected of brand communications.

O_2 also provides an excellent example of the benefits of astonishingly complete integration across channels.

The need for transformation

In November 2001, mmO_2 plc was de-merged from BT plc, creating a wholly independent holding company. The UK brand, BT Cellnet, was relaunched as O_2 in April 2002.

The new brand faced significant challenges – the market had matured, making revenue growth increasingly hard to come by. And competition for that growth was intensifying.

Tougher trading conditions
For a number of years, mobile brands had recorded significant growth on the back of a growing market. But by 2002, as penetration plateaued, revenue growth had stalled and had to be found either by enticing customers away from competitors and/or increasing average revenue per user (ARPU) – primarily by stimulating usage of non-voice services.

Competition was intensifying
The new brand had to take on well-established and well-supported competitors. Between 1994 and 2000, Orange and Vodafone had each spent around £200m on advertising.

One2One was being relaunched as T-Mobile. Then there was the imminent launch of 3 (which proved to be the heaviest advertising launch the market had seen).

The troubled legacy of BT
BT Cellnet had neither the presence of Vodafone nor the appealing image of Orange. Although well known, it lacked a clear identity and had little sense of forward momentum. Public jadedness was mirrored by low internal morale. Only 20% of staff felt that the different parts of BT Cellnet worked well together and less than half believed that management provided clear direction.

	BT Jan.–March 2001	BT Jan.–March 2002	Trend
Table 1: BT Cellnet looked vulnerable			
New connections			
Millions	1.6	0.8	
Share (%)	27.9	22.8	↓
Total subscribers			
Millions	11.2	11.1	
Share (%) post-pay	25.1	24.8	↓
pre-pay	25.9	23.6	
Non-voice transactions			
Share of text and picture messages sent (%)	18.9	27.1	↑
Data as percentage of service revenue	8.1	13.8	
ARPU			
£ (blended, 12-month rolling)	269	231	↓
As a percentage of market average	91.7	87.7	
Revenue			
Share of retail revenue (%)	23.6	21.4	↓

Source: Oftel, BT Cellnet/O$_2$

As competitors appealed to consumers more effectively and staff morale flagged, BT Cellnet looked vulnerable. Despite some success in stimulating non-voice usage, any gains in revenue as a result of this were more than offset by a fall in subscribers. Table 1 demonstrates BT Cellnet's position against key metrics.

Creating a transformatory brand

Marketing principles
Two principles have driven O$_2$'s approach:

1. Custom-building the brand for its times. Unlike T-Mobile, which effectively retrofitted onto UK operations a brand that had been developed in a different market in a different era, O$_2$ sought to build an entirely new brand, deliberately designed to maximise growth in a mature market.
2. Full integration. Market conditions dictated integration on two levels.
   - It was essential to build rapid brand awareness (to recoup the ground lost by switching from BT Cellnet to an entirely new brand).

Given O$_2$'s budgets, this would only be achieved by complete visual integration across channels.

■ The bulk of O$_2$'s marketing investment would need to be put behind revenue-driving products and tariffs. Yet at the same time it was essential to build a strong, attractive brand for the long term. The challenge for O$_2$ was how to be successful on both counts simultaneously.

The solution was to ensure complete strategic integration. The brand idea and attitude informs and shapes everything from product positioning to advertising and sponsorship, to staff conferences and trade launches.

The brand idea

From the start, customers rather than products have been at the heart of O$_2$'s approach. Consumers were tiring of pretentious or empty promises and had grown adept at identifying only those aspects of technology that were actually of relevance.

Rather than being a provider of technology or a mobile visionary, O$_2$ set out to become the most 'enabling' brand in the marketplace. The brand exists solely to provide more ways in which the customer can work, play, communicate.

Strategic integration: the brand–product–communications continuum

Other brands in this market seemed to be rather remote from their day-to-day product offering. They established an image and a personality through their brand and, almost in isolation, used their product offering (such as bonus airtime, new tariffs) in a tactical way, to drive short-term sales.

O$_2$ had neither the time nor the resource to adopt this 'parallel' approach. Rather than treating products as technical gizmos, or tariffs as tactical one-offs, O$_2$'s communications wrap them in the brand idea.

Transformation

It is now two years since O$_2$ was launched.

O$_2$ is an entirely different animal to its predecessor. It is a vibrant, healthy brand that drives consideration and growth; performance against every one of the key business metrics has been reversed.

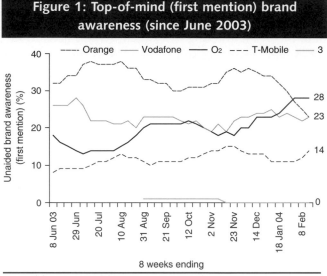

Figure 1: Top-of-mind (first mention) brand awareness (since June 2003)

Base: adults, 16–65, mobile phone owners/considerers
Source: Millward Brown

Brand awareness: O$_2$ is on the map

One of O$_2$'s most impressive achievements has been how rapidly it has established itself in the market, in contrast to both T-Mobile and 3. O$_2$ is also more salient than its predecessor. Towards the end of its seventh year of trading, top-of-mind awareness of BT Cellnet stood at 20%. After just two years, the level for O$_2$ is 28%, making O$_2$ the most salient brand in the market (Figure 1).

A relevant and compelling positioning

The consumer-led positioning of O$_2$'s products has helped make them more compelling than they would have been under BT Cellnet's manufacturer-led approach. It has also ensured that, simultaneously, O$_2$'s products have a broader impact on positive impressions of the brand:

> *Customer driven, not corporate force-feeding … In the words of one consumer, the brand appears both 'high-tech' and 'high-touch'.*
> Corr Research & Consultancy (May 2002)

> *O$_2$ has been successful in positioning itself as a fresh, contemporary, youthful and innovative player (on its own terms and relative to the rather tired and muddled landscape that is mobile communications).*
> H2 Research (April 2004)

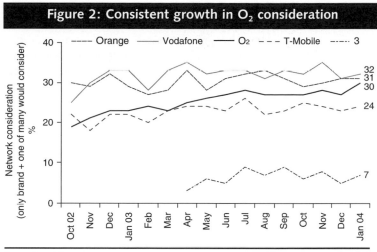

Figure 2: Consistent growth in O$_2$ consideration

Base: all mobile users
Source: NOP

This has been confirmed by tracking that shows clear blue water between O$_2$ and its traditional rivals. Only 3, with its unique 3G technology, is seen as more 'refreshingly different'.

Transformation in brand consideration
As salience and brand image have been transformed, there has been a parallel turnaround in consideration, which has grown consistently since launch (Figure 2).

Millward Brown's 'network would choose tomorrow' measure of consideration shows that O$_2$ is now the most preferred brand.

Transformation of the business
Since rebranding as O$_2$, performance against every one of the key business metrics has been transformed. The consistent increase in consideration has translated into actual behaviour (Table 2).

(It is worth noting that although O$_2$'s non-voice growth looks less spectacular than BT Cellnet's, it is actually exceptional vs the market.)

Transformation of morale
Where BT Cellnet was hindered by low staff morale, O$_2$ is aided by the enthusiasm of its staff for the new brand and its consumer orientation.

	BT Jan.–Mar. 2001	BT Jan.–Mar. 2002	Trend	O$_2$ Jan.–Mar. 2003	O$_2$ Jun.–Sep. 2003	O$_2$ Jan.–Mar. 2004*	Trend
Table 2: Key business metrics have been transformed							
New connections							
Millions	1.6	0.8	↓	0.9	1.2	NA	↑
Share (%)	27.9	22.8		24.7	26.1	NA	
Total subscribers							
Millions	11.2	11.1	↓	12.1	12.6	13.3	↑
Share (%) post-pay	25.1	24.8		25.5	26.3	NA	
pre-pay	25.9	23.6		23.7	24.2	NA	
Non-voice transactions							
Share of text and picture messages sent (%)	18.9	27.1	↑	33.1	33.4	NA	↑
Data as percentage of service revenue (12-monthly rolling)	8.1	13.8		19.4	19.4	NA	
ARPU							
£ (blended, 12-monthly rolling)	269	231	↓	247	259	272	↑
As a percentage of market average	91.7	87.7		90.8	94.4	NA	
Revenue							
Share of retail revenue (%)	23.6	21.4	↓	21.9	23.3	NA	↑

Source: Oftel, BT Cellnet/O$_2$. (Figures are for the three-month period shown.)
* Latest Oftel figures are for June–September 2003, whereas the most recent O$_2$ figures are for January–March 2004. Since Oftel is the source of competitor information, we are able to show figures up to June–September 2003 only.

Belief in the brand is confirmed by O$_2$'s internal staff survey, which shows particularly high morale among all-important retail staff.

The role of communications in transforming the business: an overview of how O$_2$'s integrated approach works

Visual integration has given O$_2$'s communications exceptional cut-through. This has been instrumental in building rapid brand awareness. It also delivers financial efficiency. Strategic integration (across the brand–product–communications continuum) has delivered product propositions that are particularly compelling. They drive not only short-term consideration, but also longer-term brand consideration. As a result, despite a heavy emphasis on what would typically be classed short-term sales-driving initiatives, O$_2$'s communications deliver the intended long-term sales effects normally expected of brand-level communication.

The role of advertising and sponsorship in transforming the business

O_2's advertising and sponsorship has been highly visible, especially when taken in the context of its share of voice.

Spontaneous awareness of O_2's advertising rose rapidly to a level enjoyed by its well-established competitors. It very quickly superseded memories of BT Cellnet advertising and is now well ahead of T-Mobile.

Sponsorship too, has been highly visible. By the end of the third series of *Big Brother*, more people associated O_2 with TV sponsorship than *Coronation Street* sponsor, Cadbury's.

Over time, O_2's combined communications have become the most memorable in the market (see Table 3).

Table 3: O_2's combined communications are the most memorable in the market	
	Total communications awareness (seen anywhere recently) 8 weeks to end January 2004 (%)
O_2	66
Vodafone	59
Orange	50
T-Mobile	46
Virgin	43
3	32

Importantly, O_2 has not simply been preaching to the converted. Getting on the radar of potential conquests is vital to share growth: 77% of those who are aware of any of O_2's combined communications are users of other networks. This level of cut-through has undoubtedly been driven by the consistent and instantly recognisable use of blue and bubbles across all O_2 activity.

> *The brand has created its own iconography – blue, bubbles and natural space.*
>
> Corr Research & Consultancy (2003)

> *Alone in this market, O_2 is synonymous with a distinctive creative device.*
>
> H2 Research (January 2003)

Figure 3: Communications gets O_2 onto the radar of potential conquests

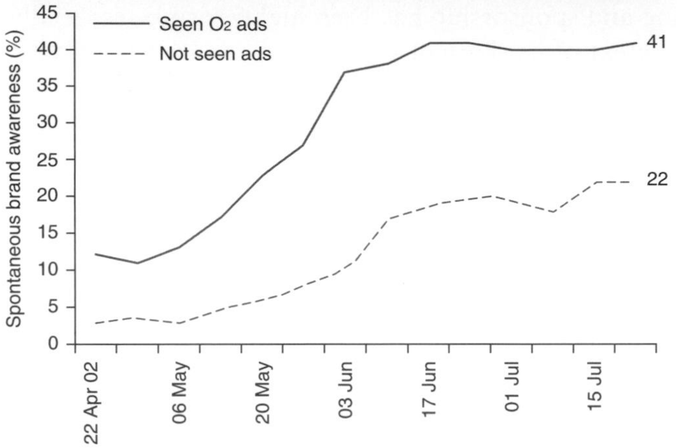

Base: high-value phone users using networks other than O_2
Source: TNS

But to what extent did this visibility impact on brand awareness?

Tracking suggests that O_2's advertising played a vital role in building brand awareness in the launch period. It is also clear that this brand awareness was generated in the minds of O_2's potential conquests (customers currently with other networks). As Figure 3 shows, among this key audience those who were aware of O_2's advertising at launch were twice as likely to be spontaneously aware of O_2.

Econometric analysis of spontaneous brand awareness confirms the significant roles played by advertising and sponsorship in building brand awareness. By the end of *Big Brother 3*, for example, around three-quarters of O_2's rapid gains in awareness could be attributed to the combined effect of advertising and sponsorship. The econometrics also show their effects are long-lasting: the gap between actual awareness and awareness without advertising widens over time as the current advertising builds on the ongoing effect of earlier advertising.

O_2's intention of communicating its products and tariffs as genuine consumer benefits, rather than just product or prices, is recognised and valued by consumers.

> *The idea of better experiences as opposed to better gizmos is understood by consumers to be at the heart of the O_2 brand message.*
>
> H2 Research (January 2003 Bolt Ons Research)

Importantly, advertising has also created the intended virtuous circle whereby product messages feed back into consumers' understanding and appreciation of the brand.

> *The advertising creates a distinctive, appealing and empathetic world for O_2 and its communications. It creates the impression of a brand that is both modern, progressive, vibrant and, crucially, believable, practical and useful.*
>
> Corr Research & Consultancy (2002)

> *Amidst the crudely tactical aspirations of the mobile telecoms market (epitomised by Vodafone) where product talk is all, the O_2 imagery is unexpected, fresh and distinctive.*
>
> H2 Research (January 2003)

This relationship between communications and brand image is confirmed by tracking, which also suggests that O_2's communications have helped drive the impression that the brand is 'refreshingly different'. Again, this is the case among potential conquests (i.e. users of other networks) as well as existing customers.

Advertising and sponsorship were instrumental in rapidly creating O_2's presence in the market and in building positive impressions of the brand. We shall now see that this translated into significantly higher consideration of the brand (Figure 4).

As so many factors influence consideration, rather than rely on tracking, we have used econometric analysis. This allows us to isolate the contribution of communications and to understand the nature of their relationship with consideration. Again we see clear evidence of not only short-term advertising effects, but also very persistent ones – and we see these coming from what are, intrinsically, product and tariff messages. The model attributes over half O_2's consideration in the year to September 2003 to advertising and sponsorship; 90% of this additional consideration is attributable to product and tariff messages.

Figure 4: Uplift in consideration generated by advertising and sponsorship

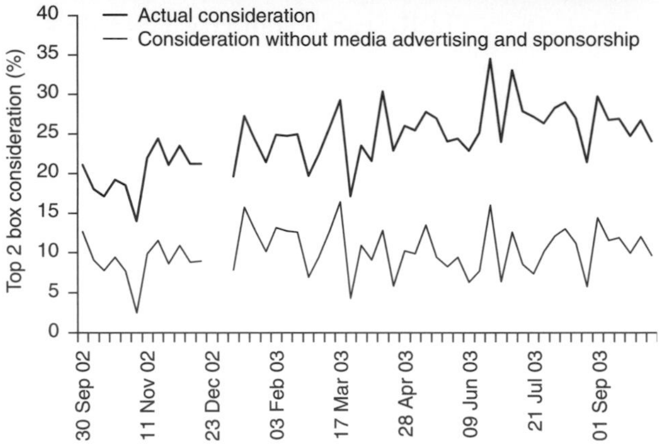

Base: incorporates non-communication effects, competitive effects and sampling error
Source: Holmes & Cook

Brand consideration has converted into an unusually high level of long-term sales

The results of the econometric analysis have very direct parallels with the consideration findings (and support the tracking findings that O_2's communications have attracted conquest customers). Again, we see that both advertising and sponsorship have not only a short-term but also a very persistent effect on sales.

Since its launch in April 2002, O_2 has generated more than a million new connections per quarter. Clearly there are many factors that have influenced this, but the econometric analysis enables us to separate the contribution of communications from that of other sources. It shows that advertising and sponsorship generated 4.1 million connections during the seven quarters from April 2002 to December 2003 (Figures 5 and 6).

As with awareness and consideration, we see the effects on sales of advertising and sponsorship dying away only slowly (by 5% from month to month). This rate of decay implies that only 46% of their total effect on sales occurs within 12 months of airtime. Thus on top of the 4.1 million extra connections generated from launch to December 2003, a further 4.5 million will occur over the lifetime of the advertising.

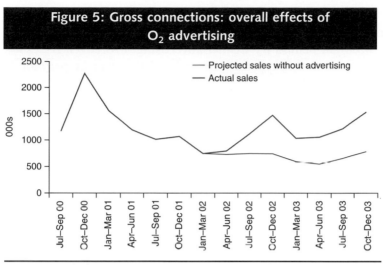

Source: Holmes & Cook

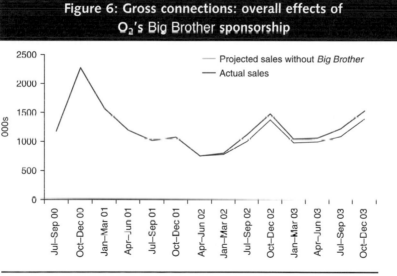

Source: Holmes & Cook

The scale of effect

To establish whether the scale of these effects might simply be typical for the market, we have compared O_2's communications performance to both BT Cellnet and two competitors.

All things being equal, gross connections attributable to O_2's advertising are 1.5 million (or 24%) higher than they would have been had the same investment been put behind BT Cellnet advertising. Moreover, BT Cellnet's advertising decayed at a faster rate than O_2's – 10% or more per month compared to 5% for O_2.

We have also compared O_2's advertising effects to effects previously reported for Orange and One2One. Comparisons need to be made sensitively, since these findings relate to the 1996–98 period when the market was much smaller. However, if new connections are expressed as a percentage of each company's subscriber base at the time of the advertising, the scale of O_2's effect is still significantly larger. This is all the more remarkable since O_2 achieved this on a lower share of voice (Table 4).

Table 4: The scale of O_2's advertising effect		
	New connections attributable to advertising (expressed as a percentage of the brand's subscriber base at the time of advertising)	SOV at time of advertising (%)
Orange (1994–98)	+8.4	30+
One2One (1994–98)	+14	21
O_2 (2002–03)	+31	18

Source: Advertising Works 10; Oftel; Holmes & Cook

The financial value of O_2's integrated approach to communications

O_2's integrated approach to communications has evidently been fundamental to the transformation of the business. We are able to place a value on both levels of integration and, more broadly, assess the overall effect of communications on shareholder value.

The value of visual integration
Millward Brown has calculated that despite an actual share of voice of 14%, O_2's effective share of voice is 33%. This implies that, had its advertising been more typical of the market, O_2 would have needed to spend more than twice as much on advertising as it actually did to achieve the same effect.

In 2002 Accenture reviewed the effectiveness of telecoms launches by assessing how long each brand took to reach its level of spontaneous brand awareness – and at what cost. No other brand achieved the same presence as rapidly or as cost effectively as O_2 (Figure 7).

> *The brand is rare in exceeding our most optimistic targets. The results are testament to the potency of the brand identity and advertising creative.*
>
> Source: Accenture MROI group

Accenture's findings provide another perspective on the financial value of O_2's communications. If O_2 had run advertising of a similar nature to BT Cellnet, it would have needed to spend three times as much as it actually did to achieve its level of awareness (and it would have taken four times as long).

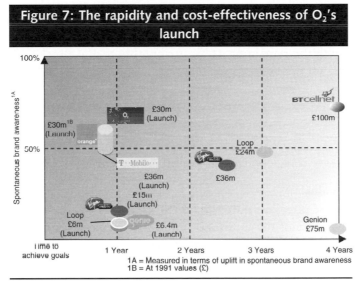

Figure 7: The rapidity and cost-effectiveness of O_2's launch

1A = Measured in terms of uplift in spontaneous brand awareness
1B = At 1991 values (£)

This analysis was conducted in September 2002 (and therefore covers O_2's first nine months, by which time it had achieved spontaneous brand awareness of 59%).
Source: Accenture MROI Group

The value of strategic integration

Because consumers generally remain with O_2 for a period of years, and because they generate revenue throughout their lifetime, only a small part of the benefit of the campaign has so far been realised. The activity that has taken place so far will continue to underpin revenue and margin for years to come.

The econometric analysis has assisted us in quantifying the relative scale of these effects. They are, first, those that have occurred from launch to December 2003 and, second, those that will come after December 2003 as a result of the advertising carryover and average lifetime value of the consumers who have been attracted to O_2.

Factors included in the payback calculation are:

- the number of connections attributed directly to communications
- the average revenue generated by each connection in any given year (ARPU)
- the average lifetime of each new connection (three to five years, depending on consumer type)
- O_2's margin
- the cost of media, production and agency fees (£78.3m).

Until December 2003 advertising and sponsorship combined generated £493m in additional margin for O_2, of which 84% was a direct result of advertising, with the remaining 16% attributable to *Big Brother*. This is a return of 6.3:1 on the money invested.

But the best is yet to come. Over the remainder of the lifetime of the advertising and sponsorship effects and new customers, a further £4.799bn in additional margin is expected. The ultimate payback is thus expected to be 62:1.

Shareholder value
The mmO_2 share price has outperformed the FTSE 100, Vodafone, Orange and BT. The success of the O_2 brand in the UK has been fundamental to this performance, with industry experts agreeing:

> As services have become more or less interchangeable, it has been the skill of marketing and not the size of the operator that has made the difference. O_2 has shaken off its leaden Cellnet image and achieved a remarkable transformation. They have not needed to be vastly big to do it. What they have had to do is understand the values that the young people in the market appreciate, deliver those and motivate the employees to live the brand.
>
> *Evening Standard* (23 April 2004)

> *A fundamental part of the value O_2 now commands resides in the brand. This is now a key asset to the company, and significantly enhances our value to shareholders.*
>
> Sohail Qadri, Head of Strategy (and plc Board Member) mmO_2

In February 2004, mmO_2 became the target of a takeover bid from KPN, which valued the company at £9.5bn. The offer was rejected. The turnaround in fortunes demonstrated by mmO_2's latest results has vindicated that decision. As the *FT* put it, mmO_2's 'miraculous turnaround' explains 'why KPN could barely contain its eagerness to capture the bride in February – and why mmO_2 refused the offer.'

Perhaps the final word should go to Hans Snook, founder of Orange:

> *They have done a superb job. They have done a superb job on branding.*
>
> *The Times* (February 2004)

Defying commoditisation in your market

Chapter 8

Richard Storey

Planning Director, M&C Saatchi

This chapter concerns one of the most damaging phenomena in business – consumer indifference.

Markets where customers are uninterested in their choice of brand or service tend to destroy value over time, rather than create it. That's because businesses in such markets learn at first hand how to deploy the single most powerful marketing weapon at their disposal – not advertising, but price.

Decreasing price to increase a brand's fortunes is a dangerous drug. While its effects are often dramatic and instantaneous, its repercussions are insidious and long-standing. Businesses that chase volume by cutting price invariably end up sacrificing value, sometimes in the short term and almost always in the long run. Indeed it has more or less become the standard opening for an IPA Effectiveness case history to outline a tale of woe about market stagnation, descent into price promotion and the rise of own-label and other cheaper brands.

The City intuitively understands this cycle, tending to mark stock down the moment price heads south. However, the alternative for businesses in commodity markets is not that palatable either. Those that are smart enough to kick the price habit are vulnerable to assaults from competitors less concerned for their own long-term profitability and more interested in making price-driven inroads. Look at the Halifax (2002) case from the eyes of its competitors and the story isn't quite so rewarding. The big banks watched their cosy inertia-based profits being eaten into by an aggressively priced challenger.

So it seems you're damned if you resort to price and damned if you don't. However, a study of the IPA case histories shows how to head off this damaging commodity spiral. By understanding the root causes of their customers' indifference, marketers are able to escape it and profitably influence consumer attitudes, behaviour and choice. But first they have to accept personal responsibility for their market's predicament.

We cause commodities

A popular cop-out for marketers is to accept that certain categories are, or inevitably become, commoditised as a matter of course.

Naturally you give far less consideration to your choice of bacon or butter than to the selection of a new car or mobile phone. Motors and mobiles matter more. They say much more about you. And your choice makes a difference in terms of both functional performance and emotional reward. It's inevitable therefore that markets with less intrinsic interest should drift inexorably towards commoditisation. So, at least, goes the argument of the weak marketer.

However, there are numerous examples across the IPA case histories of businesses – from loo rolls to utilities – that have bucked 'commodity' markets. The harsh truth is that we cause the very commoditisation that is so damaging. We cause it by not making customers care.

The end of a customer relationship is rarely caused by the particular incident that sparks the breakdown. Invariably its origins lie earlier, in a prolonged lack of care, nurturing and investment over the years. In life's marketing onslaught it's unreasonable to expect a customer to continue to care about your brand unless you actively do things to make them care. Let's face it, there are plenty of other brands, many of them outside your immediate category, who are nurturing their customers. Brands need to adopt a genuine and unmechanistic approach to customer relationship nurture (CRN, if you like).

Marketers inadvertently cause commodities by pushing an agenda that relates to their business and its marketing objectives but not the customers' view of the world. Frequently they navigate around territories that customers don't engage with, rather than finding one they actively do care about.

Research is often misused here. All too often it's deployed to screen out propositions or creative expressions that don't work. That's not the same as using it to find something that positively does.

The case histories add a striking clarity to this. They indicate that it's no good just relying on the communication of product features. Making consumers care about your brand is a bigger undertaking than telling them about your product's strengths.

Telling isn't selling

Recent learnings in psychology point to the relatively weak role of 'reasons why' in decision-making. Psychologists now believe that reasons are not why we do things, but are merely back-up to the feelings that actually motivate our behaviour. Basically we humans act because of what we feel, and support that action with whatever reasons we find to justify it.

This fits with a consistent thread running through many of the IPA case histories, namely the limited value of communications that simply impart reasons to buy. It seems that telling isn't that effective at selling.

Many of the cases in the Awards' 25-year history allude, either directly or indirectly, to the discovery of a unique 'emotional point of differentiation' (Dulux, 1984), the dramatisation of which allowed the brand to develop more emotive communication.

Add values to add value

The evidence shows that communications that evoke an emotional response are not just more effective in terms of numerical metrics (awareness, image, sales measures, etc.), they are also effective in entirely different ways. They inspire and motivate. They reinforce and validate existing behaviour. They exist beyond the moment they are consumed, often becoming part of popular culture to act as an enduring reminder. They stimulate and encourage third parties (employees, retailers, investors, etc.). And so on.

Above all, the cases demonstrate that adding emotional values to a brand adds measurable financial value to it. Here are a baker's dozen examples of such 'emotional selling points' (ESPs) extracted from the spectrum of categories represented in 25 years' worth of IPA Effectiveness competitions.

Consider each one carefully. They may be summed up in a word or two (often my own), but each offers a profound and extensive insight into a consumer point of engagement with the category. Each word probably represents the culmination of months' worth of clever analysis, thoughtful research and creative intuition.

Category	Brand ESP
Tyres	The thrill of speed
Cat food	Mischief
Toilet paper	Emotional comfort
Butter	Sophistication
Glue	Dependability
Stock cube	Centre of family life

Raisins	Childish carefree fun
Ice cream	Intimate pleasure
Finance	Clever straightforwardness
Lager	Irreverent selfishness
Jeans	Rebellion
Insurance	Nostalgic dependability
Champagne	Spontaneity

The case history writers document what gold dust these ESPs are in terms of brand and sales measures. The big question is where and how did they find them? Fortunately there are two big clues on this, the first being an observation on where to focus your activity.

The bird in the hand

Many of the case histories in established markets observe that a lost customer is pretty much a lost cause. They conclude that stopping existing customers from lapsing is more feasible and more cost-effective than attempting to re-attract customers once they have lapsed. It seems the bird in the hand is worth several in the bush.

This runs counter to the somewhat macho 'conquest' strategy popular with many of today's aggressive businesses. Indeed the Henley Centre remarks that:

> More than 4 in 5 consumers believe companies should reward loyal customers instead of offering the best deals to new customers. But companies routinely spend more money acquiring new customers than maintaining existing ones, even though retention is cheaper than acquisition.

Certainly advice that clients in commodity or near-commodity markets might take from many of the IPA case histories would be to concentrate on understanding what keeps loyal customers loyal, rather than what triggers lapsing customers to lapse or what might attract switchers from another brand. Often commissioning this kind of research might feel like a somewhat pointless affirmation of what customers already value in a brand and what will maintain current behaviour. It lacks a certain 'cut and thrust' compared to a more pointed investigation of switchers' motivations to change behaviour.

However, the insights generated from research into loyal users are frequently deeper and more profoundly motivating, precisely because the research is forced to uncover the emotional selling point(s) that cement current behaviour. In contrast, the concepts that tend to score in switcher-based research tend to be sharper, but shallower.

One staggering statistic underscores the power of enhancing loyal consumers' bonds with your brand. In 1991 one-third of Andrex (1992) buyers didn't buy any other brand of loo roll in the course of the year, despite having on average 26 opportunities to buy a substantially cheaper one. (A further third only bought a cheaper alternative on average five times.) What kept them loyal was not just a rational belief that Andrex was softer, stronger or longer, but an emotional comfort with the brand, embodied in a cute Labrador puppy.

Furthermore, there is evidence that the emotional truths derived from current users can be effectively channelled to recruit new users. Andrex documents non-users' remarkably high esteem for the brand. More topically, O_2 (2004) uncovered existing BT Cellnet customers' disillusionment with technological innovation propositions and focused instead on 'enablement' to establish a fresh thinking attitude. The case goes on to illustrate how consistent reinforcement of this property across all channels drove both brand equity growth and short-term sales.

So the first place to look for an emotional selling point is the views of existing loyal users. The second is as far upstream of the problem as possible.

Make changes upstream

It is probably fair to say that marketers nowadays spend most of their time and resources at the sharp end of the selling process. This is perhaps unsurprising, as taking your eye off the ball here is likely to lead to a bloodied nose, such as that dealt to the banks by Halifax (2002).

It's all very well studying rate of sale in multiples or price relative to competitors or gains–loss switching analyses, but you risk marketing on the head of a pin. The IPA case histories teach us about the missed opportunities of such a myopic view. Many of the big winners made a dramatic intervention derived from insights gained way upstream of the marketing coalface.

Orange (1996) famously stepped back from the day-to-day detail of a raging tariff war that in 1994 was dragging the mobile phone market towards commodity. Orange found its insight by crystal ball gazing and exciting customers about 'a wirefree future'. That bright insight was worth £300m.

Likewise, Dulux's (1984) success stemmed from looking beyond the vicious trading battle taking place on 'pure brilliant white' and taking inspiration from décor trends of the day. Interior fashions had shifted from stark, cold, clinical and daring, towards warm, human, natural and safe.

Crucially, not only did Dulux look for broader insight, it made an upstream strategic change to its product mix. Faced with an inability to win the commodity battle in the pure white sector it set itself the objective of reducing the business's dependence on that sector, in favour of creating a new higher-margin, non-commodity sub-sector (which became 'Natural Whites'). It was pure brilliance.

So, the real value of looking upstream is in making subtle but significant changes to product, packaging, pricing, business model, etc., to enhance the overall business proposition.

Interestingly, changes to the IPA Effectiveness rules in recent years have relaxed the obligation to painstakingly establish an advertising effect independent of changes to product, packaging, pricing, channels of promotion, etc.[1] One effect of this broadening of the scope of the Awards has been a greater documentation of the value of upstream changes to business models, product platforms, channel strategy, and so on. Value that was subsequently multiplied by appropriate communications.

In Skoda (2002) a fundamental shift in targeting from likely considerers to those who ridicule Skoda buyers was only able to work because of a vastly improved car. Barnardo's (2002) new mission really began to pay off when it took to the streets and began to sign up donors face to face. British Airways (2002) used communications to drive through a changed business model that stemmed the haemorrhaging to budget airlines while continuing to extract a premium from the brand's reputation. For Hovis (2002), new packaging contributed as much as advertising to a dramatic modernisation of the 'goodness' proposition.

So, in summary …

---

1. *Prior to 2000, authors had to isolate effects that were purely the result of advertising, discounting the influence of changes to product, pricing, packaging, distribution, etc., and removing the effects of below-the-line activity. Such self-interested criteria reflected a certain sniffiness among the above-the-line community to marketing forces 'beneath' their own. Nowadays we live in more enlightened times.*

Mind your Ps: find your ESP

The three big lessons to be learned here are all almost as old as the IPA Effectiveness Awards themselves. One is about exploiting marketing's 5Ps (product, price, promotion, placement and performance, for those of you from another era). If you are only really fiddling around with one or two of these, it's likely you are missing out on upstream opportunities.

Another is about the value of existing customers. Don't rely on their loyalty, actively nurture it.

The third and perhaps the most valuable lesson is the value of the Emotional Selling Point (to give an old acronym a new twist).

So how did Dulux and milk do it?

The truth about the IPA Effectiveness case histories is that nobody's that interested in how well you did. They're interested in how you did so well.

The two case histories that follow document how two different organisations did so well selling a white liquid. In each case the liquid was pretty much indistinguishable from any one else's, except by the fact that it cost appreciably more. The customer was beginning to become indifferent to which they used, or how they obtained it.

Both organisations faced up to their customers' growing apathy. They interrogated it and got upstream of it. Both managed to find an emotional centre to their product or service. Each found a sentiment that was intrinsic to their brand and used it to make people care about their choice. For Dulux, the sentiment was inspiration from nature, for milk it was the security of your milkman's friendly, overseeing eye.

These sentiments may appear weak and soppy, especially compared to 'hard' product and service claims. However, both organisations amplified and exploited them, turning them into a cumulative incremental profit of over £60m at today's prices.

That's how they did it. How will you?

Food for thought

- Commoditisation is never an inevitability: where there is a will, branding can rescue businesses from price and profit erosion in even the most undifferentiated of categories.
- Telling isn't selling: adding layers of emotion to products concentrates rather than dilutes their sales power.
- Loyal customers know brands best; tapping into their motivations not only wins their ongoing loyalty but new customers too.
- When a market is in a price frenzy, the most competitive and profitable response may well lie with alternative levers: product, promotion, placement or performance.

Other IPA case histories particularly recommended on the subject of defying commoditisation are:

Californian Raisins (1986)
PG Tips (1990)
Andrex (1992)
Anchor (1994)
Pirelli (1996)
Orange (1996)
Solvite (2000)
Milk – White Stuff (2002)
Hovis (2002).

The Milkman relaunch
How advertising halted a long-term decline in share

Grand Prix winner 1992

What could advertising do to help the brand leader in a £3.2bn market losing over a million customers a year to cheaper competitors? The brand was the milkman, its competitors the supermarkets.

The answer to the problem wasn't to confront it directly. Using advertising to dissuade customers from cancelling their milkman was too little, too late. Instead prevention proved far more effective than cure. Examining the move from milkman to supermarkets in more detail, we found advertising could have an effect in preventing the crucial first step towards cancelling. In this way, advertising profitably halted the decline in the milkman's share during 1991.

History of the milkman

Milk delivery is a British tradition dating back to the nineteenth century, when handcarts delivered door to door. After the Second World War the service expanded to its current scale. Wartime agriculture had created a huge milk surplus. The Milk Marketing Board (MMB) correctly assumed that households would use more milk if it was delivered daily.

As recently as 1980, almost 90% of households bought from a milkman. Since then the milkman has been in steady decline, partly due to

---

Abridged version of the original case study written in 1992 by John Grant (BMP DDB Needham) for the National Dairy Council.

demographic and lifestyle trends, but mostly due to competition from supermarkets, whose milk is cheaper.

Who cares if the milkman continues to decline?

The farmers
Farmers sell all their milk to the MMB, which sells it to the dairies and operates to maximise consumption of milk products. Farmers sell more milk if more households use a milkman. This is because delivery puts milk 'on tap'. Once it's there, milk tends to get used up. Milkman customers are less prone to run low and restrict consumption.

Econometric modelling has shown that for every 1% fall in doorstep deliveries, milk sales fall nearly 0.2% (source: MMD Ltd).

The dairies/delivery companies
The dairies process and package the milk and sell it either through their own milkmen or independent delivery companies, or to retailers and wholesalers. The dairies and delivery companies make 12p more profit on each pint sold through the milkman. National Dairy Council (NDC) estimates of dairy profits are as follows:

     19.5p per pint sold through a milkman
     7.5p   per pint sold through shops
     12.0p incremental profit per pint, on milk sold through the milkman

In addition they had made a massive historical investment in doorstep delivery. Thousands of milkmen and dairy employees depend on it for a living.

The National Dairy Council
In short, the whole milk industry (excluding the retailers) had a strong interest in stemming the milkman's decline. All these groups contributed a levy to our client, the NDC, to coordinate milk advertising, promotion, PR, sponsorship and education in England and Wales (separate dairy councils cover Scotland and Northern Ireland).

Why were milkman sales declining?

It was clear that the milkman was losing both volume share and customers to the supermarkets (see Figures 1 and 2). It was also clear why.

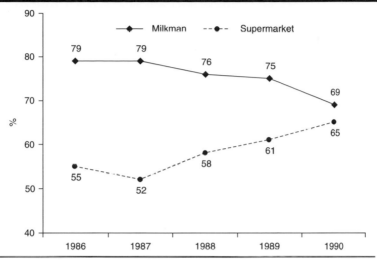

Figure 1: Sources from which milk ever bought

Source: NOP

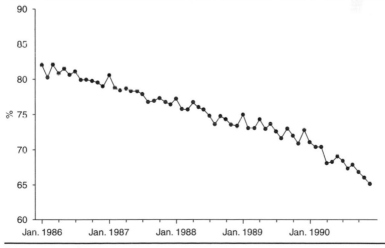

Figure 2: Milkman volume share – doorstep proportion of household milk

Source: MMB/Nielsen

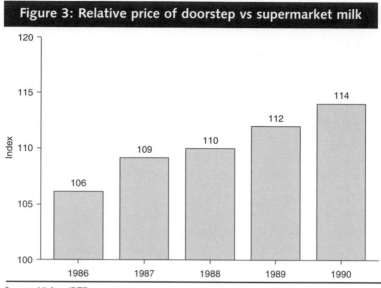

Figure 3: Relative price of doorstep vs supermarket milk

Source: Nielsen/DTF

Price

Supermarkets sell milk at virtually cost price to gain share of the £3.2bn market and generate store traffic. As the biggest household staple, cheap milk also builds their reputation for good value.

Econometric analysis concluded that the price difference between doorstep and supermarket milk was responsible for two-thirds of the milkman's decline in 1989. Since then, that price difference has continued to increase (see Figure 3).

Supermarketing

As well as cut-throat pricing and promotions, the supermarkets invested in product quality (e.g. freshness), packaging (e.g. four-pint containers), merchandising (e.g. prominent displays of low-fat milks), advertising and leafleting to publicise their cheap prices.

The growth of supermarkets, their improving image and the move to out-of-town shopping have also contributed to their increasing share.

Service

The milkman's quality of service (e.g. frequency of delivery) affects share. With declining customers a milkman cannot afford to deliver as often, leading to a vicious spiral of falling share and service.

What could be done?

Share decline had become a priority issue for the NDC. At its present rate there would be no milkman customers left within 12 years. With a widening price gap, decline was expected to get even steeper. Something had to be done.

With much out of the NDC's control (e.g. supermarket price) there were only three important factors they could influence:

1. *Price.* A substantial price reduction would be needed to influence potential cancellers. This would obviously have to be offered to all customers, not just those about to cancel, decimating profitability.
2. *Service.* Improvements might increase loyalty. Various initiatives were being tested (e.g. guaranteed early delivery). However, such changes take time (at least two years) to implement.
3. *Advertising.* Given these stark choices, the milk industry gave its full support to an advertising campaign to help stem the decline (at least until longer-term solutions could be found).

Developing a marketing and advertising strategy

The marketing objective was to slow the decline in milkman share. We calculated that saving just 0.5% share points would pay back a sizeable advertising investment of £5m:

Volume saved = 0.5% × 8.9 billion pints
             = 45 million pints
Profit saved   = 45 million × 12p
             = £5 million

Target audience

There were three possible strategies:

1. Re-acquire lost customers.
2. Stop customers from cancelling.
3. Recruit new customers.

The dairies knew from door-to-door canvassing the first was unachievable. Lost customers were very hard to get back. The last option was too small. At most, 2% of households a year are potential new milkman customers, whereas 6% cancel.[1]

This left the strategy of stopping customers cancelling. We set about finding out who they were, why they were cancelling and, more importantly, why other customers were not. Qualitative research showed that these people had regular experience of both sources, were fully aware of how much extra the milkman cost and were virtually looking for an excuse to cancel anyway, for example a row over the bill. It was unrealistic for advertising to directly persuade them not to cancel. But in the process we discovered an audience that advertising could influence.

An unexpected target

In fmcg purchasing, people very rarely go from 100% loyalty to one brand to 100% loyalty to another. There is nearly always a period of adjustment. Likewise consumers don't suddenly decide to cancel their milkman.

Most milkman customers buy from supermarkets occasionally, typically the odd pint when they run out. Our research showed that before cancelling, customers had first gone through a phase of buying more of their milk from the supermarket more regularly (e.g. stocking up for the weekends with their weekly shopping with four-pint containers).

Having regularly bought from the supermarket for some time they become confident in its constant availability, freshness and convenience 'when you are there anyway'. They become more aware of the price difference and feel irresponsible spending so much extra to have milk delivered. This crucial finding influenced our targeting strategy. It seemed the move from milkman to supermarket followed a step-wise pattern, as illustrated in Figure 4.

The key step target was the drift from occasional distress purchasing to regular supermarket purchasing. Before drifting, customers were not yet strongly affected by price and far more likely to respond to advertising.

From an annual source of purchase data we calculated that every year 6% of customers cancelled their milkman and 9% of customers drifted into regular

---

1. *While new customers were an insufficient audience for the main focus, we didn't completely dismiss this option. Later advertising carried a phoneline number to recruit new customers, coinciding with a major canvassing drive by the dairies (source: NOP, year to June 1990).*

Figure 4: The move from milkman to supermarket

Milkman customers (occasionally buy from the supermarket as distress purchases)

↓ **Drifting**

Customers still buy most from the milkman, but regularly stock up from the supermarket

↓ **Cancelling**

Become supermarket-only customers

---

supermarket buying. The data also showed that on average these drifting customers bought eight pints a week from their milkman and four from the shops. We therefore estimated the volume lost by drifting and cancelling as:

Cancelling   8 pints × 6% of 20 million households
= 9.6 million pints/week

Drifting   4 pints × 9% of 20 million households
= 7.2 million pints/week

Drifting was therefore responsible for nearly half the volume lost. Furthermore, research told us that only those who had gone through this phase of regular shop purchasing tended to cancel their milkman. Reducing the number of drifters should have an additional long-term effect of reducing future cancelling.

There was evidence for just such a long-term process in econometric modelling. MMD picked up a 'feedthrough effect', with volume share lost in one year affecting further longer-term losses.

Getting them to value their milkman again

Research revealed people tended to take their milkman for granted. They seldom saw him, apart from on payday. They had come to expect pints of milk just to 'turn up on the doorstep'. Only on probing did they appreciate the strong rational and emotional benefits of having a milkman:

- *Convenience.* Not having to carry heavy milk, not having to go and get it, not having to worry about it; it's there in time for breakfast, etc.

- *Green.* The bandwagon was in full swing, yet few had realised the familiar returnable glass milk bottles were better for the environment.
- *Low-fat milks.* Some were not sure the milkman sold these.
- *Weekend milk.* Many didn't think about extra milk for the weekend until they reached the shops, finding it heavy and bulky to get home; leaving a note for the milkman would make more sense.
- *Warm emotional values.* Friendly, helpful, traditional, a family ritual, part of the local community ('like a village bobby').

Source: BMP Qualitative

Notably even those about to cancel their milkman agonised over it, weighing up the convenience and anxious about upsetting their milkman. The brief to creatives was therefore to make people appreciate their local milkman again, to make the benefits more salient and provide a strong counterargument against drifting.

Summary of creative brief

The target audience was defined as housewives who use a milkman but occasionally buy extra milk from the shops, aged 25–45, with children and who are heavier purchasers of milk.

The objective of the advertising was to persuade them to continue buying from the milkman (or buy more from him) rather than drifting into the habit of regularly stocking up at the supermarket.

The proposition was 'Don't forget how helpful and convenient your milkman is'. The brief was supported by:

- The loveable, friendly, archetypal milkman.
- He delivers low-fat milks.
- His returnable glass bottles are friendlier to the environment.
- He's more convenient for weekend extras than carrying heavy milk home.

Media planning

TV was chosen as the only medium sufficiently impactful and involving to stage a major relaunch. The media target audience was housewives with children. Advertising ran during April–May and August–October 1991 (see Figure 5).

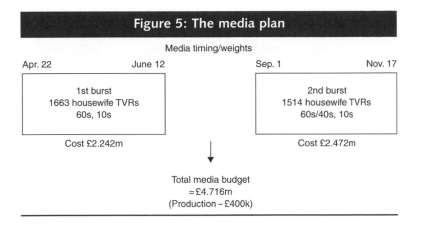

Figure 5: The media plan

Media timing/weights

Apr. 22   June 12   Sep. 1   Nov. 17

1st burst
1663 housewife TVRs
60s, 10s

2nd burst
1514 housewife TVRs
60s/40s, 10s

Cost £2.242m   Cost £2.472m

Total media budget
= £4.716m
(Production ~ £400k)

Creative development

The creative team worked out that each milkman delivers around 900 bottles a day. This impressive scale, plus the almost magical way milk appears on your doorstep, inspired the 'Daybreak' commercial, now known to most TV viewers as 'the one with the dancing bottles'.

To make the main (60-second) ad as magical and emotive as possible, rational support messages were relegated to 10-second ads, shown 'top and tail' in the break. We believe that much of the credit for the effectiveness must go to the creative team, for such a famous and distinctive, yet relevant campaign.

The campaign's effect

Halted sales decline

The milkman's share of household milk had been in long-term decline. From January 1990 to April 1991 that decline averaged 0.43% per month. However, in only eight months, we saw a very pronounced effect. Over the advertised period, May to December 1991, decline stabilised to only 0.01% per month (see Figure 6).

We also saw two significant increases in milkman share, coinciding exactly with the advertising bursts.

Advertising burst	Milkman share (%)
Apr.–May	+2.9
Aug.–Sept./Oct.	+1.5

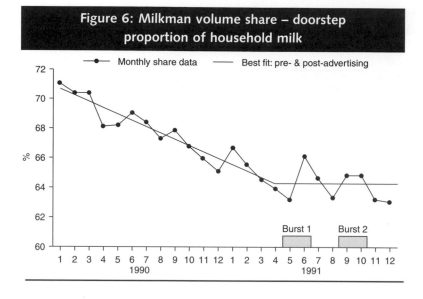

Figure 6: Milkman volume share – doorstep proportion of household milk

Halted drifting

The advertising was designed specifically to combat the 9% of households a year drifting into supermarket purchasing. We set up a continuous measure for source of purchase using Millward Brown to track 'drifting' into regular shop purchasing.

In 1991, following the advertising, drifting was halted. In fact we actually saw 'negative drifting', with some households moving back to buying more of their milk from the milkman (Table 1).

Effect on cancelling

We did not expect to affect cancelling in the first year and we were right: 7% of housewives cancelled their milkman in 1991, compared with 6% the previous year (source: NOP). However, we predicted that if we reduced drifting in the short term, the 'feedthrough effect' would reduce cancelling in

Table 1: Rate of drifting		
	June 1989–June 1990	Feb. 1991–Jan. 1992
Households drifting (%)	9	−2
(sample)	(1600)	(800)

Source: NOP, Millward Brown

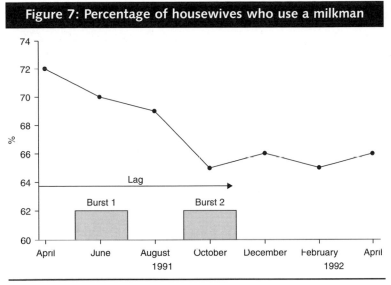

Figure 7: Percentage of housewives who use a milkman

Source: Millward Brown

the longer term. The latest data we have show the reduction in cancelling we had hoped for happening from December 1991 (see Figure 7).

Unexpected scale of effect

In 1990, almost half the volume lost by the milkman was through drifting. As we stopped drifting altogether but didn't affect cancelling, the best we might expect was to reduce share decline by nearly 50%. In fact we halted it altogether.

The explanation is an effect we had not expected. Those who used a milkman and had not drifted during 1991 bought more milk from the milkman and bought from the supermarkets on fewer occasions (e.g. by remembering to order extra from their milkman). Figure 8 shows 7% of households cancelling their milkman, but volume share declining by only 3%. For the first time milkman volume share exceeded customer share. This explains why there were such immediate sales peaks during our advertising bursts. Indeed this is how we should have expected the 10-second 'rational' ads to work.

We can estimate the size of this effect from the fact that volume share declined by only 3% in 1991. From share of customer data we would have expected a volume decline of 7%.

Figure 8: Milkman volume share vs share of customers

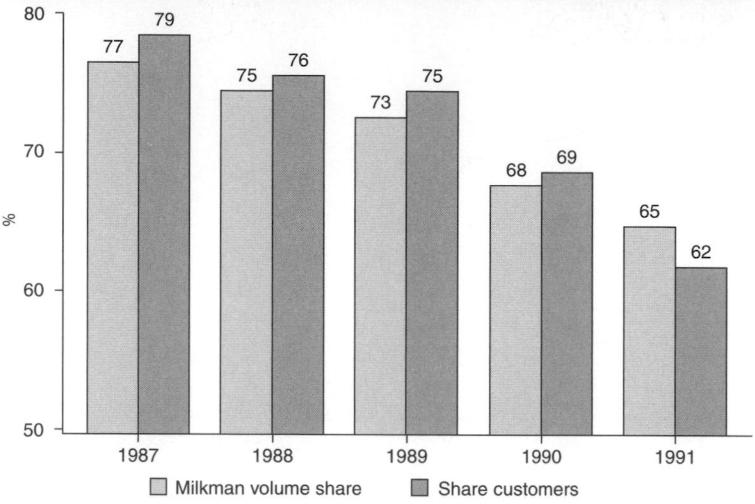

Source: NOP, MMB, Nielsen

Extra volume saved = 4% × 20 million households × 8 pints
                   = 6.4 million pints
Per customer   = 6.4 million pints ÷ 62% of 20 million households
                   = ½ pint

This equates to every remaining milkman customer buying on average an extra pint from the milkman instead of from the shops every two weeks.

Effect on consumer measures

Qualitative research (BMP Qualitative) conducted among housewives who bought from a milkman after the first burst reported that:

- It was most respondents' favourite TV advert – 'straight away you have a smile on your face when it comes on, even if you're down.'
- The Disney-like imagery and music transported the viewer into childlike feelings of security and pleasure; feelings linked to the milkman – a magical figure with everything under control.
- Overall, the advertising made them feel good about and appreciate having a milkman, and inclined to use him more.

Table 2: The top ten spontaneous recall		

Q: Thinking back over the past week, which commercials can you remember seeing or hearing?

	Account	Agency
1	Milk	BMP DDB Needham
2	Persil	JWT
3	Coke/Coca-Cola	McCanns
4	Radion	Ogilvy & Mather
5	Carling Black Label	WRCS
6	Fairy Liquid	Grey
7	Guinness	Ogilvy & Mather
8	British Telecom/BT	JWT
9	PG Tips	BMP DDB Needham
10	TV Quick	Lowe Howard-Spink

Source: Marketing, 27 June 1991

Table 3: Awareness levels (end of first year)		
	Spontaneous awareness (%)	Proven recall (%)
'Daybreak' campaign	60	67
Previous highest scores	48	62
Average (last three campaigns)	42	48

Source: Millward Brown

This helped the advertising become one of the most liked and noticed campaigns on TV (Table 2).[2]

In its first year, our milkman advertising achieved higher levels of spontaneous awareness and proven recall than any milk campaign in the previous ten years (Table 3).

Prompted communication statements show an unprecedented strength and depth of message take-out (Table 4).

---

2. It also received recognition from the advertising industry, winning Gold awards from the Creative Circle and British Television Awards.

Table 4: Prompted communication (housewives)		
	Pre-advertising Jan./Feb. 1991 (%)	Post-advertising Oct./Nov. 1991 (%)
The milkman is the best way to buy fresh milk	29	56
The milkman delivers semi-skimmed milk	9	39
Milk delivery is environmentally friendly	7	40
The milkman can handle difficult orders	4	33

Source: Millward Brown

Effect on milkmen

A survey (Gordon Simmons Ltd) carried out among 70 milkmen at the end of the first advertising burst found that:

- Awareness and communication were strong.
- Milkmen believed they could and should live up to the cheerful, friendly and helpful image portrayed.
- One-third reported sales increases recently; very few reported a decline.

Isolating the advertising effect

We can eliminate all other factors that could possibly have arrested the decline in milkman share.

Price

The price difference between milkman and shops continued to increase during the second half of 1991, when the campaign was on air. If anything, milkman share should have declined faster (Table 5).

Distribution

Nothing untoward happened during 1991 to affect milkman distribution. Supermarkets actually gained distribution due to store openings and Sunday trading.

Table 5: Relative price of milkman vs supermarket milk		
	Jan./Apr. 1991	May/Dec. 1991
Index	112	115

Source: DTF, Nielsen

Table 6: Telephone ad hoc 'service' survey – sample 1000		
	Pre-advertising, Mar. 1991 (%)	Post-advertising, Nov. 1991 (%)
Over the past three months, would you say that the service your milkman has given you has:		
Improved	7	8
Stayed the same	91	90
Deteriorated	2	2

Source: BMRB

Service

There has been a general drive within the milk industry to improve service, in response to falling sales. As a result there have been slight improvements in the perceptions of the service. However, there was no significant change in these improvements before and after the advertising (Table 6).

Other activity

There was no other national marketing activity supporting the milkman in 1991. Any local activity would have been seen by customers as a service initiative. We show above that there was no significant perception of any service improvement.

Isolating the effect

An increase in the major factor influencing milkman share (i.e. relative price) should have increased the decline during the advertising period. Instead the decline in the milkman's share was halted in the advertising period with clear increases in milkman share coinciding exactly with both advertising bursts. *No other influencing factors* could have caused this.

Estimating the size of effect

Short-term effect

Average milkman share following the advertising (May–December 1991) was 64.2%. Assuming share would have continued to decline at 0.43% per month without the advertising, share for the period would have been 61.7%. We calculate the additional volume due to the advertising as:

Additional share points	= 64.2% – 61.7%
	= 2.5%
Eight months, total milk volume	= 5.95 billion pints

Therefore additional milkman volume   = 2.5% × 5.95 billion pints
                                      = 150 million pints
Additional profit   = 150 million × 12p
                                      = £18 million

In addition, we know that milkman usage brings extra volume because milkman customers use more milk: an extra 0.2% in milk volume for every 1% of extra milkman share. We can therefore estimate the amount of extra milk consumption due to the incremental 2.5% share:

Additional volume = 2.5 × 0.2% × 5.9 billion pints
                  = 30 million pints

Extra profit   = 30 million × 15p

                  (NDC estimate of average profit for milk)
                  = £4.5 million

In total the extra profit was therefore £22.5m, exceeding our objectives and our wildest dreams of what we could achieve.

The total advertising spend was £5.1m. Advertising therefore paid for itself by more than a factor of 4 in 1991.

Longer-term effect
Slowing drifting in the short term feeds through to a reduced rate of future cancelling. We have seen some earlier evidence that this was happening. In the longer term this saves even more volume and profit, and further contributes to the industry's long-term objective of turning around the decline.

Summary

The milkman was losing share rapidly to cheaper supermarkets. We were briefed to develop advertising to stem this decline, the obvious solution being to stop customers from cancelling. However, it did not appear realistic that advertising could do this.

We discovered a crucial first step towards cancelling when milkman customers started regularly purchasing extra milk from the supermarkets. This migration accounted for nearly half the volume lost in the short term. It also gave us a way to nip future decline in the bud.

Highly creative advertising was used to remind this audience of everything they appreciated about their milkman. This saved 150 million pints by stopping consumers drifting into more regular shop purchasing. There also was an unexpected effect in increasing the amount of milk bought from the milkman by those customers who did not drift.

No factors other than the advertising could have caused the halting of the decline.

The campaign generated £22.5m in extra profits in 1991, paying for itself by more than a factor of 4.

There is also evidence that the effect led to reduced cancelling in the longer term.

Conclusions

Tackling what seemed a terminal decline within a £3.2bn market was a huge task.

There was no guarantee of success. A previous attempt to stem decline in 1984 by targeting those who were about to cancel had had no discernible effect.

We halted the decline in only eight months by targeting prevention rather than cure through outstanding creative advertising.

Hopefully, with our advertising continuing, the milk industry may find a lasting solution to this problem.

Postscript

This case was based on 1991 data. In 1992 the 'Daybreak' campaign continued and all data indicated the advertising was just as successful and profitable in its second year.

In 1993, the campaign was curtailed in favour of other milk marketing activity and, unfortunately, milkman decline returned.

ICI Dulux Natural Whites

Grand Prix winner 1984

Dulux Natural Whites, a new paint range from ICI, was launched in February 1982 and advertised from March 1982. The range exceeded its objectives, holds brand leadership of a new market sector and has reached a 17% volume share of the total white emulsions market after two years.

Consumers identify advertising as their source of awareness and propensity to buy. Its role in the continuing success of Natural Whites is demonstrated here.

Leadership of a slowing paints market

Before 1980, the retail decorative paints market had grown dramatically (from 90 million litres in 1970 to 115 million litres in 1980) because of three key factors:

1. Consumer expenditure increased, along with propensity to decorate.
2. The overall stock of houses grew considerably.
3. There was a significant move away from wall coverings to paint, which is seen as more convenient and cheaper.

Throughout the 1970s Dulux held brand leadership, averaging 28% volume share, reaching 29% in 1980. Total Dulux volume therefore grew 35%, ahead of the market.

Abridged version of the original case study written in 1984 by Kevin Green and Richard Dodson (Foote Cone & Belding) for ICI.

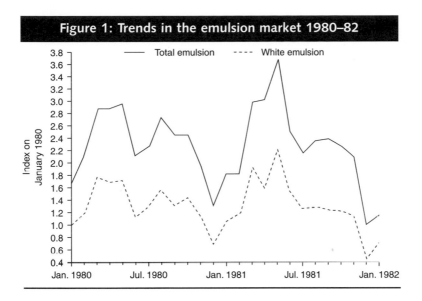

Figure 1: Trends in the emulsion market 1980–82

The growth of specialist DIY chains created strong price competition, meaning that value growth of the market was less dramatic. Moreover, from 1980, house building slowed, as did the move away from wall coverings. As a result, although consumer expenditure continued to rise, the decorative paint market remained static in volume (see Figure 1). Dulux was facing static volumes and declining value.

Problems with Brilliant White

In white paints, Dulux's share only increased from 25% to 26% by 1980. In the largest and most dynamic market sector – emulsion – share suffered a severe decline to 23% (Figure 2). This was largely caused by strong price promotion (see Figure 3).

For some time there had been no product improvements in Dulux Brilliant White emulsion. White paint was becoming a commodity and purchasing Dulux had assumed lower priority. Brilliant White emulsion was competing in a heavily promoted sector, with multiple DIY retailers dictating pricing.

Dulux's dilemma was that share growth through more aggressive pricing would simply lead to reduced profit margins. Dulux needed not only to re-establish dominance in whites, but also restore profit levels in this high-volume sector.

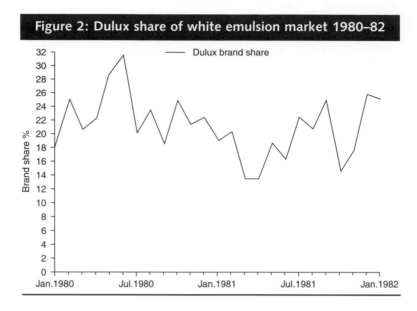

Figure 2: Dulux share of white emulsion market 1980–82

In addition, reactions to Brilliant White commercials in 1981 were qualitatively milder and weaker compared with the early 1970s. Whites advertising was beginning to be criticised for coldness and lack of impact or humanity.

By 1981, stark use of Brilliant White was no longer fashionable. Although still used on most decorating occasions, it was no longer considered to make

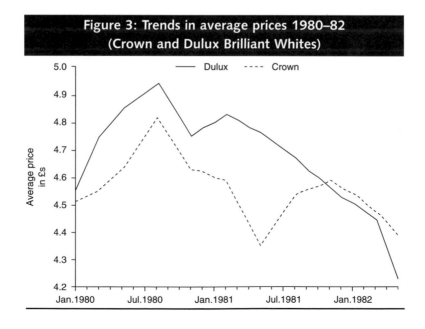

Figure 3: Trends in average prices 1980–82
(Crown and Dulux Brilliant Whites)

a marked contribution to the overall décor. It had become an automatic, habitual choice. The question was, would it be possible to excite consumers about white paint again?

Action

Beyond competing on price grounds in the short term, Dulux sought a way of reducing its reliance on the whole Brilliant Whites sector. In the absence of a new product-based story, differentiation would have to come primarily from the creation of an image, and therefore be advertising-led. A number of actions were put into effect.

A major market research exercise enhanced knowledge of why consumers used white paint and their attitudes towards it. A detailed review of potential product improvements indicated a number of technical improvements available. However, none was felt to warrant the consumer paying a premium or meet the objective of reducing the overall price sector of the market.

A review of paint markets around the world revealed that most other countries were suffering from heavy price competition in Brilliant Whites, although most had a much lower dependence on it. Other countries sold more coloured paint from in-store tinting machines. Another clue came from overseas in the shape of a colour card including a range of tinted whites. Consultation with décor experts indicated that tinted whites could combine the excitement of colour with the reassurance of white.

Towards a positioning – whites or colours?

A tinted whites range would be exciting, unique and aesthetic, and might meet our longer-term objective. Further qualitative research was therefore conducted to investigate the concept and identify where to position it.

Admirers of the new range referred to it as 'near whites' and 'delicate colours'. There was little doubt as to its likely role: a substitute for Brilliant White, light and airy, but less stark and harsh, a safe option in an integrated colour scheme.

The lack of courage of the target audience must not be forgotten. We were talking to users who felt that magnolia was far too dangerous and bold.

Reassuring them that the tinted shades would bring successful results would have to be a job for advertising. However, for two reasons, it was vital that the new range was not simply an alternative to Brilliant White:

1. Other research revealed that consumers were demanding more:

   It's nice to have something that's not dead white.

   It'd make you want to change your colours to match, whereas with real white, it just goes with anything.

2. In strategic terms, we had to move away from the passivity of brilliant white, otherwise the new range would assume the same unimportant background role, with choice of brand being equally unimportant.

Dulux's positioning

Consumers believed that the leading brands offered the same range of paints, based roughly on the same technology. Any attempt to differentiate on rational grounds was viewed with active suspicion. Reinforcing superiority to other brands would therefore entail an emotional point of differentiation, centred around the feelings that accompany redecorating and the assurance of a beautiful end-result.

In 1980, qualitative research identified the most motivating and differentiating proposition for Dulux as an emotional one of 'personal renewal'.

The creation of Natural Whites

A creative consultant produced a range of three tinted whites: Apple White, with a hint of green; Rose White, with a hint of pink; and Lily White, with a hint of cream. The advertising brief was to develop a distinctive approach that would set the range apart from other paints and communicate the subtlety of the concept. It was to be more cosmetic and less functional than previous advertising. The brief also asked that point-of-sale material reflect the advertising idea.

The agency developed the concept and worked with packaging designers to develop appropriate can liveries. A number of names were developed, including Natural Whites. An animatic of the creative approach was produced, together with a number of concept cards and paint panels. These were qualitatively researched. The Natural Whites concept elicited encouraging results.

Dulux research and development then produced three shades, reproducible on a large scale. They were both clearly discernible from Brilliant White, yet not pastel colours.

Natural Whites were not, in any structural way, a new product. They were a new colour concept. As such, they would be extremely easy to copy. (Indeed lookalikes appeared within nine months.) For this reason and because of the dependence on a small number of major national retailers it was not possible to area-test prior to the national launch.

Pricing policy was developed on the basis of research. It appeared consumers would pay 15% more for tinted whites than Brilliant White. This was fundamental to meet profit objectives. Volume forecasts were prepared on the basis of sales in line with Dulux's best-selling pale colours, Magnolia and Buttermilk. These forecasts justified a launch spend of £2,800,000 on advertising, and £400,000 on POS and display material.

The first cans were duly released on 1 February 1982. Within three months, the range had achieved 75% sterling distribution nationally. The advertising began in March 1982.

Launch strategy

Marketing aim
The aim of the campaign was to increase Dulux share of whites in the face of heavy promotion from Crown and cheaper paints, particularly own-label.

Advertising objectives
The advertising objectives were to reawaken consumer interest in white paint, lifting it from a low priority, commodity area with decisions taken on the basis of habit and price, to a more positive, conscious choice. Within this, to increase interest in and commitment to Dulux white paint.

Target audience
The target audience was users of white paint, premium or commodity. They feel less than happy about their continued use of white, but are not prepared to make a move into the far riskier area of colours.

Demographically, a very broad sample – BC1C2, under 55. Women play the major role in decision-making.

Proposition
Now there's an exciting but safe way to transform your home.

Reason why?
Dulux has a new range – Natural Whites – which offer white with a touch of natural colour: Rose, Apple and Lily.

Tone of voice
Soft and reassuring.

Executional consideration
Include the Dulux dog, an extremely effective and emotive branding device.

Media strategy

The media strategy was to launch at competitive weight, gain high awareness rapidly and then maintain a strong presence, using a combination of television and posters.

A number of factors influenced the scheduling of television advertising (Figure 4). The requirement for a 60-second time length was paramount. The range is based on a concept, rather than product development, and therefore needed strong creative-led communication. However, this was not allowed to influence the setting of TVR targets to preserve competitive weights.

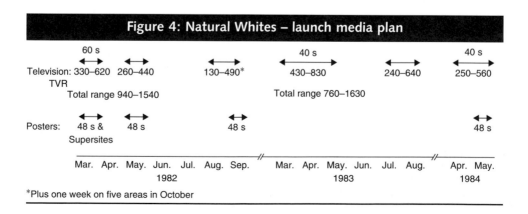

Figure 4: Natural Whites – launch media plan

*Plus one week on five areas in October

The majority of television exposure was concentrated just prior to and through the main sales period and to support the important August Bank Holiday period. To increase impact, Natural Whites advertising was scheduled to appear in discrete bursts without overlapping other Dulux products. To increase and prolong the presence of the campaign, a mixture of 48-sheet and supersite posters were used.

The advertising

The launch commercial used animation, a completely new form of expression for Dulux. The focus was on three images created for Rose, Apple and Lily White. These images were used in all creative material, from the can design through to advertising and POS.

As well as illustrating the concept, the approach provided a strong but reassuring emotional point of differentiation for the range.

Evaluation of results

Success relied on the communication of the concept of Natural Whites in a way that reassured risk-averse consumers.

Not having a test area makes it extremely difficult to isolate individual contributions to the product's success. In particular, the correlation between sales and distribution-linked variables opens a debate as to which factor is causal. Therefore we shall demonstrate the success of the launch in broad terms first and then look in more detail at the individual factors involved.

The base data for our analyses are garnered from ICI's bespoke consumer and retail panels.[1]

---

1. *ICI's Marketing Research Services operates a field force of over 300 interviewers and has run a consumer panel of some 4500 households since 1969. In addition, this group also carries out a check of price, distribution and display (PDD) in some 700 retail outlets three or four times a year, plus various ad hoc studies.*

Overall launch success

The launch was successful against all criteria.

Reduced dominance of Brilliant White

The dominance of heavily price-promoted Brilliant White in the emulsions market was reduced from 58% in 1980/81 to 51% in 1983. Figure 5 illustrates the growing importance of Natural Whites and the decreased reliance on Brilliant Whites.

Increased Dulux white share

Natural Whites obtained an 18% share of white by 1983, while Dulux Brilliant Whites lost only 1%. As a result Dulux increased its share in the white emulsions sector from a low of 18% to 36% in 1983, Dulux's highest ever brand share for a decade.

At the same time Dulux maintained share of the colours sector (29% in 1981 and 29% in 1983).

Despite fluctuations in monthly emulsion brand shares (Figure 6), the trend is clear. By growing its Natural Whites share, Dulux grew its total share of white. This is borne out in the emulsion market split and Dulux brand shares for the period (Table 1).

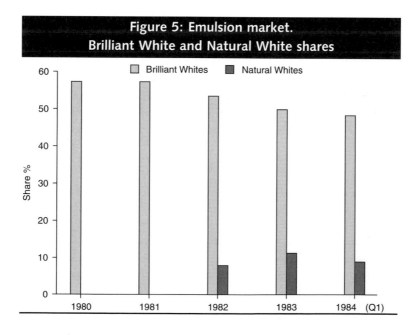

Figure 5: Emulsion market.
Brilliant White and Natural White shares

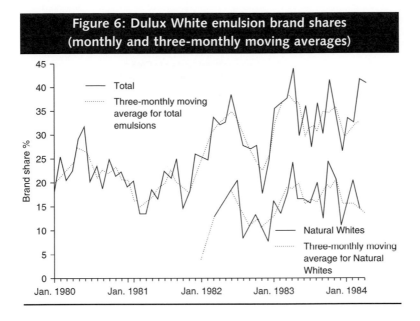

Figure 6: Dulux White emulsion brand shares (monthly and three-monthly moving averages)

Price premium
The above share gains were achieved on the back of a price premium.

Natural Whites maintained an average premium of 17% above Crown Plus Two brilliant white and 13% above Dulux Brilliant White (the two premium brands in the white sector). (See Figure 7.)

Table 1: Emulsions market 1980–83				
	1980 (%)	1981 (%)	1982 (%)	1983 (%)
All emulsions:				
Colours	42.5	42.2	37.9	38.1
Brilliant Whites	57.5	57.8	53.9	50.6
Dulux Natural Whites	–	–	8.2	11.4
White emulsion:				
Dulux Brilliant Whites	23.3	18.4	16.6	17.4
Dulux Natural Whites	–	–	13.3	18.5
Dulux total	23.3	18.4	29.9	35.9
Colours:				
Dulux	34.0	29.0	30.0	29.0

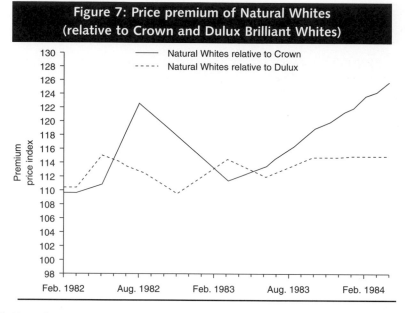

Figure 7: Price premium of Natural Whites (relative to Crown and Dulux Brilliant Whites)

Insulation from competitive response

Both share and premium have been maintained despite launches of competitive lookalikes during the summer of 1982. In addition there was heavy discounting on Crown Brilliant White during autumn 1982.

Neither of these competitive responses affected the long-term growth of Natural Whites, although short-term effects are discernible.

New Dulux users

Natural Whites attracted new, younger users to Dulux. During April and May 1982, a Natural Whites users study revealed the following profile. The results are compared with a 1981 Dulux Emulsion user profile (Table 2).

Only 61% of Natural Whites users claimed Dulux was previously the brand they most frequently purchased. Importantly, 84% of users claimed they had

Table 2: User profile comparisons		
	Natural Whites (%)	Dulux Emulsion (%)
Male	35	49
Female	65	51
Under 35	37	28
35–54	43	38
55+	20	34

decided to buy Natural Whites before entering the store. Some 79% of users claimed to have first heard of the product through TV advertising.

Another major finding was that only 11% of users were dissatisfied with the shade (most of these thinking it too pale) – an indication of successful communication of product reassurance in the advertising.

Profitability

Above all, the launch was profitable. Over the period 1982–83, Dulux invested more in advertising than in whites historically. The net effect was a major gain in white emulsion sales. Against this was a small loss of sales from colours caused by the resulting shifts in the emulsions market. Margins achieved on Natural Whites were higher than those on Brilliant Whites, albeit lower than colours.

The approximate gross profit contribution can be calculated from the total market volumes and the gross margins for Natural Whites, Brilliant Whites and colours. For reasons of confidentiality the precise numbers cannot be divulged. However, the contribution from Natural Whites – less that lost on Brilliant Whites, the small colours decline and launch costs – is still substantial. This ignores the current strength, which will maintain very substantial benefits well into the future. Dulux has continued to exploit and develop the Natural Whites range. Gloss and non-drip gloss finishes have subsequently been introduced. Natural Whites were added to the Dulux Weathershield exterior masonry paint range, and to the Dulux Professional Decorator range. The range has also been extended by a further three shades – Bluebell, Apricot and Barley White – presented in a similar way to the three originals. Additionally, a range of wallcovering borders has been introduced to match all Natural Whites.

The new market will provide yet more opportunities in the future.

Regression analysis

The success of Natural Whites is demonstrated conclusively by the results above.

Although the whole concept revolves around the communication of the emotional stance as well as other variables it is necessary to show that the growth of brand share was closely related to the advertising. We have done this using standard linear regression techniques. Of the numerous variables investigated, the most significant were found to be:

- Advertising, indexed to 1980 levels.[2]
- Share of shelf footage in store.
- Relative price for both Natural Whites and Dulux Brilliant White relative to Crown Plus Two.

Several analyses were performed investigating Dulux share both before and after the Natural Whites launch. For brevity not all these are discussed here, but the key findings are given below. The results of the final analysis over the whole data period are shown in the Appendix. The main conclusions were as follows:

1. Prior to the Natural Whites launch both relative price and Dulux Brilliant White advertising had significant effects on brand share.
2. After the launch Natural Whites advertising and Natural Whites share of shelf footage also showed significant effects.
3. The Dulux Brilliant White price elasticity reduced after the launch from approximately 0.8 to 0.6.
4. Advertising expenditure produced short-term sales effects equivalent to one brand share point for each £100,000 (1980 prices) for both Dulux Brilliant White and Natural Whites.
5. Each 1% of shelf footage allocated to Natural Whites accounts for about 1.5 brand share points.

Summary

The success of the launch is attributable to three key factors:

1. Thorough analysis and interpretation of the market situation.
2. Identification of a real opportunity.
3. Development of a consistent and highly appealing creative package.

The launch reduced the Brilliant White sector of the market, stemming its descent towards commodity. It created a third market sector in the UK retail decorative paints market, enabling manufacturers to improve their profit margins and bringing a new dynamic to the marketplace.

---

2. *This was used rather than audience measure since the media schedule consisted of multiple media.*

Appendix: regression analysis

Dependent variable: Dulux brand share (white emulsion)
Independent variables: Relative price
                        Share of shelf footage (SSF) (Natural Whites)
                        Advertising expenditure (Brilliant White and Natural Whites)

Figure 8 shows the plot of actual brand share and the estimated brand share from this regression analysis.

Table 3: Regression analysis data

	Coefficient	t-statistic
Constant	79.5	3.5
Relative price	−56.5	51
SSF	1.6	7.9
Advertising Brilliant White	0.01	1.3
Advertising Natural Whites	0.01	2.3

Goodness of fit: $r^2 = 0.62$

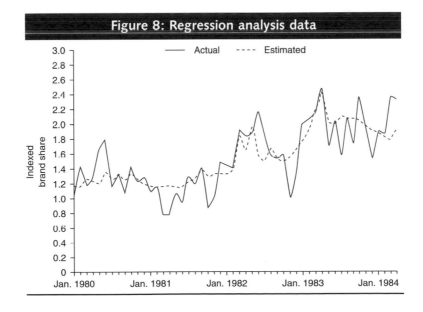

Figure 8: Regression analysis data

Adding value to your brand through communication

Chapter 9

Neil Dawson

Executive Planning Director, TBWA\London

What can we learn from comparing brands from product fields as diverse as premium cars and tea with differences in levels of involvement, frequency of purchase, target audience, consumer usage and communications role? The answer, based not just on this comparison but also a wider inspection of the full IPA dataBANK, is quite a lot – a brand is still a brand regardless of category.

Both BMW (1994) and PG Tips (1990) demonstrate the power of communications to add value to create a strong brand. The rewards for this are immense: £2.7–£3.2bn in extra sales for BMW and an additional £2bn sales revenue for PG Tips. They show us that long-term brand building is much more than an act of faith – in particular, the importance of ongoing measurement to provide short-term understanding and confidence to stick with an approach for the long term.

Looking back at them in 2005, they also seem to exemplify two different models of marketing communications. PG Tips is the receding model: mass-targeted, TV advertising-led and offers limited integration. In contrast, BMW with its targeted, print-based, heavily integrated 'look and feel' approach is almost a portent for the way marketing communications is increasingly approached today. In this sense it represents the emerging and in many sectors the dominant model. This is not a function of difference of category. Even in traditional fmcg markets targeting and integration are now widespread mantras.

Despite such difference, both these and other similar cases from the IPA dataBANK offer us valuable insights into 'added value' and the role communications plays in creating it.

How 'added value' works

Strong brands are valuable financial and strategic assets to companies because they offer dependable streams of profit. They do this by creating strong relationships with consumers that exist beyond the functional product or service itself. Feldwick and Baker (1990) define it thus:

> *A brand is an entity with which consumers (and all other relevant parties) have a relationship based upon factors over and above its functional performance.*

This relationship is built on any number of physical and emotional interactions over time. And it is characterised by what are often called the 'added' or 'extra' values of the brand. These are the intangible feelings, associations and imagery which mean that consumers see them as more valued and more valuable. Strong brands are thus able to command repeat purchase and a price premium.

This notion of brand relationship is useful *as a metaphor*. Think of our relationships with other people. We expect a fairly high degree of consistency from friends and family. When we go into our local pub we look for familiar faces of people we know. However, it is important not to think of this relationship too literally from a consumer perspective. Most of us do not want a close relationship with a manufacturer or mass service provider and would reject the notion that we could ever have one.

The important role of communications

Communications are obviously not the only factor within the brand relationship. Product or service quality, value, distribution and packaging are all key factors. The relative influence of these will vary by category: product and value are critical in cars; but in retail, convenience of location is of paramount importance. But there is strong evidence from the IPA dataBANK that communications plays an important role in building, maintaining and controlling the added values over time. In a world of increased competition, parity products and services, cut-throat pricing and growing dependence on intermediaries, communications is undeniably one of the key avenues available to establish the added values.

Added value requires simplicity

If the added values characterise the brand relationship then you have to be precise about what these values are and how you are driving them. The focus and simplicity of strategy and execution is striking; Table 1 gives some examples.

BMW had two key objectives and four key values that were deployed via a sniper strategy in which each ad focused on a value relevant to a particular segment.

Table 1: Examples from the IPA dataBANK of added value through simplicity of strategy and execution		
Brand	**Year**	**Title**
Stella Artois	2000	Reassuringly profitable
Solvite	2000	How incredible advertising power helped Solvite add real value
Orange	1998	The FTSE's bright, the FTSE's Orange
Roses	1994	Thank you very much
Oxo	1992	Oxo cubes and gravy granules
Andrex	1992	Sold on a pup
O_2	2004	It only works if it all works

Having appropriated a generic territory, the Chimps and their relationship with PG Tips became the simple thread which ran through all advertising that followed. Communications drove consumer affection and warmth for PG Tips through the Chimps.

Added value demands consistency

Both papers demonstrate an overall consistency of campaign approach over significant periods of time. The Chimps ran for 35 years and were still being deployed ten years later as part of a relaunch of PG Tips in 2000. BMW reports 15 years of consistent advertising and this also continued post-1994.

Recent thinking by Wendy Gordon drawn from the world of neuroscience confirms the importance of repetition for brand associations:

> *Cells that fuse together are wired together. The more frequently an association between things is repeated, the more likely it is that the connections between neurones strengthen – i.e. there are physiological changes that take place that increase the likelihood of certain patterns occurring in response to a stimulus.*

If our relationships with brands are like those we have with people, then the importance of this consistency in communications cannot be underestimated. We take time to get to know people and the more we see them, the more we feel confident about their characters. However, this does not mean they have to remain exactly the same. Indeed, if they did they'd soon become boring.

Added value also demands being the same but different

Both brands managed to remain attractive and relevant to consumers over long periods of time. Communications helped to establish and maintain the strong relationship. They also successfully delivered 'new news'. For BMW this encompassed a wide range of models varying dramatically in price and performance. For PG Tips, this included successfully launching tea bags in 1967 and relaunching the brand with Flavour Flow tea bags in 1981.

This resolution of the apparent conundrum of being the same but different was achieved by establishing a unique and ownable creative theme that was flexible enough to accommodate the desired 'new news'. Over time the creative theme became the consistent thread that strengthened the brand relationship. In the case of BMW, this creative theme is the focus on the car and the precise, clinical and technical tone that harnessed the energy of all communications to the brand; whereas for PG Tips, the creative icon of the Chimps created affection and warmth for the brand. Part of the appeal of the Chimps was due to their ability to change with the times and reflect trends within society.

In each case, the advertising that built the brand became an integral part of it in the mind of the consumer. And the creative itself was continuously innovative, rather than being only the vehicle for product innovation.

Related to this, both campaigns may now be seen as long-running, but at their inception they were founded on an innovation, overturning the conventions of the marketplace and being highly disruptive.

Table 2 gives examples of other brands that achieved added value through being the same but different.

Strategically there are different ways to add value

The two papers adopt fundamentally different strategic approaches.

The BMW strategy is based on product 'truths' intrinsic to the brand. These were used to build a desirable image of exclusivity and expertise. Despite creative focus on the car, the campaign was ultimately about the user image.

Table 2: Examples from the IPA dataBANK of added value through being the same but different		
Brand	**Year**	**Title**
Orange	1998	The FTSE's bright, the FTSE's Orange
Oxo	1992	Oxo cubes and gravy granules
Tesco	2000	How every little helps was a big help to Tesco
Andrex	1992	Sold on a pup
Alliance & Leicester	1990	First-time buyer mortgages
Barclaycard	1996	Put it away Bough
Roses	1994	Thank you very much
BA	1994	10 years of the world's favourite advertising
VW	1992	VW Golf 1984–90
BT	1996	How BT made advertising work smarter not just harder
Stella Artois	2000	Reassuringly profitable

In contrast, PG Tips appropriated the generic chimp association of the tea party and over time built affinity through association and reinforcement. In this sense it is based on extrinsic values. As the paper highlights, the logic for this is that functional performance in the tea market is generic.

While each approach was demonstrably effective for the brand in the particular marketplace at that time, increasingly added value seems to be more often driven by the creative communication of 'intrinsic product truths'. This may well be in part a response to an increasingly cynical and marketing-fatigued consumer. These truths may be rooted in latent or underexploited truths or product innovation and improvement. This is not to say that 'added' emotional values are any less important; only that they have to be strongly integrated with rather than simply associated with the product.

'Added value' is not dependent on outspending the competition

The campaigns also demonstrate different approaches to the issue of media investment. PG Tips demonstrates how the combination of consistency of creative vehicle and high levels of media weight on TV can build added value and lead to payback over the long term. Using this strategy, PG Tips was able to withstand being intermittently outspent by competitors. Furthermore, the brand was less sensitive to short-term reductions in advertising support because of the strength of the added values.

Table 3: Examples from the IPA dataBANK of different strategic routes to added value		
Primarily intrinsic		
Brand	**Year**	**Title**
Boddingtons	1994	By 'eck
Skoda	2002	It's a Skoda, honest
Stella Artois	2000	Reassuringly profitable
BA	1994	10 years of the world's favourite advertising
Solvite	2000	How incredible advertising power helped Solvite add real value
Croft Original	1990	One instinctively knows when something is right
Andrex	1992	Sold on a pup
Primarily extrinsic		
BT	1996	How BT made advertising work smarter not just harder
Orange	1998	The FTSE's bright, the FTSE's Orange
Roses	1994	Thank you very much

BMW invested at lower levels than competitors of similar share. Despite this the consistency of the campaign led to levels of ad awareness as high as the mainstream volume manufacturers such as Ford and Vauxhall. This consistency flowed both from creative and media execution. The aforementioned sniper strategy demanded a large number of executions united by a consistent creative theme targeting different segments. Creative media planning focused initially on consistent presence in leisure and weekend supplements and was followed by TV in the latter period of the campaign.

While the specific data are not available for all papers, it is evident from the dataBANK that with notable exceptions such as BT, many of the added value cases referred to here did not rely on a dominant share of voice and indeed were often heavily outspent by competitors (see Table 3 for some examples).

Increasingly, added value demands integration

Referring back to the receding and emerging models of PG Tips and BMW, it is clear from the IPA dataBANK that advertising has become part of a far wider mix of communications activity. Ideas are leveraged across multiple channels in order to build consistency and maximise impact in as short a space of time as possible (see Table 4). The reasons for this are well documented: competitive pressure, media fragmentation, consumer disinterest, the increasing cost of TV as a medium, the growth in

Table 4: Examples from the IPA dataBANK of added value through integration – papers using four or more channels		
Brand	**Year**	**Integration method**
Skoda	1998	5 channels (TV, press, poster, direct marketing and radio)
Stella Artois	2000	4 channels (TV, poster, sales promotion, PR)
Orange	1998	9 channels (TV, radio, press, poster, internet, direct, sales promotion, PR, coupons)
BA	1994	4 channels (TV, press, poster, cinema)
Tesco	2000	4 channels (TV, radio, press, poster)
O_2	2004	9 channels (TV, radio, press, poster, sponsorship, sales promotion, PR, trade, internet)

understanding of the effectiveness of other communications elements and a general cynicism among clients about the vested interests of ad agencies in television as a medium. This trend is epitomised by the O_2 mantra in 2004: 'It only works if it all works'. In the space of two years this has built added value for O_2 with a predicted ultimate payback of 62:1 over the lifetime of the campaign purely in terms of sales effects of advertising and sponsorship.

One further observation on this is whether the PG Tips Chimps would have endured for 45 years had they been 'leveraged' in the manner of, say, 118 118 or indeed O_2 (2004). With the drive to maximise impact by delivering the message across multiple channels comes the price of more rapid creative wear-out.

Building added value depends on broader company culture and approach

Specific similarities and differences of strategic, creative and media approach are highlighted above. But there are also some unifying characteristics of the kind of companies involved. These are 'organisational' truths that drive their behaviour:

1. *They exhibit high levels of confidence in and commitment to marketing communications.* This allowed them to overcome competitive pressures, economic downturns and short-term blips. Remarkably the BMW case demonstrates long-term sales growth and success for a premium marque in a period that includes the most significant recession in living memory. In 1967 PG Tips used the Chimps to gain

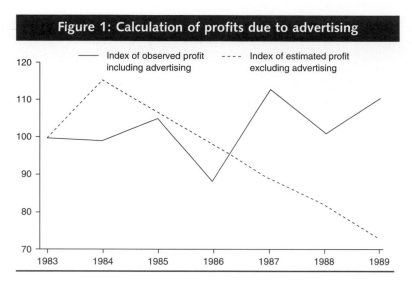

Figure 1: Calculation of profits due to advertising

— Index of observed profit including advertising

- - - - Index of estimated profit excluding advertising

leadership in tea bags within four years, despite new rival Tetley launching in tea bags first without a packet heritage.

2. *They take a long-term view of the business metrics.* This is most clearly demonstrated by a chart from the Oxo 1990 case history (see Figure 1). Considering this simple analysis of brand profitability with or without advertising support, Feldwick and Baker (1990) point out the following.

   Taking a year view (1983–86) cumulative profits would have been around 10% higher without *advertising. But taking a 6-year view (1983–89), as the base level without advertising erodes, cumulative profits work out 10% higher* with *advertising than without. More importantly, actual profits in 1989 – which represent the base level for* future *profits and the basis for any brand valuation exercise – are some 50% higher with advertising than without.*

3. *They enjoy continuity of people and/or culture.* Brooke Bond (owned by Unilever) is part of a long brand-building tradition. BMW had three marketing directors over the 15 years covered by the paper. Both worked in long-term partnerships with their agencies. In a world of increasingly aggressive competition, ever-faster technological change and pressure for short-term business results this is not a call for a return to the good old days of corporate stability and long tenure. It is simply an observation that building added value requires commitment and attention from all concerned. Nor is it necessarily the case that

BMW and PG Tips represent a bygone era. Recent cases such as Tesco, Stella Artois, Orange and most recently O$_2$ refute this.

4. *They are committed to measuring the right things.* All of the papers referred to here, by their presence in the IPA dataBANK, are demonstrations of evaluative excellence. Any commercial endeavour cannot simply be an act of faith. Successful businesses have to act in both the short and long term. Knowing what success looks like and knowing how to measure it is a simple lesson for us all.

Key considerations to add value through communications

- What is the long-term (5+ years) vision and strategy for the brand?
- What are the business objectives and over what time period?
- Is the strategy and creative theme simple?
- What is the foundation of the strategy (intrinsic vs extrinsic)?
- How does the creative theme deliver consistency over time, 'new news' (positioning, product or innovation) and across channels?
- What are the implications of your strategy for media budget and share of voice?
- How will success be measured and what measures are in place?

References

Feldwick, P. & Baker, C. (1990) *'Longer and Broader' Effects of Advertising. Some Observations and Recent Evidence.* ESOMAR.

Gordon, W. (2002) Brands on the brain: new scientific discoveries to support new brand thinking, in Baskin, M. and Earls, M. (eds), *Brand New Brand Thing.* Kogan Page.

PG Tips
How the Chimps kept PG Tips brand leader through 35 years of intense competition

Grand Prix winner 1990

In 1955, Brooke Bond relaunched an existing brand, Pre-Gestive Tea (so called because of the tea's claimed dietary and medicinal properties) as 'PG Tips'. The relaunch may have modernised the brand's image but it did not increase its market share: through to late 1956 it remained number four brand in the market.

Thirty-five years later, PG Tips is the dominant brand leader. How was this success achieved and maintained? Many changed factors over the period might have affected the brand's performance. What the British eat and drink, fashions in the tea market, and society itself have all changed substantially. The only two unchanging factors have been the advertising campaign for the brand – which first started in 1956 – and the high level of media support given to it ever since.

This case history aims to show the following:

1. That PG Tips reached its dominant position by 1958, because of interest generated by the Chimps advertising.
2. That it then maintained brand leadership by assimilating added value, enabling it to represent a more valued consumer purchase, even though its absolute price has always been higher than that of competitors.

Abridged version of the original case study written in 1990 by Clive Cooper, Louise Cook and Nigel Jones (BMP DDB Needham) for Brooke Bond Foods.

3. That the Chimps campaign is primarily responsible for this added value.
4. An attempted quantification of the financial contribution of 34 years of the Chimps campaign.

The Chimps campaign

The original Chimps idea was chanced on when a copywriter, charged with creating the first PG Tips TV commercial, visited London Zoo in Regent's Park in 1956. The zoo's chimpanzees were enjoying a tea party in front of a large crowd. The first Chimps commercial, with a voiceover by Peter Sellers, was screened nationally in autumn 1956.

This 60-second commercial aimed to boost awareness of PG Tips, and to develop an original, inimitable property for the brand. The belief at the time was that the obvious enjoyment of the crowd at the zoo could be replicated in viewers' homes when they saw the commercial – hopefully establishing a stronger relationship between brand, advertising and consumers.

No one then thought the Chimps advertising would be so effective so quickly. In two years, the brand had overtaken Brooke Bond Dividend and Lyons, and displaced Typhoo as brand leader. Evidently a hot property, PG Tips retained brand leadership while confidence in the Chimps' long term campaign potential grew.

Consistency has been maintained ever since. Similar creative executions have run over the whole 34-year period (by 1989, the Chimps' 30th anniversary, over 100 commercials had been made). The brand has also maintained a consistent media presence: PG Tips has always held the dominant share of voice in the tea market, only slightly varying its advertising spend in real terms from year to year, whereas competitive budgets have fluctuated considerably.

Having rapidly found a winning formula, the agency has not of course simply churned out more, very similar Chimps commercials. Viewers continually need new ideas, and also the period has been one of rapid social change: consequently the Chimps have had to reflect trends in society in order to avoid getting 'dated'; this has required constant change within the creative vehicle.

PG Tips performance 1955–1958

While complete data from the period do not survive, the brand's volume share seems to have grown from about 10% to 23% in its rise from fourth to leading brand. In today's values, even in the contracted current market, the 13% gain would represent a sales value of £50m.

Analysing possible growth factors

By elimination, the only variable that can have caused the rise was advertising. The only other possible factors would have been the following:

1. *The name change* to 'PG Tips'. However, consumers were already abbreviating Pre-Gestive as 'PG', and the formal change occurred without effect on volume, a full year before advertising – and share growth – began.
2. *Taste*. The product blend was not changed at the time the advertising first broke.
3. *Distribution*. The brand was already strongly distributed. (Before own-label emerged, the stocking of four brands was quite normal.)
4. *Price*. The brand sold at the same price premium to other brands both before and after the campaign began.

Evidence for advertising as the key variable

It should be noted that the brand's growth coincided with a period of very rapid ITV penetration growth: the Chimps was the first tea brand TV advertising.

Noting that the main purpose of this paper is to demonstrate long-term effects, it seems evident, however, that the advertising was also responsible for propelling the brand into an initial leadership position. Hence the advertising had a dramatic short-term sales-increasing effect in its first three years.

The tea market 1956–1989

Particularly from the 1960s, tea has generically been eroded by coffee and substitutes, its overall volume consumption steadily shrinking from 156 million kg in 1964 to 110 million kg in 1989. Structural changes within the tea market since the 1950s have included the introduction of the tea bag, and the steady emergence of own-label.

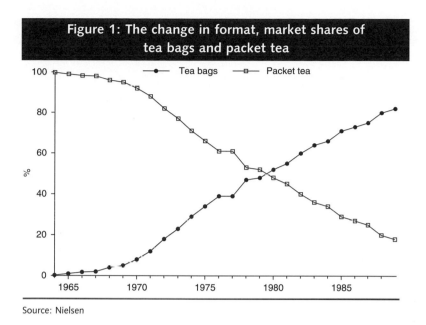

Figure 1: The change in format, market shares of tea bags and packet tea

Source: Nielsen

Tea bags

Until 1963, all tea was sold in packets – loose leaves for brewing in a pot. The arrival of tea bags (Figure 1) heralded a format change that now dominates, with bags today accounting for 80% of tea volume.

The rise of own-label

As in many markets, own-label has significantly eroded the volume of branded teas (Figure 2). It can be seen that PG Tips has both benefited more than other brands from the introduction of tea bags (even though they were launched by a competitor) and has lost less than other brands to own-label over the last 34 years, because it assimilated added value.

PG Tips performance 1959–1989

The brand has continued as leader, with a high and stable share, certainly ever since 1968, when surviving data began. It has faced intense competition pressure over the period, with other brands being relaunched (e.g. Quickbrew in 1986) and intermittently out-spending PG Tips. In addition, competitors have used every conceivable promotional weapon to erode PG Tips' share. None of these tactics has dented the brand's position for any length of time.

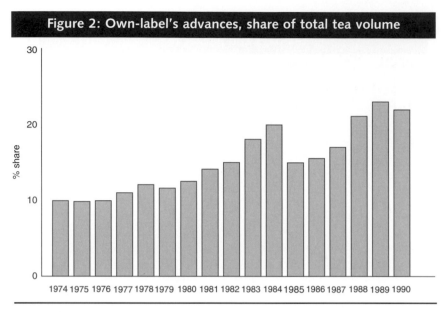

Figure 2: Own-label's advances, share of total tea volume

Source: Nielsen

The concept of added value

The brand's stable dominance derives from having assimilated, over the years, increasingly perceived 'added value' – supplementing the functional benefits of the product. (It has already been noted that the latter are essentially generic.)

Evidence of added value
It can be shown that this accrued 'added value' is sufficient to motivate consumers to buy the brand despite price and other factors, and takes many forms.

Branded vs blind product tests. Consumers always find it difficult to distinguish in this market between competing products in blind taste tests. Thus in a typical 1983 test consumers rating different teas on a seven-point scale showed a variation of only 1% or 2%. But in branded tests, after eliminating brand size factors, PG is consistently perceived as the best tasting (PG index 100, Tetley 85, Typhoo 40).

Price premium. Added value attributed to the brand enables it consistently to support a price premium over functionally similar competitors, without share

loss, as evidenced by an overview of PG Tips' price premium over time from
(1) Nielsen, (2) recent econometric analyses and (3) the consequences of
external effects on price.

According to econometric analyses using data from the tea bag sector (which
now holds 80% of the market), modelling PG Tips and Tetley against
relevant variables, PG is markedly less sensitive than Tetley to price changes
by both branded and own-label competitors. A 1% increase in PG's price
relative to Tetley leads to a drop of 0.4% share points. A similar increase in
Tetley's price has a much greater (1.4%) effect on its share.

The external effects of both rocketing coffee bean and tea lead prices in 1977
had negative effects on both beverages. In coffee, cheaper chicory-based
blends grew to 30% of the market. The coffee brand leader Nescafé was
especially hard-hit. Tea market volume dropped 10%. However, PG (unlike
Nescafé) retained a 23% brand share.

Resilience in the face of short-term media withdrawal

Econometric analysis shows that reduced adspend compared to competitors
produces a very small short-term decline for PG Tips – a drop of 100 TVRs
compared to Tetley results in a loss of 0.07% share points for PG. Tetley is
markedly more sensitive a drop of 100 TVRs relative to PG results in a
share loss of 1.7% share points for Tetley. (A downside to this inbuilt
strength is that short-term share-building through increased media weight is
relatively expensive: Tetley's share, for instance, is more upwardly responsive
to its advertising.)

Further evidence of relative insensitivity to short-term declines in share of
voice is seen in the brand's performance after the 1979 ITV strike, when
print and radio were the only media available. Its share of voice fell to
12.3% against a more usual value of 20–30%, but its market share remained
stable at 25% that year.

Salience and consumer perceptions

PG Tips is consistently well known and well perceived. Thus throughout the
1980s it had higher spontaneous recall than the nearest competitor. Indexed,
the average score across the decade was: PG, 100; Typhoo, 91; Tetley, 58. It

Table 1: Brand attributes, March 1990			
Average percentage agreeing:	PG Tips	Tetley	Typhoo
Particularly popular	100	83	83
Particularly good quality	100	54	76
Best taste	100	85	40

Source: Millward Brown

also consistently outperforms these other brands on perceived popularity, quality and taste (see Table 1).

Capturing the tea bag sector

The history of the UK tea bag sector began in 1963 when an entirely new tea brand, Tetley, first introduced bags (Tetley has never offered packet tea). For three reasons, Brooke Bond was slow to introduce a competing PG tea bag: early sector growth was slow, suggesting little consumer demand; the volume implications of bags were negative, as loose-tea users tend to use more tea; and it was not in the brands' immediate interest as market leader to promote a variant.

PG Tips tea bags were introduced in 1967, four years after Tetley's launch, when bags still accounted for only 1.4% of total tea sales, but had been growing 50% year on year. Tetley dominated the bag sector with a 71% share. However, PG Tips tea bag sales grew steadily after launch (Figure 3), and when other tea bag brands proliferated it was Tetley that lost share.

Tea bag brand media expenditures are not now available for 1967 or 1968. However, Tetley outspent PG bag expenditure by 22% in the three years 1969–71, yet by 1972 PG Tips had become brand leader in the bag sector. The existing perceived added value of the PG Tips brand evidently swung the balance, and left Tetley the more vulnerable to heavy later competition. (The two brands were equal in quality terms; distribution and price if anything favoured Tetley.)

Resilience in the face of own-label
Similarly, and for the same reasons, PG Tips has been remarkably resilient since the onset of own-label (see Figure 4), despite its relatively higher premium price over own-label compared with competitive brands.

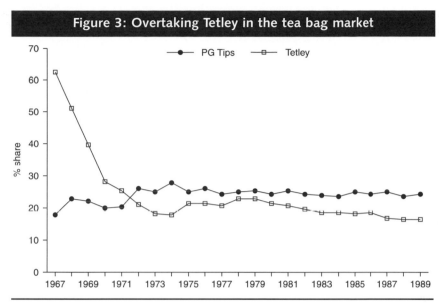

Figure 3: Overtaking Tetley in the tea bag market

Source: Nielsen

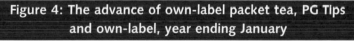

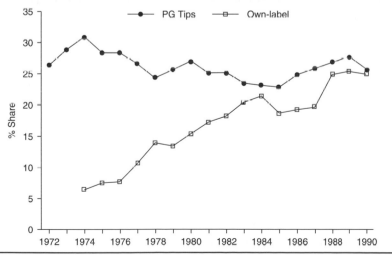

Figure 4: The advance of own-label packet tea, PG Tips and own-label, year ending January

Source: Nielsen

Isolating the effects of the Chimps campaign 1959–1989

Just as it has been shown that the Chimps advertising created the brand's initial leadership in the 1950s, it can be demonstrated that the 'added value' sustaining it through the market events outlined above also derives from this campaign, on three grounds. These are that:

1. Other potential causal factors provide no plausible alternative explanation.
2. Only its distinctive creative approach, and advertising investment level, distinguish the brand from less successful competitors.
3. Considerable 'soft' evidence, showing how the advertising works, correlates with aspects of the brand's values – which can be indirectly measured quantifiably.

Eliminating other factors

Many aspects of the PG Tips brands are matched by competitors, and therefore could not be the source of its perceived added values. These are:

- *The product*, which while excellent, and blended to a standard rather than to a raw material price, is indistinguishable in blind product tests (see above).
- *Promotions* for the brand appear to have been neither heavier nor of greater value than competitors'; if sometimes more effective, this would be an effect of innate added value rather than a cause.
- *Sterling distribution* has been comparable and high for all three major brands (in March 1990 all three had 90%+ sterling distribution), so availability has not been a factor.
- *The brand's pricing* has been at a consistent 1% premium over its closest brand competitors; against own-label the premium has been widening over time: in September 1989 it was 57% more expensive, compared with 24% in September 1971.
- *Packaging* is technically a less easily eliminated variable, but there is no evidence that the brand has a significant design edge over competitors – indeed the opposite.
- *Repeat purchase*, if a function of added value at all, seems originally to have been generated and thereafter sustained by the Chimps advertising, and must therefore be counted as a secondary effect.

In sum, this process of elimination leaves consistent advertising and consistent advertising weight as the only identifiable drivers of 'added value'.

Comparison with other brands' performance

A number of competitive brands have suffered in the marketplace over time (Table 2) but enjoyed comparability with PG Tips in terms of product, pricing and distribution before their decline. The significant difference is that these brands chopped and changed with regard to the content of their advertising, and sustained generally lower levels of advertising support overall.

Table 2: Long-term share trends – standard tea bags				
	1975 (%)	1980 (%)	1985 (%)	1990 (%)
Tetley	21.2	21.1	18.1	17.2
Quickbrew	10.8	9.5	6.4	4.6
Typhoo/Freshbrew	11.1	9.0	6.4	7.1

Note: we have only historical data for Typhoo and Freshbrew combined
Source: Nielsen, year ending January

The mechanics: how advertising works

Further circumstantial evidence as to how advertising has built the brand's added value may be seen in aspects of consumers' reaction to it:

- *Awareness and appeal*. The Chimps campaign enjoys higher recall than all other tea campaigns. It also seems to be the most efficient campaign in generating awareness on the basis of the predicted awareness effects of TVRs in a previously unadvertised region. Finally, attitudes to the Chimps campaign are highly favourable compared with market norms.
- *Specific brand benefits*. A core message of all Chimps advertising has been along the lines of 'There is no other tea to beat PG ... it's the taste'. It seems evident that the entertaining and lovable context of the advertising enables this message of quality to be accepted.
- *Assumption of tea values*. Interestingly many consumers describe the advertising almost in terms used to describe their preferred tea – as a 'pick-me-up'.

Excluding all other variables, the financial edge, or corresponding cost benefit that appears to have been achieved by the Chimps, may be considered in the form of three specific consequences, as follows:

1. *Financial benefits of long-term brand leadership.* Noting the well-documented difficulty of accurately isolating commercial advertising effects, it is nevertheless possible to identify what revenue would have been lost had the brand remained number four – its position in the 1950s. On this basis, the Chimps have arguably helped generate an additional £2bn sales revenue across the last 20 years. At the most conservative estimates, the profit generated must be markedly higher than the total advertising cost over the whole 34-year period. These costs over the past 20 years have been £86m for media as measured by MEAL and £6m for production – a total of £92m – at 1985 prices.

2. *Financial benefits of price premium.* The extra revenue above what PG Tips would have generated at average branded prices (1985 values) is some £125m over the last 20 years.

3. *Financial benefits of capturing the tea bag market.* Were PG Tips, without the Chimps, to have remained second brand to Tetley, then (again at 1985 prices) its profits would have been £200m less – disregarding the disproportionately larger advertising cost of supporting a number-two brand.

Conclusions

Over the 34 years since its first TV promotion, PG Tips has been an extraordinarily successful and resilient brand – remaining clear market leader for the whole of the period, seeing off fierce competitive challenges (particularly Tetley and its tea bag innovation) and sustaining a significant price premium.

Throughout this time, the brand has consistently employed the same advertising theme – the Chimps – and, except for short periods, has sustained consistent advertising investment and share of voice. Other than this, the brand has had no significant edge over its competitors, whether in terms of product quality, distribution, promotion or packaging.

It has been shown that after building the brand's initial market, the consistent Chimps advertising and expenditure level went on to build 'added values' for PG Tips, which have sustained its strength and continued to generate huge profits over and above the advertising investment.

BMW
How 15 years of consistent advertising helped BMW treble sales without losing prestige

Grand Prix winner 1994

An objective of these awards is 'better understanding of how advertising works'. This case study shows how consistent advertising for BMW over a long period of time has built an exceptionally strong brand.

Creating the perception of a strong personality requires consistency. We say that a person whose behaviour is inconsistent from day to day (one day jolly, but the next day sad; one day confident, but the next day insecure) has a disturbed personality. But we say a person whose behaviour is consistent day in and day out has a strong personality. It follows that consistent advertising campaigns are more likely to build strong brand personalities.

This case history also suggests that the so-called 'death of brands', which has excited some commentators, has been greatly exaggerated. It shows that high consumer demand for the BMW brand helped BMW (GB) and its dealers to sell more cars, at high margins, than would be expected.

BMW's business objectives

BMW (GB) was established in 1979 as a wholly owned subsidiary of BMW (AG). It replaced a distributor that also sold other 'performance' marques

Abridged version of the original case study written in 1994 by Tim Broadbent (WCRS) for BMW (GB) Ltd.

such as Maserati. Its objective was to treble volume sales by 1990 (from 13,000 new cars a year to 40,000) while maintaining high profit margins.

Advertising objectives

A primary advertising objective was to create a richer brand image. BMWs were mainly known as performance cars, reflecting the models imported in the 1970s. It was necessary to reach beyond the 'enthusiast' consumer segment in order to achieve the sales target.

A secondary objective was to improve BMW's reputation as a manufacturer of prestige cars, even though people would see more of the less exclusive models on the road as sales grew.

The advertising strategy

BMW's strategy has been shaped by four concepts: core brand values, sniper strategy, centre of gravity and BMW tone of voice.

Core brand values

Research indicates that the BMW brand is selected before individual models.

The brand was, in the past, very demanding of its driver as he or she was expected to share the potency of its performance imagery. Broadening its image allowed more types of driver to desire BMW and rationalise its high price.

Increasing the brand's prestige helped sell more affordable models; as a younger marque than Mercedes or Jaguar, BMW at that point lacked the prestige conferred by heritage.

> A BMW *doesn't give me any prestige to arrive outside the Polygon Hotel in, I'll be honest. The BMW is not – well, the mechanics are brilliant, but it does nothing for me.*

> I, *rightly or wrongly, regard that Mercedes have had a quality motor car for a good while, and BMW are trying very hard to catch up the Mercedes image. But they are a younger company who are coming along, if you like, behind a position that Mercedes have been in for a while.*

> *I don't think they're in that [Mercedes/Jaguar] club yet.*
> Car clinic qualitative research, Communications Research Ltd
> (July 1980)

Consumer research and 'product interrogation' with BMW engineers in Germany ('interrogating the product until it confesses to its strengths' is a cornerstone in the WCRS strategic process) identified four core brand values. These values shape all BMW communications, though their expression in advertising has evolved in response to social, economic, environmental and competitive changes. The four values are as follows:

1. *Performance.* This has evolved from 'cars that go faster' to 'cars that are rewarding to drive', as pure 0–60 mph acceleration has become less relevant (and socially acceptable) in today's driving conditions.

2. *Quality.* This has evolved from 'cars that are well made' to 'quality that permeates every aspect of BMW ownership, from initial design through to servicing', as standards of car construction have risen among all manufacturers.

3. *Advanced technology.* This has evolved from 'the latest technology' to 'the most relevant and thoughtful technology', as other manufacturers – particularly Japanese – have packed their cars with hi-tech gizmos.

4. *Exclusivity.* The product of these values has evolved from 'rarity and snob value' to 'values not available elsewhere – only BMW could make a car like this', as the number of BMWs seen on the road has increased. The evolution of core values ensured that BMW, the ultimate yuppy driving machine of the 1980s, remains a relevant and socially acceptable brand in the recessionary 1990s.

Sniper strategy

BMW advertising in Britain is notable for the production of a large number of different advertisements every year. Each ad shows a different aspect of core brand values, aimed at a particular group in the marketplace, hence the term 'sniper strategy'.

Research is used to identify particular groups of prospective customers and establish which attributes are most important to them. For example, an ad about quality would help sell a 3 Series to an older man who values this attribute most, while an ad about 3 Series performance would be more attractive to a successful young executive.

Since 1979, 253 colour advertisements in leisure and weekend magazines, and – more recently – 24 television commercials, all reflecting core values, have created a richer image for BMW in Britain than elsewhere. This approach differs from other car advertisers, who make fewer advertisements and show each one more often. But BMW cars are not mass produced, so neither are BMW advertisements.

Centre of gravity

This concept recognises that the BMW brand is made up of many models varying dramatically in price and performance but sharing a driving experience that can be identified as BMW (see Figure 1). Placing greater advertising emphasis than sales warrant on more advanced models raises the centre (average perception) of the brand higher. This benefits the less expensive models in the range by adding to the intangible desirability of owning a BMW; it militates against hardnosed comparisons of price/specification/performance with 'ordinary' cars. For example, a BMW 316i buyer would currently have to spend an extra £2000 to match competitive specification, and he or she could easily choose a faster car at the price but then they would not own a BMW.

Many ads have stressed the similarities between the less expensive and more expensive models in the range.

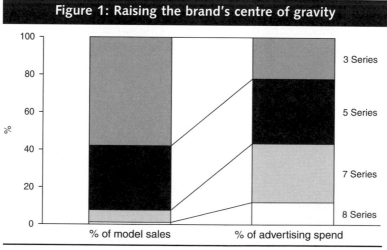

Figure 1: Raising the brand's centre of gravity

Base: 1990, a typical year that had no major new car launches

BMW tone of voice

The BMW advertising produced over the years by WCRS looks and feels remarkably similar because of its consistent tone of voice. The 'BMW world' is not warm. There are few humans or signs of humans, because humanity can suggest fallibility, whereas BMWs are shown as precise, cold, technical icons with jewel-like perfection.

The car is the master of each ad. The advertising idea is based on facts about the car. The art direction is a neutral frame in which the idea exists. There are no contrivances to add superficial glamour, such as stately homes, sunsets or glamorous blondes. Assumptive wit is used to puncture pomposity and create a feeling of belonging to the 'BMW club' among those who enjoy the joke.

These values have been consistent across all BMW communications, creating a campaign that is better known than would be predicted from BMW's relatively modest advertising budget. Since 1980, BMW has spent £91m on advertising (at MEAL prices), which is a modest sum against sales of £6.3bn.

Summary of BMW's strategy since 1979

BMW (GB) approached the challenge of trebling sales volume at high margins by using advertising to build the BMW brand. It changed the perception of BMWs from performance cars to a richer view of the brand.

This was achieved by advertising additional 'core brand values', and by the sniper strategy of communicating many aspects of BMW values in a large number of advertisements.

The marque's prestige was enhanced by raising the brand's 'centre of gravity', associating the values of top-end BMWs with more affordable models. Its consistent tone of voice harnessed the energy of all BMW communications to the overall brand. The question is, did this strategy work? In the following sections we show that it worked superbly.

BMW's business success

BMW (GB) set out to treble sales. This has been achieved. Market share has almost trebled too, as BMW sales outperformed the market (see Figure 2).

Further, the company set out to achieve growth with high profit margins. This has also been achieved.

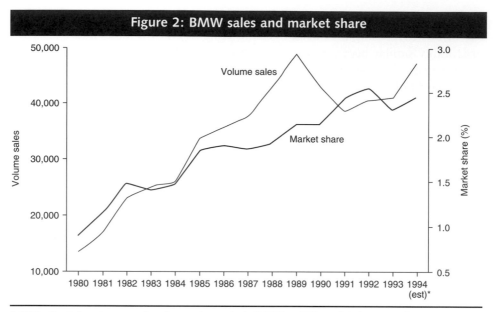

Figure 2: BMW sales and market share

* 1994 estimate based on percentage increase in year to April 1994 vs 1993; market share to April 1994
Source: BMW, SMMT

BMW (GB) has made profits every single year since 1980. Annual profits depend on the prevailing sterling/Deutschmark exchange rate; however, total company profits since 1980 amount to just under £400m (source: BMW company reports).

What are the causes of BMW's exceptional sales success?

To answer this question, we shall first show that price, distribution and improved products could not be solely responsible for BMW's sales success; then we shall show that richer brand imagery has created exceptionally strong consumer demand.

A detailed account of the proof is available in the full paper; however, the key elements are listed below:

1. Factors that could not explain BMW's sales success.
   - Lower prices, distribution changes and improved product can be excluded as factors.
   - Specifically, sales success is not just due to better products because the same cars have sold better in Britain than in other countries (Figure 3).

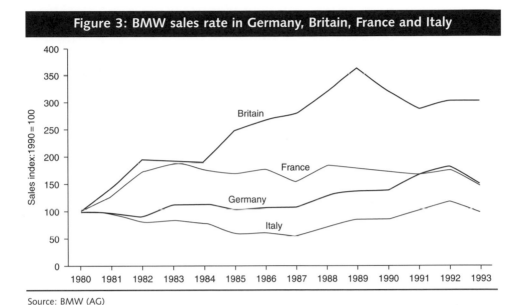

Figure 3: BMW sales rate in Germany, Britain, France and Italy

Source: BMW (AG)

2. The strength of the BMW brand in Britain.
   ■ Despite the number of BMWs increasing from 81,000 in 1980 to 455,000 in 1993, BMW imagery has improved and it has become the strongest marque in Britain, stronger even than Mercedes on key attributes.
   ■ Consumer demand is second only to Vauxhall, far stronger than BMW's market share.
   ■ BMW owners are more likely to repurchase than Audi owners, despite the latter being equally reliable cars.
   ■ Dealers believe BMW is the best franchise.

3. How advertising consistency created an exceptionally strong brand.
   ■ BMW's advertising is better known than would be expected on its relatively modest budget (Figure 4).
   ■ Consistency is a signal to consumers about the company that is responsible for the cars and how they are advertised. BMW is seen to have a view of how quality cars ought to be. 'This impression of dedicated determination has been created by the consistency with which BMW has advertised the excellence of its cars for 15 years' (source: Cragg Ross Dawson, The BMW Brand, March 1994).

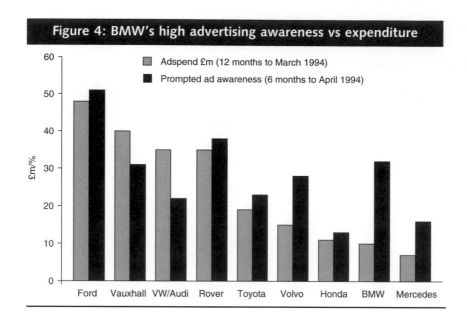

Figure 4: BMW's high advertising awareness vs expenditure

The value of the BMW brand

You pay £9000 for the car and £5000 for the badge.

Competitive car owner, 1990

Since 1979 BMW prices rose higher than market prices; BMW's distribution rose by only 10%; yet sales trebled, which is a much higher rate of growth than in other European markets that sold the same cars.

The BMW brand in Britain is stronger than it was in 1979; is now stronger than other leading marques such as Mercedes; Britain is the only market in which BMW is stronger than Mercedes; Britain is the only market in which the brand has become as strong as it is in Germany, if not stronger.

The only reasonable explanation for BMW's sales success in Britain is that the exceptional strength of the brand has created exceptionally strong consumer demand; and it has been explained how the consistency of BMW's advertising has created the impression of a company dedicated to the manufacture of good cars.

The remaining issues are to try to place a cash value on the extra strength of the brand in Britain, and then to relate this value to the cost of the advertising that helped create the extra brand strength.

There are two empirical methods of estimating how much of BMW's sales are due to the strength of the brand. First, suppose that BMW had average rate-of-sale increases – the same as the market rate-of-sale increases during 1980–93. Second, suppose that BMW sales in Britain had grown at the same rate as they did in Germany, France and Italy during the period 1980–93. Calculating BMW's hypothetical sales under both these suppositions eliminates some of the variables that would mask how much influence the stronger brand has had on sales. The effect of product improvements is eliminated in the comparison between other countries and Britain, because all markets received the same improved products. The effect of economic recession hitting European car markets at different times is eliminated in the average market rate-of-sale comparison, because the recession in Britain hit BMW at the same time as other marques.

Figures 5 and 6 show what volume sales would have been under both suppositions, compared to actual volume sales. It can be seen that in both cases sales would have been significantly lower. Table 1 shows how much sales revenue would have been lost. The table shows that extra strength of the BMW brand has probably been worth around £2.7bn–£3.2bn in extra sales over the past 15 years. These numbers are so large and surprising it may be worth repeating that only two reasonable assumptions have been tested: that BMW could have had average rate-of-sale increases, or that

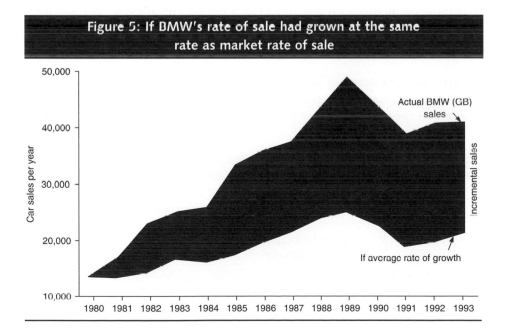

Figure 5: If BMW's rate of sale had grown at the same rate as market rate of sale

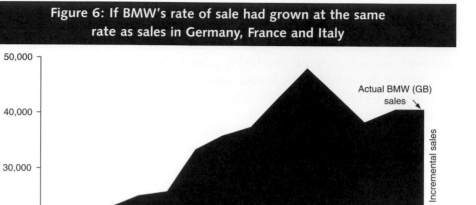

Figure 6: If BMW's rate of sale had grown at the same rate as sales in Germany, France and Italy

BMW could have had the same sales growth as in other major European markets.

What these calculations do not allow for is improvements in dealer quality. There is no way to quantify dealer quality over time and across markets, therefore it can only be assumed to be a constant for these calculations.

However, improvements in dealer quality generally relate to better conversions of prospects to sales. What advertising does is deliver new prospects in the first place. In 1993, for example, BMW's advertising created

Table 1: Sales revenue			
	Actual sales 1980–93	If BMW's rate of sale increased at the same rate as all cars' rate of sale	If BMW had same sales growth as in Germany, France and Italy
Sales volume	466,327	263,989	255,440
Sales value	£6.3bn	£3.6bn	£3.1bn
Actual sales higher by		£2.7bn	£3.2bn

35,000 enquiries, nearly all from non-customers, which helped dealers sell to the 14,600 new customers won last year. So far this year (to 20 May 1994), advertising has been responsible for 99% of dealers' 'hot' and 'medium' prospects.

Conclusions

It has been demonstrated in all previous IPA car case histories that a sudden twitch to the needles of research dials coincided with changes in sales. However, the research deck is stacked against a similar demonstration here.

What it is possible to show is that BMW's advertising set out to enrich the brand's appeal, and that this has happened, and this has only happened in Britain, and that only in Britain have sales trebled.

BMW's advertising expenditure through WCRS has been £91m. As this has helped create brand values worth some £3bn in extra sales, the value of BMW's brand-building campaign seems beyond question.

Using advertising to orientate your organisation

Chapter 10
David Golding
Planning Director, Rainey Kelly Campbell Roalfe/Y&R

The Lancaster Bomber has famously been described as 10,000 rivets flying in close formation. As well as capturing the essence of this great and heroic airplane this is a pretty apt description of many organisations. Many a CEO must have felt like a mini Guy Gibson as he or she bravely tries to pilot all their staff, suppliers and partners in the same profitable direction. Anything that can make this formation tighter, more committed and more manoeuvrable has to be a good thing.

But advertising is rarely front of mind as a tool in this endeavour. More likely companies will invest in numerous 'live the brand' awayday sessions as they try to motivate all the different stakeholders in their business to really get behind where the business is aiming to go, and how it's intending to get there. These are usually very useful but they are limited in their reach – only so many staff/suppliers/analysts etc. can attend conferences or workshops. So how can CEOs truly and powerfully communicate their ambition, vision and passion for the business to as broad an audience as possible? Well, they might try an advertising campaign. Or at least they might after reading the Tesco and Barnardo's IPA Effectiveness Awards papers from 2000 and 2002.

There are several landmark case studies that all MBA students are taught. Few finish business school without a pretty good idea of the inner workings of Dell, Federal Express or Amazon.com. One other famous case involves Sears Roebuck, the US retail giant, which has proven the link between improved customer and staff satisfaction and bottom-line returns. And I believe that in these two IPA Effectiveness Awards papers we have two more important pieces of hard proof to augment the Sears study. Both underline how an organisation, galvanised by a motivating, publicly stated philosophy, can become more successful than any CEO, analyst or marketing director could have imagined.

These two papers recognise the explosive effects that advertising can have across whole organisations. They are not alone: other IPA winners not reviewed in this book have added to this knowledge and I refer to some of these later. However, by looking at how the Tesco and Barnardo's campaigns touched so many in their respective enterprises we can start to see how advertising is a force that acts for good not just on people as consumers but people as employees, volunteers, opinion-formers and ambassadors.

So, if you're an MD or CEO of an organisation and you'd like to get your advertising working to motivate all the stakeholders in your business, what can you learn from Tesco and Barnardo's?

The value of making a public statement of brand intent

Both these case studies illustrate the power of setting an organisation a mission and then making that mission a public statement of brand intent.

There's much written about mission statements: just skim-read a copy of James Collins and Jerry Porras's book *Built to Last* and you'll get a pretty clear idea about the good, the bad and the uglier missions adopted by various different organisations.

In the cases of Tesco and Barnardo's, the respective advertising agencies played a significant role in helping to define and then articulate powerful statements of brand intent. In the case of Barnardo's, the charity set itself the clear goal of 'giving children back their future'. For Tesco it was the recognition that Every Little Helps in making the whole shopping experience more rewarding for customers.

These are two different missions but both are hugely powerful organisational ideas. These aren't just promises to the customer: they are guiding beacons for everyone associated with both enterprises.

For Barnardo's, that new focus on children's futures led to widespread changes in how the charity went about a broad range of fundamental practices. New approaches were taken to how lobbying was undertaken, how public relations were handled, and even to what projects were proposed. All of these activities were redirected towards the delivering of positive futures for disadvantaged children. In short, everyone in and around the organisation became future-focused, contextualising their roles in terms of how they contributed to creating better futures for disadvantaged children.

For Tesco, the emphasis on incremental improvements to the customer experience has been equally fundamental, with 114 new initiatives being put in place between November 1993 and March 1995 alone. And these initiatives covered the whole organisation, whether they involved front-line staff behaviour (e.g. bag-packing services), store infrastructure (e.g. parent and child parking) or head-office financial strategies (e.g. Clubcard).

The focus here is not simply to highlight the value of having a clear company mission, but instead to see how advertising can unite an organisation. The two are linked. It is doubtful whether either statement of brand intent for

Tesco or Barnardo's would have been so impactful if they hadn't formed the central premise of the advertising campaigns developed around them. A plaque on the wall in reception simply doesn't act with the same force as a powerful and public advertising campaign.

Tesco and Barnardo's certainly put their brand missions at the heart of their advertising campaigns. In its campaigns, Barnardo's showed both sides of the future: what a child could become with or without Barnardo's help. Tesco equally presented what Every Little Helps means to customers in a clear, observable and direct way: in each ad 'Dotty' experienced the benefits of each initiative. Other brands too have been highly successful in putting their mission statements at the centre of their advertising. Those recognised by the IPA Awards over the years range from BMW's desire to produce the 'Ultimate Driving Machine' through to Stella Artois's determination never to compromise quality for price.

However, for Tesco and Barnardo's the advertising amplifies a brand statement into a truly organisational idea rather than just an advertising tagline. A core reason for this is how staff are shown to respond to the advertising.

Staff watch, and learn from, their employer's advertising

As well as articulating the driving aims of the organisation, these cases illustrate the real value that advertising can bring to staff motivation and loyalty.

Staff love seeing themselves in advertising. They might be bad actors, and they might not be right as ambassadors for lots of brands, but where they are featured the benefits to morale and motivation can be marked.

The Tesco case in particular demonstrates how staff feel more a part of the brand through their role in the advertising. They see how what they do matters to customers. And, crucially, they get a guide to how they should be acting. This sense of 'free' staff training is a huge learning experience from which so many service brands could benefit. Advertising as illustration of best practice is arguably much more effective than the standard 'John Cleese' training videos because it is so public a demonstration. Staff get to see customer expectations and can respond accordingly.

The Barnardo's case similarly proves how the advertising motivated key front-line teams, in this case the social workers involved with Barnardo's projects. Here it was achieved less by showing how to behave and act, and more through illustrating the perils that face the disadvantaged if they don't do their job to the best of their abilities.

Beyond these two examples the Halifax paper from 2002 is another very strong illustration of how staff reacted positively to being featured in advertising. The Halifax actually set out to target 'colleagues' as well as customers with its 'Howard' campaign and the results in terms of staff engagement with the campaign and its message are very compelling.

Like the ads, like the boss

So featuring staff in communications can be a powerful motivational and training tool. However, regardless of whether you follow this path, these cases demonstrate how important it is that staff like the ads you do create. If staff like the ads created for their company they will feel more positive about working for it. If they hear friends and family saying good things about the advertising then this too adds to a sense of pride.

When developing and researching advertising it is important to think about how staff will respond to it. Add a couple of focus groups to those you're planning to do with consumers and explore how the advertising makes staff at various levels in the organisation feel about the company they work for. In short, follow the advice of the Halifax and make staff a defined target audience group for the advertising.

When launching a campaign, help make staff feel privileged as a preview audience and help them to see, understand and engage with the campaign. In this way not only will they enjoy it more when they see it in the media but they will become more active ambassadors, urging friends to look out for 'their new ads' – with a staff base the size of Tesco's this is no small PR drive.

Ads that recruit customers can also recruit staff

Both Tesco and Barnardo's are brands that had image problems before their respective campaigns were devised. Tesco's perception as *the* pile 'em high retailer was a significant millstone around its neck as the grocery market moved more towards the quality side of the value equation. Barnardo's was *the* orphanage charity as orphanages became less commonplace across the UK.

When I say '*the*' I mean only perceptually. Tesco at the start of the 1990s had made huge leaps forward in store and product quality, while Barnardo's had started its move from orphanages to far wider and deeper work with children as early as the mid-1960s. And yet these changes were eclipsed by entrenched brand images.

Like so many brands, therefore, both Tesco and Barnardo's needed to employ advertising to help the public reappraise their offering, to close the perception–reality gap. And both papers clearly demonstrate how effective the advertising has been in achieving this and thereby delivering a greater customer base as a result. Other papers that present very clear evidence of advertising closing a perception–reality gap include Skoda (2002) and the M&S lingerie paper (2004).

However, both Tesco and Barnardo's also go on to demonstrate how improvements in public image have important ramifications for the recruitment of the right people to work for the organisation.

Tesco has found it significantly easier to recruit the best graduates and marketers following the Every Little Helps campaign. The highest-calibre people are more willing to consider working for the highest-profile, most forward-looking and dynamic organisations.

Equally, Barnardo's has, as the case states, 'been able to recruit much younger volunteers in sectors of the community where it had no record of fundraisers before'.

Advertising can influence the influencers

Connecting with customers and motivating staff are important functions of a good advertising campaign. However, there remain stakeholders beyond these two audiences that are important to an organisation's performance. Here we're talking about business partners/suppliers, the City, regulators and policy-makers.

Whether the advertising is simply seen by these audiences as part of a broad consumer campaign or presented more directly to them using a more targeted approach, a consumer-orientated campaign can drive powerful reactions among a non-consumer and non-staff audience.

As the Barnardo's case presents so well, advertising can significantly help set the agenda within which much classic lobbying activity can thrive. By raising a brand's profile as well as its ambitions, those engaged by the lobbying arm of a company will be better able to contextualise any specific messages they are presented with.

Equally, business partners – whether they be suppliers or corporate partners – respond well to a brand that is seen to have an improving public perception. A brand with a purpose, direction and commitment, illustrated through popular and high-profile advertising, is typically the sort of brand many would want to work alongside.

Food for thought (for CEOs)

- Examine your corporate mission statement. Could it form the basis of powerful, simple and effective advertising? Does it really motivate staff? Can a powerful idea be crafted to build upon anything that exists already in the company?
- Go public. If your statement of intent is a beacon for every stakeholder in your company, then stating it and celebrating it in your advertising will make it shine much more brightly.
- Include staff among the key target audiences when developing a campaign. Monitor staff reactions to the advertising as the campaign develops.
- Align HR and marketing to see how the advertising that is developed can be merchandised among the organisation to augment other 'live the brand' initiatives.
- Ensure corporate PR specialists are fully aware of the advertising as it is being developed. How does it impact upon/dovetail with their plans? Work to understand how to use your consumer-based advertising campaigns against other stakeholders.

Tesco
How 'Every Little Helps' was a big help to Tesco

Grand Prix winner 2000

The radical transformation of Tesco's fortunes from lacklustre number two to Britain's largest retailer has been well documented. Between 1990 and 1999, Tesco's turnover increased from £8bn to £17bn and its share rose from 9.1% to 15.4%, overtaking Sainsbury's to become market leader in 1995.

Of course, Tesco made radical structural changes. However, a fundamental turnaround in its brand image was essential to making these changes meaningful to consumers and other stakeholders alike.

Think back to 1990. Tesco still had its unappealing 'pile it high and sell it cheap' reputation. Incredulity would have greeted the suggestion that people might buy gourmet food and wine from Tesco or entrust it with their savings. From a company with flagging credibility, Tesco is now one of the nation's most trusted brands.

Advertising has been a consistent but relatively minor component of Tesco's total investment. However, strong evidence shows it has played a crucial role in transforming consumers' perceptions of Tesco, particularly those consumers who could not experience Tesco's in-store transformation (because, at the time, they did not shop there). Moreover, its transformed image has allowed Tesco to expand into a wide range of non-grocery sectors, where brand credibility is a key requirement.

Abridged version of the original case study written in 2000 by Ashleye Sharpe and Joanna Bamford (Lowe Lintas) for Tesco plc.

The advertising has also helped improve Tesco's image in the minds of three further audiences:

1. Tesco store staff – whose competent delivery of Tesco's initiatives was vital.
2. The marketing community – an important source of new talent to drive Tesco's development.
3. City analysts – who directly affect Tesco's share price.

A complex task

How do you establish the effect of advertising on the fortunes of an organisation with over 160,000 employees in more than 600 stores, each with around 20,000 lines, which regularly introduces new initiatives? The evidence that exists demonstrates clearly the effect of the advertising on image, behaviour and, ultimately, sales. Econometric modelling is a key component of this evidence. Unusually, we have used it to help understand the effect of advertising on *image* as well as sales.

There are two phases to Tesco's transformation: pursuing and achieving market leadership (1990–95); consolidating this position (1995 onwards). We have interesting conclusions about the role of advertising during phase one, though the bulk of available evidence covers the period from 1995 onwards. For simplicity, we have concentrated on the effects of TV brand advertising only.

The pursuit of market leadership (1990–1995)

In the early 1980s, Tesco was still 'piling it high and selling it cheap'. Yet it had set its sights on market leadership. It initiated a major programme to counteract its key weakness – quality. This was Sainsbury's strength.

From around 1983, Tesco started to upgrade its stores and the quality and range of what it sold. Yet even by 1990 it had failed to dent Sainsbury's dominance. Although the changes in-store were evident to existing customers, they had not affected Tesco's image among non-shoppers. As a result, few new shoppers had been persuaded to give Tesco a try in the period from the beginning of the Quality programme (1982) to the launch of the new campaign (1990).

The opportunity for advertising

The opportunity for advertising was to persuade non-shoppers to think again about Tesco by presenting it as a credible alternative to Sainsbury's. Equally importantly, people had to *want* to shop there on an emotional level – to be happy to be seen carrying a Tesco carrier bag.

The 'Quest for Quality' (May 1990–December 1992)

The first campaign, the 'Quest for Quality', ran from 1990 to 1992. It adopted a deliberately light-hearted approach. It starred Dudley Moore as a Tesco buyer who scoured the world in pursuit of an elusive flock of French free-range chickens, en route discovering other surprisingly high-quality products to add to Tesco's range.

The campaign was very impactful – peaking at 89% awareness. Non-shoppers even remembered the campaign more than they remembered advertising for the competitor stores they shopped at. The key message was understood and helped people begin to believe that Tesco was improving its quality.

'Every Little Helps' (November 1993–March 1995)

In 1993, having achieved significant improvements to product and store quality, Tesco embarked on a newer and bigger strategy. It understood that shopping is so much more than just the products you buy – and realised that none of its competitors was making serious attempts to improve the *whole* experience of shopping. Tesco capitalised on this by launching 114 new initiatives, which included mother and baby changing facilities, removal of sweets from checkouts, the 'One in Front' checkout-opening system, a new Value range and Clubcard.

The new strategy required new advertising since 'Dudley' was so closely associated just with the *products* that Tesco sold. The advertising idea was that while not everything in life goes perfectly, Tesco was doing its best to make at least one aspect – doing the shopping – a little easier. A new line, 'Every Little Helps', was used across all executions to capture Tesco's new consumer-orientated philosophy of always 'doing right by the customer'.

What happened?

Tesco's turnover increased by 38%, enabling it to overtake Sainsbury's in early 1995. In contrast to the period before 1990 when Tesco's in-store changes had not affected *non*-shoppers' image of Tesco or their willingness to shop there, 1.3 million extra households were persuaded to choose Tesco between 1990 and 1995.

Significantly, this penetration growth is not simply the result of more stores and increased floor space. Tesco's floor space grew by over four million square feet during the 'Dudley' and 'Every Little Helps' advertising. Nonetheless, the penetration gained per additional square foot was significantly higher during the latter than in the initial years of Tesco's expansion programme.

Consolidating leadership (mid-1995 onwards)

By 1995, as intended, 'Every Little Helps' had become the driving philosophy that steered every initiative that Tesco made. The advertising that was developed concentrated on customers' attitudes to Tesco. And this was no ordinary customer. The new campaign centred on 'the mother of all shoppers', Dotty Turnbull, who regards each of Tesco's initiatives as an opportunity to put the store to the test. In testing it to the limit, Dotty gives Tesco and, importantly, its staff, the opportunity to shine.

What happened?
Over the period of the 'Dotty' campaign, Tesco has strengthened its brand image vs Sainsbury's considerably. This is reflected in its widening share advantage over Sainsbury's (see Table 1). The growth was principally because more people were encouraged to shop at Tesco and, in contrast to the previous five years (where loyalty was static), those who did shop there also became more loyal. As before, penetration grew at a higher rate than the additional floor space might have suggested.

Table 1: Widening the market share gap between Tesco and Sainsbury's		
	1995 (%)	1999 (%)
Tesco	13.4	15.4
Sainsbury's	12.2	12.1

The value of advertising's effect beyond customers

Since the beginning of the 1990s Tesco's advertising has also helped change the image of Tesco for the better in the minds of two other important audiences: the staff and professional marketers. We have also assessed the advertising's direct impact on Tesco's share price by exploring the effects of advertising on a third audience – City analysts.

The impact of Tesco's advertising on store staff

It has been well documented that a failure on the part of advertising to meet the approval of staff can also have disastrous effects on *their* loyalty. Tesco has over 160,000 staff. The effect of the advertising on them is fundamental to the success of the 'Every Little Helps' strategy and to securing their loyalty.

Since 'Every Little Helps' was introduced in 1993 the advertising has been a very public statement of the kind of experience Tesco will deliver in store. The strategy can only be successful in securing loyalty (and satisfying new customers) if consumers see it in action. Hence, it is essential that staff believe in the advertising and deliver accordingly.

Tesco staff see the advertising as consumers, but the advertising is also used as a more motivating way to train staff in the 'Every Little Helps' philosophy than a memo or pep talk from a store manager. The new customer-orientated strategy was launched to the staff in a video, which used the advertising to demonstrate what was meant by the new strategy.

Ads have run on a loop in staff canteens and they are regularly featured in further 'First Class Service' training videos and the 'First Class Success' service bulletins that are issued to staff. This is an efficient way for Tesco to train its staff, since the advertising is effectively a 'free' training tool. The alternative of investing in separate video material for training can cost anything between £50,000 and £250,000 per film.

Using advertising to train staff is not only efficient, but also effective. Staff feel this way, and consumers see the results for themselves:

> *It makes you feel you should prove yourself. ... staff want to be the image that's shown in the ads.*

> *It sets an example to staff. It's informal training.*
>
> Tesco staff interviews

There is also another important issue here: advertising helps build loyalty by demonstrating that Tesco values its staff. With 160,000 staff, the costs of losing staff are significant. Most executions in the 'Dotty' campaign have deliberately given staff a key role in sorting out Dotty's demands. Research has shown that the campaign helps demonstrate how much Tesco values the staff's contribution to its business and, in doing so, it makes them feel more positive towards Tesco.

Furthermore, qualitative research reveals that the campaign makes staff feel more positive about working for Tesco:

> *Yes, it makes me proud. People turn around and say 'oooh, it's your shop'.*

> *It adds to the feeling that you're working for the best in the field.*

> *I think the atmosphere at work is jolly because of Dotty.*

> *Twenty-six years ago I'd say I worked in a shop. Now I say I work for Tesco.*
>
> Tesco staff interviews

The value of advertising in attracting better-quality marketers to Tesco

Headhunters agree that a company's image is important in attracting the best people – and that advertising is one of the factors that influences this.

> *Public image plays a key role in attracting potential employees. [This] is affected by all forms of communication, including consumer advertising.*
>
> Norman Broadbent International

Clever marketing has been instrumental in Tesco's success and it is essential that it continues to attract the best marketing talent around. Although retailing is not regarded as a particularly attractive sector in which to work, Tesco's positive public image has helped it shrug off the limited attractions of retail, enabling it to attract new talent easily. The advertising has been instrumental in transforming this image. It also directly affects the way marketers feel about Tesco as a potential employer.

Last year, for the second year running, Tesco was voted Britain's most admired company by its peers.

The advertising has also been influential in encouraging graduate applications to Tesco.

Tesco advertising's direct effect on share price

It would be expected that the advertising effect we have identified would indirectly impact upon Tesco's share price – all other things being equal, improvements in sales and market share ought ultimately to result in improvements in share price.

We canvassed City analysts' views of Tesco's corporate image, Tesco's advertising and the relationship between the two. The quotes below summarise our findings. It appears that the advertising has, indeed, shaped their views.

> *Clearly something has allowed Tesco to move forward into other markets more successfully than its competitors; ostensibly that is its brand, which has been served well by a consistent, high-profile advertising campaign.*
>
> Simon Champ, Dresdner Kleinwort Benson

> *Tesco advertising has been very sound. The basic approach has been to have a central theme of 'Every Little Helps', and personally I think it's worked. The key to Tesco's advertising has been to implement changes and then communicate these, gently reinforcing over time. Consistency is essence in retail. The brand has been consistent. The advertising has been consistent.*
>
> David McCarthy, Saloman Smith Barney

These findings have been corroborated by the *Financial Times*:

> *Analysts identify the new advertising campaign, 'Every Little Helps' – a more understated campaign [that] played on what people would recognise as Tesco's strengths, while on the other hand saying to its customers 'We recognise that you have got problems' – as 'one of the initiatives crucial in giving Tesco a competitive edge'.*

The advertising pays back

Direct payback

Using econometric modelling, we have calculated that the 'Dotty' campaign delivers an incremental £2.206bn of turnover (excluding VAT) across fiscal years 1995–99. Using Tesco's average operating margin over that same period, of 5.9%, we have calculated that the campaign delivers an incremental operating profit of £130m.

So every £1 spent on advertising generates an incremental £38 of turnover and £2.25 of operating profit. Thus the campaign pays for itself more than twice over, delivering a 225% return on investment. This is a significant payback to operating profit given that the 'Dotty' campaign has accounted for less than 1% of Tesco's operating costs over fiscal years 1995–99.

Additional revenue opportunities afforded by Tesco's image transformation

Expansion in non-staple categories is essential to Tesco's continued growth. We believe that the advertising has helped transform Tesco's brand image to the point that it is able to operate more successfully in grocery categories such as wine and gourmet food (via the launch of its premium range, 'Finest') where brand affinity is particularly important. This transformation in Tesco's credibility has also enabled it to expand into new non-grocery categories.

In conclusion, it would seem that 'Every Little Helps' has indeed been a big help to Tesco.

Giving Barnardo's back its future

Grand Prix winner 2002

This is the story of how babies injecting heroin and adults committing suicide changed the face of Britain's oldest children's charity for ever. Of how integrated communications turned a generation of brand rejecters into brand supporters, and influenced diverse audiences from MPs to students. How one of the most ambitious recruitment programmes ever conducted by a UK charity has ensured millions of pounds in donations for years to come. This is the story of how Barnardo's divorced itself from its orphanage past and embraced the future.

The brand problem

The importance of donations
A crisis in donations is probably the worst set of circumstances a charity could find itself in. Donations are a measure of its popularity and as such a source of pride. Donations are also of strategic importance:

- Donations income spells independence. Increased reliance on state funding compromises a charity's ability to lobby and campaign among MPs, a major area of the charity's work.
- Money from donations gives Barnardo's the opportunity to work in areas too politically sensitive to be funded by the state.

Abridged version of the original case study written in 2002 by Dan Goldstein (Bartle Bogle Hegarty) and Mary Daniels (Barnardo's) for Barnardo's.

■ The state pays only for existing services and does not joint-invest in new projects.

Donor age profile

The reason Barnardo's donations income was under threat lay in the profile of the charity's donor base. The people donating to Barnardo's were old: over half were over 65, a profile peculiar to Barnardo's.

The vast majority of Barnardo's donor base was recruited via the charity's direct mail programme. These people were affectionately referred to as 'Dorothy Donor'. Dorothy presented the charity with a series of problems:

■ Dorothy wasn't going to be around for ever – it was estimated that 5% of the donor base was dying each year.
■ Dorothy was giving one-off cash gifts when prompted to do so by direct mailers; only 3% of the donor base was giving via the more committed standing order/direct debit routes.
■ Dorothy was also a less valuable donor, giving less money in the way of donations than younger age groups.

It was clear that Barnardo's needed not only new donors but a new profile of donor:

■ younger
■ committed in their method of payment
■ longer term
■ higher value.

The 'lost generation'

In the past, Barnardo's was a children's charity famous for its orphanages. However, in 1966 Barnardo's began closing its orphanages. Over the next 35 years the charity was relatively quiet, with little communication about its new areas of work. This had a profound effect on how the charity was seen, particularly among younger age groups. For these people, 88% spontaneously associated Barnardo's with homes, orphanages and institutions – functions that appeared irrelevant to them in today's society:

> *I think for all of us, we have a mindset that says Barnardo's equals homes that are no longer needed. I personally wouldn't give money to keep children in institutions.*
> Male 35–45 (source: Plus Four Market Research Limited, March 1999, creative development research for recruitment direct mail)

Barnardo's orphanage past was a barrier for younger people. For them the charity was outmoded, old-fashioned and irrelevant – and hence less deserving. When Barnardo's approached Bartle Bogle Hegarty (BBH) in 1998, it was this generation of brand rejecters that the agency was tasked with recruiting into the brand.

The brand challenge

A new brand vision

The brand challenge was a considerable one – to replace Barnardo's orphanage past with a new vision. This vision had to represent the diverse work that the charity did today: 'What was the role that this 130-year-old organisation performed?', 'What did it do?', 'What was its purpose?'. The process employed by BBH in the development of the new vision involved:

- interviewing the heads of each major department within Barnardo's
- interviewing children that had benefited from Barnardo's work
- visiting the projects themselves and interviewing the social workers
- exploring Barnardo's rich history.

BBH identified a common and powerful theme. It was based on the unique way in which Barnardo's approached childcare: where other charities intervene in the immediate circumstances Barnardo's works to ensure the child's long-term 'emotional health'. Through this process Barnardo's changes the future for children. This thought became the absolute basis of how Barnardo's sees its role today:

> Barnardo's purpose is to help the most vulnerable children and young people transform their lives and fulfil their potential.
> Barnardo's Corporate Plan 2000/05

For communicating the new purpose, BBH needed to distil the vision further and expressed it as: 'Giving children back their future'.

Internal communication

The next task was to communicate Barnardo's new purpose to all 12,500 people that work for the charity. BBH, together with the marketing and communications department, ran 'Brand Roadshows' that travelled the country and visited each of the 16 regional offices. Within each office the new vision was presented to the heads of each department who in turn ran their own workshops for their own staff. By autumn 1999 all the people working for Barnardo's understood that their efforts were in the pursuit of a single definable cause: children's futures.

The new vision quickly began to shape the way in which the diverse functions within the charity operated:

- *Lobbying and influencing.* MPs were subject to literature and reports using children's futures as the context for their policy recommendations.
- *Public relations.* Journalists were courted on points of view and issues affecting the future welfare of children in the UK.
- *Corporate volunteering.* The charity began motivating corporate volunteers with 'future branded' literature.
- *Corporate relations.* Barnardo's now approached big consumer-facing companies with a brand partnership proposition not just as a 'good cause'.
- *The projects.* When pitching for funding, Barnardo's made sure that councillors were aware that the issue at stake wasn't money but 'children's futures'.

For the first time in decades there was a definable 'cause' by which Barnardo's could rally these audiences.

The communications plan

The task was to turn the lost generation of brand rejecters into active brand supporters.

The communications model
All marketing and communications activity changed its content and branding to 'Giving children back their future'. The relaunch consisted of three core activities:

1. Advertising was to reposition the brand as modern and deserving to the 35 to 55 year olds. It also needed to impact on opinion formers.
2. Face-to-face recruitment: a new channel to bring in new donors.
3. Direct mail continued recruitment and maintenance of Dorothy Donor.

Advertising

The advertising dramatised the 'future thought' in all its power. Children were shown acting out their future lives as a result of their disadvantaged childhood: a four year old robs a bank; a six year old solicits as a prostitute; an infant injects heroin. The copy described the troubled circumstances of their childhood, explaining how their lives took such a destructive path.

A second campaign showed images of dead adults. The copy described the childhood event that led to their death.

The advertising was in many ways designed to shock because it had to. The communication needed to shake entrenched views about Barnardo's. The advertising ran in broadsheet press titles – the message was of a serious subject matter, one that was felt to be in line with a broadsheet's editorial tone.

Divorcing oneself from such a historic past was a brave step, but the Chief Executive, Roger Singleton, captured the organisation's feelings about the importance of the relaunch: 'We are fiercely proud of our past, but what concerns us most is our future.'

Face to face

A new channel needed to be employed, one that was better set to recruit a younger age group in the volumes required. With this in mind, face-to-face recruitment was conducted by a specialised recruitment agency. It was an ideal choice for the recruitment of 'high-quality' younger donors. Face-to-face:

- recruits only committed donors – people paying a monthly fee by standing order
- could be targeted to find this audience
- is a two-way conversation with people
- communicated modernity.

Direct mail

The content of the direct communications to Dorothy Donor changed in line with the new brand vision – from mailers to telemarketing scripts.

How the relaunch impacted on the business

Total income
Since 21 October 1999 Barnardo's total income has increased by £46.6m on the equivalent 29-month period before the relaunch. The fastest-growing source of income was from the 'direct marketing' programme: this represents all the money generated from the direct mail and face-to-face activity.

As a whole, direct marketing increased its contribution by 86% over the same time period prior to relaunch.

Face-to-face performance
To date (February 2002), Barnardo's has both recruited and retained 107,205 people via this method, and the programme continues with no sign of exhaustion. The addition of over 100,000 face-to-face recruits shifted the entire age profile of Barnardo's donor base to a younger segment (see Figure 1).

The communications activity had also increased the quality of donors: by February 2002, 29% of donors were committed (see Figure 2).

Direct mail performance
Even recruitment and retention of Dorothy Donor has improved since the brand relaunch.

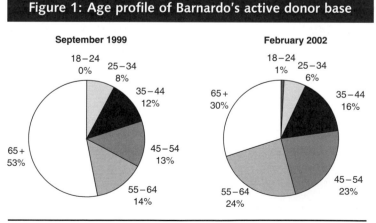

Figure 1: Age profile of Barnardo's active donor base

September 1999

February 2002

Source: Claritas

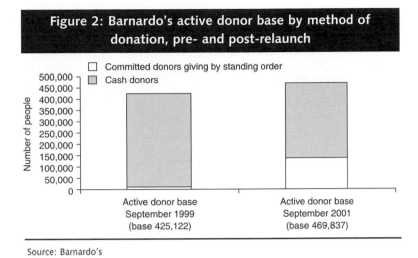

Figure 2: Barnardo's active donor base by method of donation, pre- and post-relaunch

Source: Barnardo's

Advertising performance

Of all communications it was the advertising that had attracted the most awareness – just five months from the start of the campaign, with just 147 press insertions. Barnardo's experienced the greatest leap in awareness of all UK charities.

As well as increases in awareness, Barnardo's benefited from significant image improvements including being seen as more deserving (Figure 3). As the perception of the charity's deservedness increased, so too did people's

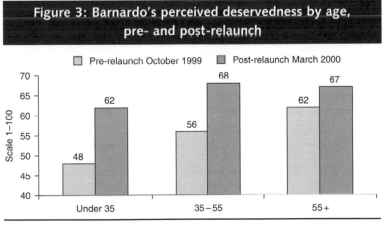

Figure 3: Barnardo's perceived deservedness by age, pre- and post-relaunch

Base: 292 (October 1999), 403 (March 2000)
Source: Quadrangle Tracking Study

propensity to donate, the most dramatic change being among the 35- to 55-year-old age group.

Total communications effect

As well as repositioning Barnardo's in the minds of potential donors, the total communications effect can be demonstrated throughout the major areas of Barnardo's the organisation.

Public relations

The advertising was the major communications channel to influence journalists, among which the campaign had a high awareness, second only to the big-spending NSPCC (Figure 4). It also created brand reappraisal among the journalists themselves.

> *The turnaround of Barnardo's from old news to headline news is remarkable. From an institution that we would never have turned to for comment, Barnardo's has become a continued source of breaking stories.*

Katie Weitz, Features Editor, *Sunday People*

The campaign's provocative and shocking content made Barnardo's the subject of a national debate, which took place in newspapers, magazines and on TV. The number of articles about Barnardo's rose 40% on the 12 months prior to the advertising.

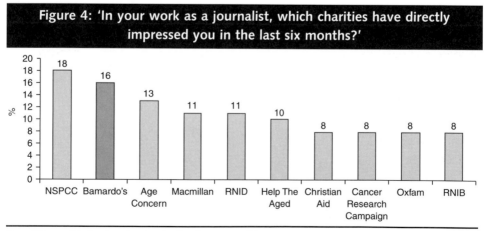

Figure 4: 'In your work as a journalist, which charities have directly impressed you in the last six months?'

Base: 61 journalists (local, regional and national: across media)
Source: Charity Media Monitor, NFP Synergy/Future Foundation (January 2002)

Lobbying and influencing

An important part of Barnardo's work is the lobbying of MPs on issues of policy affecting the welfare of children in the UK. The brand vision 'Giving children back their future' has provided a simple definable cause, which has been incorporated into all policy recommendations and literature targeted at MPs:

> *The advertising is part of putting forward our case to politicians*
> *across the board. One could say that the advertising is part of*
> *our delivery of the argument; it has contributed and added to*
> *our ability to impress.*
>
> Nigel Bennett, Director of Lobbying and Influence, Barnardo's

Corporate relations

Partnering with a modern Barnardo's is now seen as beneficial to how other brands are perceived by their own consumers, namely the 35- to 55-year-old age group. As a result, Barnardo's has been partnered with bigger brands, committing more money than ever before.

> *As the deservedness of Barnardo's increases, so too do the*
> *benefits of our partnership. The impressive rebranding of*
> *Barnardo's has led us to review our work with the charity; which*
> *can be evidenced by an increase in financial commitment as well*
> *as plans to lift the profile of the relationship Barclays has with*
> *Barnardo's.*
>
> Simon Gulliford, Marketing Director, Barclays

Argos named Barnardo's its charity of the year for 2002 and a 'major high-street retailer' named Barnardo's its charity of the year for 2003. The value of these partnerships alone is estimated to be worth £3–5m for Barnardo's.

Volunteering

Since the relaunch, Barnardo's has been able to recruit much younger volunteers in sectors of the community where it has had no record of recruiting fundraisers before. One such example is the student sector, where Barnardo's is now the principal charity operating:

> *Barnardo's is cool. To raise money for them is more interesting*
> *than Oxfam or another ******* 'save the whale' campaign.*
>
> Dan Ferguson, Student President and
> Rag Week Organiser, UEA

Local authorities
The advertising has been warmly received by the social workers in the projects themselves.

> *The women who use our services felt the rebranding really got the message across that Barnardo's work has changed over the years and that now we work with very complex and difficult family problems.*
>
> Project Leader, Domestic Violence

It is the social workers that negotiate with the local authorities for state funding. Anecdotal evidence suggests that the total communications effect has helped enhance these relationships.

> *The rebranding of Barnardo's has ensured that the organisation has raised its profile as a market leader among those national charities tackling social issues that for many others remain taboo. As a local authority it is important we have confidence in potential delivery agents in order to get the best service possible for those young people trying to survive in a hostile world. Barnardo's has enabled us to do that in Bradford.*
>
> Joyce Thacker, Head of Youth Service,
> Bradford Metropolitan District Council

Payback: communications' contribution

To be ultra-conservative in our payback calculations we will use only the income generated by the face-to-face recruits.

Barnardo's total expenditure since October 1999 on the advertising (including agency and production fees) and the cost of the face-to-face activity = £8,766,779. This means the return on the advertising and face-to-face investment is £10,212,756. Or this can be expressed as a return of £2.16 on every £1 invested.

Conclusions

This paper has demonstrated how an integrated communications campaign has turned around Barnardo's fortunes. For Barnardo's, the relaunch has been a resounding success, and some of the measures of that success have been outlined in this paper, namely:

- greater public support
- recruitment of younger donors
- a complete change in Barnardo's donor profile
- recruitment of more valuable donor relationships
- increase in income from direct mail
- recruitment of younger volunteers
- rise in corporate sponsorship
- enhanced relationships with local authorities
- improved perceptions among journalists
- enhancement of lobbying power among MPs.

Influencing the size of your market

Chapter 11

Guy Murphy

Deputy Chairman, Bartle Bogle Hegarty

Sex and the City. Changing Rooms. Jamie Oliver. To most people these are simply famous things in our culture. But for those businesses that rely on the health of the markets for sex toys, DIY and home cooking, they are much more. These names represent some of the most important catalysts for their commercial success. This can tell us a lot about how to design communications to create a rosy future for categories, not just brands.

This chapter proposes a view that in contrast to a battle for market share, growing markets require brands to create or to leverage popular culture – broadening what traditionally constitutes 'marketing communication'. It will argue for traditional media plans to be superseded by cultural communications plans, and communications experts to be seen as engineers of social change.

The shrinking pie phenomenon

Who should take particular responsibility for the health of a market? The obvious answer is the brand with the highest market share – that is, the one to gain the most from the 'pie' getting bigger. A decade ago this would have been the right answer but nowadays market leaders don't dominate markets as they once did. The universal growth of own-label and increased branded competition has seen to that (see Table 1).

So growing a market doesn't provide such a disproportionate benefit to one brand as it once did. Why grow the market when you only have 15% of it? Especially when your nearest competitor is just a few share points behind you, and own-label has a collective share of 40%? The danger is that even brand leaders continually put share gain ahead of market health. Everyone worries about having more pie than anyone else and no one is worrying about how much pie there is in the first place.

Table 1: Brand leader market shares

Commodity	% value 1983	2003
Batteries	50	34
Vodka	49	35
Vacuum cleaners	35	23
Rice	26	16
Breakfast cereals	18	7

Source: Mintel

Brand management has developed a culture where competitiveness is the dominant code. We all want to 'eat the big fish' and learn the 'art of war'. Incremental gains from competitors are the objective.

Market management invites a more collective agenda. Every player should take responsibility for market health for the greater benefit of all in the long run. This could represent real transformational performance for businesses.

Some academic studies, especially about advertising, can encourage a view that market growth is too ambitious. They claim advertising increases market share but not market size. (A theory vociferously used by the cigarette industry.) However, the key issue is not whether advertising *has* influenced market size, but whether it *can* influence market size.

The vast majority of advertising is unlikely to have influenced market size because it has been specifically designed to do something else instead – that is, grow share. To discover that advertising generally hasn't grown markets is only to discover that advertising hasn't *accidentally* grown markets while it attempts to steal share. It is more relevant to look at the effectiveness of advertising that was intended to influence market size. The two papers that follow, from BT and HEA, show their success in doing that. So it is simply not true to say that advertising does not influence market size.

'Market brands'

It seems important to start thinking of markets themselves as brands. This would give them a status, a sense of being something important that we should actively be trying to influence. Let's call them 'market brands'.

Markets have strong emotional and rational properties, just as individual brands do. Just look at how we feel about the GM food market, for example. If Levi's wanted to grow its market it would be looking at the market brand 'jeans'. If Gordons wanted to grow its market it would be looking at the market brand 'gin'.

Market brands necessarily occupy a bigger space in our lives than any individual brand. They represent a bigger set of stuff in the world. They are the very categories by which we classify what's around us. Fashion, fast food, books, cars, films, toys, clothes, pubs, hotels, cosmetics ... These are the sometimes wonderful, sometimes mundane, building blocks of how we spend our time. So our relationship with them is different to our relationship with individual brands. The relationship is broader and more deeply felt. For example, our relationship with the market brand of 'cars' is very different from our relationship with any one brand of car. How we all feel about traffic congestion, speed cameras and 4×4s on the school run is not the same as how we feel about Fords or Renaults. *It is more culturally important.*

This has several implications.

The competition for market brands is other market brands that fulfil a broadly similar consumer need. Once you pitch market against market you are talking about some important choices we make. You are asking people to shift their priorities. At its most extreme you are in fact pitching part of our life against another part of our life. For example, to get people to go on more premium holidays is to invite them to spend less money on something else that offers a sense of improved lifestyle, for example a new car, a new entertainment system, a better kitchen Ultimately, the competition is for what is more important in life – a holiday or a kitchen.

So the playground for market brands is, in fact, life. Maintaining market health is a cultural task. Your market has to become more important in our lives to be more robust. That might sound like a tall order if your market is yellow fats or toilet rolls, but that's the task nonetheless. Marketers embarking on this journey should see themselves as trying to manipulate culture: being social engineers, not brand managers; manipulating cultural forces, not brand impressions.

Building market brands

Market brands are built through a much wider variety of sources than consumer brands. To understand this it is helpful to ask the question, 'What communication has contributed to the overall impression of my market in our culture?' This provides a much more appropriate starting-point than the more usual question, 'What communication shall I use to build my brand?' Table 2 shows some common answers to this question for several market brands.

Lager has the place it does in our culture primarily because of the 'lout' it has become associated with. Olive oil has a place in kitchens because of the rise in popularity of Mediterranean cookery and a growing awareness of healthy-

Table 2: Communication that builds markets	
Cars	**Youth fashion**
Car reviews	Wearers
Word of mouth	Word of mouth
Drivers	Celebrity endorsement
Film placement	
Lager	**Olive oil**
Drinkers	Recipes
Drinkers' behaviour	Celebrity cook endorsement
Pubs	Health journalism
Advertising	

Source: BBH

eating issues. Youth fashion persists as a vibrant market because of who wears it. Building a market brand requires looking at *these kinds of drivers themselves as communication*.

Where do consumers learn about this market? Who do they trust to tell them? Who is using products from this market in popular culture? Answers to these kinds of questions define the communications channels to use. This is very different from looking at communications channels in terms of advertising, promotion, sponsorship and direct mail, as one might for an individual brand.

Market brands need a *cultural communication plan*. Instead of the rows on the media plan saying 'advertising, point of sale, sponsorship and direct mail', the rows on the cultural communication plan should include 'word of mouth, film placement, celebrity usage, PR, six-part mini TV series'.

Cultural communications planning

The importance of everyone
Who should communications talk to in order to build markets? Consumer brand-building would answer that question with reference to the potential buyers of the brand, and those who might influence the purchase. That universe would then be segmented again to identify the group of people (e.g. men, lapsed users, youth) who promise the greatest return on investment. The guiding principle is that of reduction of audience size: 'you can't talk to everyone'. The holy grail is a tight definition of the target audience.

Building market brands requires the opposite principle: expand the audience.

Culture is a shared experience shaped to a greater or lesser extent by us all. Market brands that want to become a bigger part of the culture need to embrace a dimension of universal understanding and appreciation. Everyone is an influencer of how market brands are perceived and valued. Segmented appeal, most appropriate for consumer brands, should be replaced with the need for fame.

Kettle talk

Getting 'kettle talk' (the British version of the US 'water-cooler conversation') is vital. It is considered a flattering *side-effect* of good communication if it is referenced by the media or in day-to-day chit-chat. In building market brands, however, 'talkability' must be seen as a touchstone of success, not just a nice-to-have. Making a category of product a greater part of our lives dictates that it must become a greater part of what we think about and talk about. Our culture lives through conversation.

This cultural infectiousness isn't just a function of having good PR for a campaign, but must be literally *designed into* the communication itself. It must be deliberate, not accidental. The communications brief must make this an objective. Communication development must be very mindful of what is going to invite press and public comment. Sometimes this can be a response to the creative content itself (*Super Size Me*), or the placement of the communication (Fathers 4 Justice protest on Buckingham Palace), or both (Eva Herzigova in a Wonderbra on 48-sheet posters).

To fan the flames of interest it is possible to create the word-of-mouth reaction either through influencing journalists (without compromising editorial integrity, of course) or by 'planting' word of mouth to be overheard as real word of mouth (chat rooms, radio phone-ins, conversations in pubs, etc.).

Content

Cultural communication planning requires a focus on content – the bits between the advertising, the bits that represent life – rather than branded messaging.

The effect that branded communication has on popular culture is minute compared to the effect of the broader media of TV programmes, films, music, sport, celebrities, etc. This is not just because there is a lot less of it, but because content has a credibility with people that branded communication does not. *Ground Force* has done a lot more to increase the British public's love of gardening than all of the branded communication from B&Q and Homebase.

To make a market brand more important in our lives it must be represented in the content of our popular culture. This is made possible by the fact that market-building communication doesn't need branding. The messaging should be generic to the market and doesn't need to be associated with any individual brand within that market. If you want people to think that milk is more important in our culture, they don't need to know or remember the brand Dairy Crest.

Exposure

Fading celebrities clamour to appear on *I'm A Celebrity ... Get Me Out of Here!* because it reaches a broadcast audience. For better or for worse, series two winner Phil Tufnell is now a part of our entertainment culture. He would have had less success appearing on niche programming about cricket.

Similarly, to get market brands to become a greater part of culture they need to communicate using *broadcast* channels, despite the fact that most of the audience may never purchase the category. The shared experience of broadcast communication builds a shared appreciation. Advertising in the Superbowl is valued because it is a talking point in US culture, not because the TV audience is a perfect match for a brand's demographic.

Becoming part of culture may also require a new way of thinking about *when* a market brand should be communicating. The creation of culture is an ongoing process that may require a more consistent presence across the year. Being 'off-air' at all may not be right.

However, some times of year are more culturally important than others. The summer period, especially the school holidays, represents relative inactivity in the political and media worlds. The seasonality of our culture may be more important for communications planning than the seasonality of sales. The traditional media question of 'burst versus drip' may miss these points.

The practicalities

The different approach that market brands need to adopt to become a greater part of our lives requires a new way of organising the development of communications.

The lead times for creating content are often much longer than traditional branded communication such as advertising. The traditional timelines need to be altered accordingly. Communication planning must be constantly looking at the next two years, not the next two quarters.

New working relationships are required. Media owners remain vital partners, but it is those responsible for commissioning and editorial who are key to creating content, rather than the media sales departments. The relationship between commissioning editors and marketers (and their agents) is an embryonic and sometimes uneasy one. Time is well spent understanding and nurturing this new dynamic.

Evaluation of communication activity needs a different approach. One has to measure the health of the market brand, rather than the health of an individual brand. But this may not best be done using traditional tracking studies and evaluative measures. Is it more important to know how many column inches a market brand is receiving rather than a communication awareness score? We should be looking at everybody's view of a market not just the potential buyers'. It may be the evaluative tools from the PR and entertainment industry rather than the advertising industry that should lead the way.

Summary

This chapter describes the task of growing a market as the collective responsibility of all the players, not just the market leader. Markets are brands too. They must become a bigger part of our lives to demand a bigger slice of our attention and our disposable income. From this theory flows many implications for communication.

The IPA case histories that follow were written some years ago and obviously the world has changed since then. However, they show how markets have been successfully moved by communication: BT moved the 'phone calls' market up, and the HEA moved the 'illegal drugs' market down. They both illustrate the point that communication must pervade our culture to have the greatest success.

Food for thought

- The traditional notions of media are too narrow. The drivers of our culture (entertainment, news, celebrities, etc.) become the channels through which to communicate a market brand.
- Word of mouth is critical. It must be designed into the communications and not left to chance.
- The target audience is everyone. Segmentation may sacrifice effectiveness for efficiency.
- Content (versus branded communication) must form a large part of the plan.
- The 'always on' rhythms of our culture dictate the flighting of communication through the year. Think cultural seasonality, not sales seasonality.
- Rewrite the timing plan to have two years of communication in development at any point in time.
- Think of yourself as an engineer of cultural change and not just a builder of brands.

BT
It's Good To Talk

Grand Prix winner 1996

Perhaps the word campaign does it an injustice ... it is actually a piece of social engineering.

Marketing Week

Having looked through the *Advertising Works* books, we have not found an example of a brand leader using advertising to grow an already buoyant market. We believe that this paper will be the first to do so.

We will show that BT's past three campaigns designed to stimulate calls have done so, but that 'It's Good To Talk' has been by far the most effective, and has achieved a return on investment of 6 to 1.

The need to grow the market

Following privatisation in 1984, one of Oftel's rulings was that BT should reduce its 'basket' of individual call charges. For BT's residential division, the only way out of this enforced revenue decline was to grow the market. Its response was threefold:

1. To encourage adoption of products likely to stimulate calls (e.g. second phone points in homes, and answerphones).
2. To step up R&D to create new call stimulatory services (e.g. Call Return – 1471).
3. To use the power of advertising to stimulate calls.

Abridged version of the original case study written in 1996 by Max Burt (Abbott Mead Vickers.BBDO) for BT.

The evolution of BT's call stimulation advertising

'Beattie': targeting heavy users, prompting more calls from women
'Beattie' attempted to highlight the different types of call in people's 'portfolio' (e.g. enquiries to shops, consolation calls) in order to prompt people into making similar ones. The target audience was heavier callers – mid-market 25- to 45-year-old housewives. The campaign chose a loquacious housewife as a role model for heavier phone usage.

'Get Through To Someone': strategic shift; positive role models, particularly men
The campaign differed from 'Beattie' by providing a more sensitive portrayal of positive phone behaviour. However, it was similar in that it was designed to work by prompting people into action by reminding them of a certain type of call. Lighter-calling men, who BT felt offered call growth potential, were also targeted.

While 'Beattie' and 'Get Through To Someone' had some success in *prompting* calls, little had been done to change the *underlying negative attitudes* that restrict many people's calling levels, and little emphasis given to promoting the positive value of phone communication. BT's expression of this latter point was:

> *You get more out of your life, and your relationships, by communicating [through BT].*

BT wanted to engineer a positive change in the way that our culture values phone communication.

'It's Good To Talk': major strategic shift, addressing underlying barriers to calling
The thinking behind 'It's Good To Talk' (IGTT) stemmed from research done in 1993. Women tend to spend more time just chatting on the phone because they view the pleasure this can give as an end in itself. Men, however, view the phone more as a means to an end, a functional instrument for delivering rational messages. Men's usage tends to be less frequent and their conversation tends to be more short and sharp.

Some men therefore find it difficult to understand women's behaviour, and in a large proportion of households try to restrict their partner's usage. In other words, they act as 'gatekeepers' to the phone. They use cost as justification for this and cite much of women's usage as a waste:

*She spends her time just whittering away about absolutely
nothing. I just can't understand it, and I tell her to get off the
phone 'cos it's just money down the drain you know. She'll see
her friend anyway when she picks our daughter up from school.*
AMV Qualitative

By standing over their families, tutting while they are on the phone, they
reinforce the phone's image as a 'whirring meter'. Many women therefore
feel guilty about their style of use and the cost, and restrict their own calling
levels and their children's.

We identified two opportunities.

- *Opportunity 1: promoting the value of female-style phone
  communication.* We concluded that there was great potential for call
  growth if we could raise the value of female-style communication in
  men's eyes, by directly comparing its benefits to male-style functional
  usage.
  - It would legitimise women's behaviour. This would free up restricted
    female users by softening the attitudes of the gatekeeper, and provide
    women themselves with ammunition for defending their usage.
  - It would encourage men to reappraise their own behaviour.

- *Opportunity 2: reducing price perceptions.* Given the prominence of
  cost as the gatekeeper's justification to restrict usage, we needed to
  affect price perceptions. Call prices were dropping regularly each year.
  The number of people believing that prices were high had, for much of
  the last nine years, been rising. (Research showed that consumers do
  not know the cost of calls, and derive their perceptions of telephony
  costs from the quarterly bill. In addition, competitors were fuelling
  BT's high price perceptions by marketing themselves as cheaper
  alternatives.) To counter this, BT had started advertising special offers
  and major tariff changes. Price perceptions had started to fall but
  research revealed that people still overestimated the cost of a call by
  about 400%. We concluded that, in order to bring price perceptions
  down more steeply, we needed to address these vast overestimates by
  relating the cost of individual calls to other purchases people make.

Summary of the advertising brief
To persuade people to make more and longer calls, primarily by targeting
households in which male gatekeepers put pressure on key callers, namely
their partners and children, to phone less.

We would achieve this by demonstrating the value of female-style calling, and illustrating that individual calls are as low in cost as other everyday purchases.

Our eventual aim was to ease the tension between gatekeeper and key caller, thus releasing pent-up demand. We also thought that, if men believed the benefits, they would increase their calling levels too.

Creative solution

The creative solution fell into two categories: television and non-broadcast media.

As regards television, our messages needed to be skilfully delivered, not only because we were challenging deeply ingrained attitudes, but also because some people hold a grudge against BT. We needed a campaign spokesman whose objectivity could increase the credibility of our messages: 'one of us' rather than a BT stooge. Bob Hoskins was chosen.

With regard to the second category, namely non-broadcast media, the strategy behind the TV executions was echoed in a national press campaign. To reduce price perceptions a poster campaign, comparing call costs to everyday low-cost items, was created.

Overall, BT invested £44m in IGTT between May 1994 and June 1995.

Evaluating the three campaigns

BT call growth history

As mentioned earlier, after privatisation BT had adopted a number of market growth measures. As far as calls-per-line were concerned, this strategy seemed to work. Figure 1 shows how before privatisation they were flat, but started to rise subsequently.

From April 1986 it was also possible to measure average conversation durations (see Figure 2). *Total* volume (calls-per-line × durations) had risen 23% since 1986.

What we did: the approach

Proving advertising effectiveness here is a complex task because the telecommunications market has seen huge changes over ten years. Beyond the

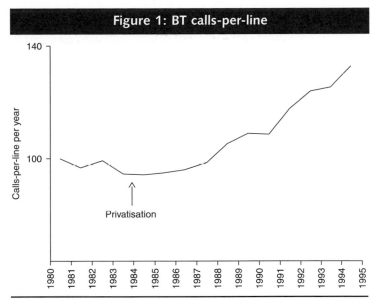

Source: BT/The Planning Business

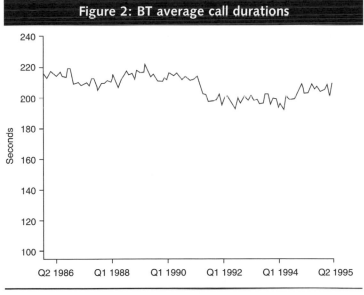

Source: BT

reduction in call charges discussed above, there has been a dramatic increase in the penetration of products and services.

BT now faces direct competition from new entrants and indirect competition in the form of mobile telephony. Econometric analysis was a necessity.

First, in order to simplify the number of variables used in the analysis, we needed to strip out the effect of products and services which are known to affect call volume. Second, given that the marketing objective was to grow the market (as measured on BT lines), we needed to decide if competition, which is mostly about switching customers from BT to cable or Mercury, was of relevance to our assessment.

If we could remove the effects of these, econometric analysis would then be left with the simpler task of disentangling the effects of price, advertising and the economy. In other words, we were going to clear the ground for econometric analysis and this is now discussed in the following subsections.

Stripping out the effect of products and services
BT is in the unique position of having highly accurate 'purchase' data on every customer. We used this to measure the effect of product/service acquisition on phone bills.

As well as customers' bills, BT holds details of equipment hired and services subscribed to. With this information we set up 'before-and-after' panels comprising approximately 4500 households for each product/service. By comparing, over three quarters, the bills of 'acquiring' households with those of demographically matched control groups who were 'non-acquirers', we quantified the effect that products/services have on bills.

Could competition have grown call volumes on BT lines?
We concluded that there were only two ways in which the above could come about:

1. If households that switched were lighter users, this would have resulted in an apparent increase in the average call volumes of the BT households remaining. This was not the case. Analysis of the final bills of households who BT knew had defected to the competition shows that call volumes in these households are, on average, 5% *higher*. We therefore accounted for this in our analysis.
2. Mobile phone penetration has increased dramatically over the period,

and households now make additional calls to mobiles. But all of the data we are using to make our case *exclude* calls from fixed lines to mobiles. However, we also asked ourselves whether calls involving mobiles generate extra fixed-line to fixed-line calls. A further BT panel analysis showed this not to be the case. We therefore concluded that mobile competition could not have led to an increase in call volumes on BT lines.

The econometric analysis

BT's business is complicated. There are over 40 different chargebands covering the many international destinations, premium-rate calls (e.g. chat lines), as well as the more common local and long-distance calls within the UK. We have concentrated on UK local and long-distance calls, which account for over 99% of volume.

Even with this restriction the analysis was a complex one because we needed to construct eight different models, measuring both the impact on calls-per-line and durations for four combinations of rates and destinations, over the nine years of the three campaigns (Figure 3).

We decided to use price perceptions as the variable, on the grounds that, in this market, consumer demand is likely to be influenced by what people *think* prices are rather than what they *actually* are.

The effect of the economy

We chose consumer expenditure, not only because the amount spent on telephone bills forms part of consumer expenditure, but also because phoning shops and businesses is a direct expression of economic well-being.

Figure 3: The eight different models

1. Calls-per-line 2. Durations	Local calls, standard rate
3. Calls-per-line 4. Durations	Local calls, cheap rate
5. Calls-per-line 6. Durations	National calls, standard rate
7. Calls-per-line 8. Durations	National calls, cheap rate

The advertising variable

An important decision was how to represent the well-known fact that advertising can have both immediate and lagged effects. We felt this would certainly be true of telephony advertising, stimulating a call to a friend, which would subsequently generate a cycle of return calls, which might peter out over time.

To model this effect, we assumed that only a proportion of a TVR has its effect in the period of spend. The rest of the effect is spread out over subsequent periods.

Other variables

We found only one that made a significant contribution, and this was that *durations* affect *calls-per-line* (discussed further below).

The results of the models

The models produced had a good fit with the data, accounting for a large percentage of the variation in call volumes (see, for example, Figure 4).

Qualitative interpretation

The models tell us much about how the markets work. Our overall confidence in the analysis was enhanced because the models suggested that

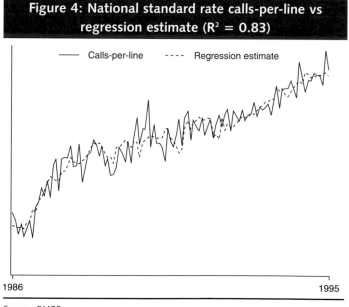

Figure 4: National standard rate calls-per-line vs regression estimate (R² = 0.83)

Calls-per-line - - - - Regression estimate

1986   1995

Source: BMRB

the markets work in ways that fit both with common sense and qualitative research:

- That durations affect the number of calls-per-line makes sense, because if you are an inhibited caller and make a long call, you will restrict the number of calls you subsequently make.
- We found that price perceptions and consumer expenditure affected local *durations*, but not local *calls-per-line*. We would expect this as, given the lower perceived cost of a *local* call, people are less inclined to think twice about picking up the phone, but as the conversation progresses the 'whirring meter' worry increases.
- On *national* calls, price perceptions and consumer expenditure have an impact on calls-per-line *as well as* durations. This also makes sense. Given the higher perceived cost of *national* calls, people are likely to think more carefully each time they pick up the phone.

Quantitative results

The net effect on total call volumes for each of the three campaigns is shown in Table 1.

Table 1: Net effect on total call volumes		
Campaign	Eventual % revenue return from 100 TVRs	Index (campaign 1 = 100)
1. Get Through To Someone	0.44	100
2. Beattie	1.05	236
3. It's Good To Talk	1.75	398

Source: David Cowan Associates

The analysis demonstrated that all three campaigns had a positive effect, but that IGTT achieved by far the highest return. The models showed that if 100 ratings are spent in a month then, for IGTT, the eventual return over time is 1.75% of monthly sales.

Putting 'It's Good To Talk' under the microscope

Direct evidence of IGTT's impact

One of the problems of econometrics is that it inevitably involves an element of 'black box', where results arise out of 'correlations and best fits'. It is always reassuring to have direct evidence of effect. In this case, we have such evidence.

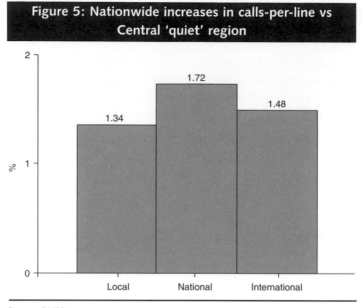

Figure 5: Nationwide increases in calls-per-line vs Central 'quiet' region

Source: BMRB

For the campaign's first three months, BT kept the Central TV region 'quiet' by withholding all ITV airtime (with C4, press and posters, Central received only 37% of the nationwide spend). Central's calling patterns are typical of the rest of the country. Even though this control region was not absolutely 'silent', a substantial increase in calls-per-line was seen nationally compared to Central (see Figure 5).

Unfortunately, BT did not have the technical capability to measure durations regionally. Nevertheless we still have direct evidence of IGTT's effect on durations by looking at the national picture. Since the middle of 1994 there has been a prolonged rise in durations for the first time since records began. This coincided precisely with IGTT (see Figure 6).

Calculating payback
We have shown that IGTT has generated a 1.75% sales uplift for every 100 TVRs spent. This amounts to an incremental value per TVR of £33,000. To arrive at an overall advertising-generated income over the period under discussion, we make the following calculation:

£33,000 (value per TVR) × 10,566 (total number of 30-second equivalent TVRs) – £44m (media) and £8m (production) = £297m

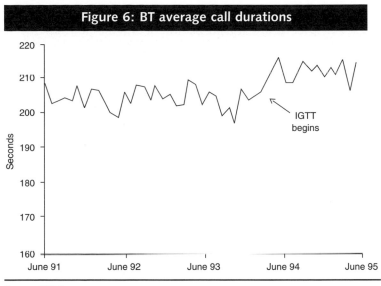

Figure 6: BT average call durations

Source: BMRB

Given that no further variable costs are incurred, this £297m is almost entirely incremental profit, and represents a return on investment of nearly 6 to 1. In fact we believe this is an underestimate of IGTT's contribution. Our analysis excludes any effect on BT's international calls, or its seven million business lines (research shows that many personal calls are made at work). We see no reason why IGTT will not have affected these calls too.

Putting the result in perspective

In the context of other advertisers, IGTT performs well. It is when this performance is combined with the huge size of BT's market, that the absolute return becomes so vast.

Beyond the strategic and creative relevance of the campaign, there are other reasons why BT's advertising is likely to be particularly effective. There is very low wastage of advertising monies because almost the whole audience uses the phone and, unlike most markets, there is a point of purchase in nearly every house.

Could anything else have caused the uplift in call volumes?

1. *Other BT activity*. Other significant marketing activity either declined or remained constant during IGTT. Both BT's *corporate* and *business* divisions reduced the adspends behind their campaigns by

approximately 50%, and there was no significant change in the strategies or level of investment behind below-the-line activity.

2. *Competitive advertising activity.* Because Mercury withdrew from the residential market during the period, other advertising in the telephony market was almost all to enrol mobile users. None of this is likely to have stimulated the BT network. In any case, year on year, media-inflation-adjusted adspends from these advertisers actually *fell* by 6% during this time.

3. *Weather.* There is some evidence to suggest that bad weather encourages people to stay indoors and, hence, call more. However, over the period, temperatures and sunshine hours were *higher* and rainfall *lower* (source: Met Office). If anything, this would depress calling.

Demonstrating IGTT's effects through consumer data

This can be done by a breakdown into five subheadings:

1. *The campaign was widely noticed.* In awareness terms, the campaign made a great impact. Soon after it broke, it reached number one in *Marketing*'s Adwatch survey, and remained there for 22 of the next 30 weeks – a record.

2. *People claim to use the telephone more.* BT's tracking study has two behaviour statements relating to the advertising. Over the advertised period, agreement with these statements rose.

3. *The advertising has worked in the way intended.* We could not track 'gatekeeper' *households*, because BT's advertising monitor interviews *individuals*, not family units. Instead, we looked for changes among demographic groups most likely to approximate to our target audience. When the two behaviour statements discussed above are analysed by age and sex, we found that the biggest rises in claimed behaviour came from the group whose phone usage we would expect to be most repressed, namely women, especially those aged 35+ (Figure 7).

    Movement was greatest among men, and especially older men, suggesting a particular softening in gatekeepers' attitudes towards chatting on the phone. Correspondingly, if the gatekeeper has a more relaxed attitude, we would expect women to feel less guilty about using the phone. There has been a small but significant reduction in the proportion of women feeling 'guilty about chatting on the phone' (48% to 44%).

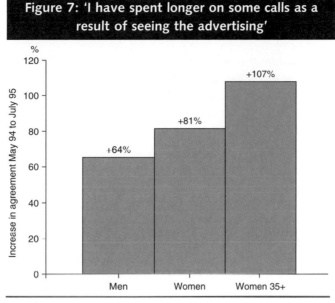

Figure 7: 'I have spent longer on some calls as a result of seeing the advertising'

Source: BMRB

4. *There has also been a steep fall in price perceptions.* We earlier described how important price perceptions were, because they fuel 'gatekeeper' prejudices and create guilt among would-be callers. Figure 8 shows that, although the percentage of people saying call charges were high had been gradually falling since mid-1992, it began to fall steeply once our campaign began.

5. *So is IGTT 'social engineering'?* Beyond the effects we have demonstrated on its intended target audiences, other evidence suggests that the campaign has worked in a wider way, and on a much 'higher' level, to raise the topic of good communication onto the agenda of 'things we should all be better at'.

   The campaign has unarguably generated a *huge* amount of media coverage. But, more importantly, when It's Good To Talk is referenced in the media, as often as not the point being underlined is a serious one: that we should be better communicators.

   By raising the topic of good communication, BT is benefiting. As the following quote illustrates, an increased understanding of the fact that it is good to talk, is leading more people to use the phone.

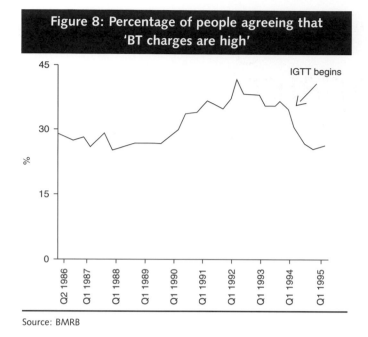

Source: BMRB

My son's schoolteacher tells her class every day that it's good to talk, and now when he wants to use the phone and my husband kicks up a fuss, he says, 'But Daddy, it's good to talk you know.' What can you say? It's true.

The Planning Partnership/AMV Qualitative

In conclusion

BT has historically invested heavily in advertising. This paper demonstrates how strategic and creative relevance made a large budget work harder to create a step-change in call volumes. Latest data show the campaign's continued success beyond the period under discussion.

We have calculated a payback of 6 to 1. In fact, the campaign's return will be far greater than this in the long term. It's Good To Talk is changing attitudes towards telephony, and the future benefit of this to BT will be huge.

BT's eventual goal is to change perceptions of telephony from a cost that should be minimised, to an investment in quality of life that should be valued. By helping to achieve this, the campaign is growing the market, and convincing the nation that it *really is good to talk*.

HEA drugs education campaign
How advertising turned the tide

Grand Prix winner 1998

What do you imagine is the biggest internationally traded commodity in the world? Oil? Tourism? No, it's drugs, and it accounts for 8% of world trade.

Drugs represent an enormous problem, touching many lives – young people, their families and communities, teachers, medical professionals and law enforcers. The social costs of this problem run to £4bn per year in the UK alone.

More under-25s engage in drug use than in any other illegal activity. An estimated £13bn of drugs circulate on Britain's streets each year. That makes our drugs market as big as the total beer market, bigger than tobacco, and three times the size of confectionery or soft drinks.

This is the story of Goliath, £13bn of drugs trade, being attacked by little David, our £2.3m per year advertising budget. Goliath has started to lose his footing. The tide of drug use in England has finally started to turn.

1995 was crisis point

The drugs problem had reached epidemic proportions. The 1990s had seen an explosion of drug use among young people. In just five years the

---

Abridged version of the original case study written in 1998 by Lori Gould and Rachel Walker (Duckworth Finn Grubb Waters) for the Health Education Authority.

proportion of 14 to 15 year olds in contact with drugs had doubled. Not only was young people's drug use accelerating out of control, it had also changed beyond recognition.

Typically the word 'drugs' conjures up images of heroin or crack addicts in inner-city no-go areas. While these drugs are a continuing part of the picture, they represent a serious but isolated problem, the practice of a tiny minority. Penetration of both heroin and crack were only 1% of 11–25s according to the National Drugs Survey (NDS) 1995.

The new problem we faced was a much wider one – huge numbers of young people using illegal and dangerous drugs like speed, ecstasy and LSD for recreational purposes. NDS found that 56% of 16–25s had at some point tried drugs, nearly half of them starting before they turned 15. Recreational drug use was no longer a counterculture, it was a majority activity.

Ecstasy opened the floodgates

The arrival in the late 1980s of the 'wonder drug' ecstasy changed the UK drugs scene beyond recognition. It soon became an entrenched feature of the clubbing scene: 84% of clubbers had used it.

This new drug, and the dance culture that surrounded it, had an impact on recreational drug use as a whole:

> *I believe that E [ecstasy] was the catalyst. It made drug taking acceptable. If they couldn't afford E, they'd take trips [LSD] or smoke cannabis instead.*
>
> Worker at Lifeline

Style magazines, music and literature fuelled this normalisation of drugs, endorsing and celebrating dance drug culture.

You're either with us or against us

The adult world, fuelled by the media, was in a state of panic. But their perspective contrasted sharply with young people's view of recreational drugs. Young people dismissed parents and other authority figures as ignorant, out of touch and incapable of offering unbiased advice. Drugs were entrenched and defended inside a youth culture fortress that was impenetrable to outsiders. Something had to be done. But what?

Evidently nothing that teachers, the police, parents or the authorities had said or done had stemmed the tide of drug use. Successive governments had been attempting to suppress drugs supply for decades, but the government now acknowledged that the only way to impact on the accelerating drugs problem was to tackle demand. The 1995 White Paper *Tackling Drugs Together* defined our task as simply to 'reduce demand for drugs'.

Our understanding of the use of heroin and crack suggested that advertising was an inappropriate weapon, being inextricably bound up with social and personal problems. Recreational drug use became our target.

The problem was twofold

The flow into drug use was too great, and the flow out not big enough. We could tackle the problem at either end – stop people starting, or get more people to stop. The easier task seemed to be to stem the flow of people into drugs use. Adopted exclusively, however, this would be a long-term solution. We had to accelerate the flow out of drug use as well.

Although our primary objective was reducing the numbers using drugs, we had to acknowledge that there would always be some who continued to use. We had a responsibility to ensure that while they continued to take drugs, these people harmed themselves as little as possible (see Figure 1).

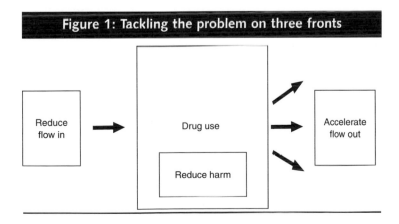

Figure 1: Tackling the problem on three fronts

Reduce flow in → Drug use → Accelerate flow out

Reduce harm

A unifying insight

Adults assumed that young drug users are victims of pressure from wayward friends or evil pushers at the school gates. Our investigations found this to be simply untrue: young people decide for themselves whether or not to take drugs, weighing up the pros and cons. The vast majority of users are introduced to drugs by a friend. Those who do use dealers see them as suppliers not pushers.

The fortress of youth culture was full of tales of the excitement drugs could offer. The problem was not pressure – it was that the balance of evidence within their world was overwhelmingly in favour of drugs.

What could tip the balance?

We needed to let young people conclude for themselves that taking drugs was not a good idea, and to find new and compelling reasons that could make them think again. We discovered one thing that had the power to change their minds. When drug users were asked what would make them stop using drugs, by far the biggest concern was 'worries about my health' (source: NDS 1995).

Yet too many were dangerously unaware of the health risks that recreational drugs carried. Millions knew of no health risks whatsoever associated with the most commonly used recreational drugs.

The power of the truth

Our investigation revealed a host of health risks carried by recreational drugs (see Table 1). Additionally, scientists had found evidence that ecstasy could permanently damage serotonin-releasing chemicals in the brain. This could potentially lead to severe depression later in life.

We had found the key to demotivation in this market: by giving facts about health risks, we could help young people make their own better-informed decisions about drugs. Better-informed people are less likely to engage in risky behaviour, as health education work in the fields of HIV and contraception testifies.

Now we just had to find a way to get people to listen to us.

Table 1: Risks of recreational drugs		
Ecstasy	**LSD**	**Speed**
Depression	Flashbacks	Heart arrhythmia
Paranoia	Bad trips	Heart damage/strain
Kidney damage	Can't escape once started	Unpredictable
Liver damage	Lasts up to 12 hours	Comedown/fatigue
Brain damage	Unpredictable reaction	Paranoia
Dehydration	Long-term mental illness	Psychological addiction
Comedown/fatigue		Need more each time
Anxiety		Tiredness
Heart damage/arrhythmia		Depression
Unpredictable reaction		Inability to sleep
Mental illness		
Stroke		
Paralysis		
Coma		

Infiltrating the fortress of youth culture

Our cynical audience would refuse to listen to us if they suspected that the government was responsible. We had to find a way past the defences of the youth culture fortress. So we adopted an open, honest tone that allowed people to make up their own minds. We recommended that the government take the unprecedented step of letting us acknowledge the positive effects of drugs, to demonstrate our insider knowledge. This was crucial to the campaign's credibility.

We used teen magazines to reach 11–15s and dance radio stations to reach 16–25s – private, trusted sources of information, and environments where talk of drugs is appropriate.

In an ideal world we would have featured every drug in advertising. But we had to be selective, in order to give each drug sufficient weight to educate effectively. We used the following criteria to ensure that our advertising addressed the most widespread and pressing problems:

- drugs that people were likely to come across (i.e. be offered)
- drugs that they were likely to use or consider using
- drugs that carried lots of health risks, about which people knew very little.

We therefore focused on ecstasy, speed and LSD.

Opening up a dialogue

Having encouraged people to question their current levels of knowledge and given them reasons to think twice, our plan was to establish a dialogue with young people, answering any further questions one to one.

The National Drugs Helpline (NDH) had been operating since April 1995, but in England it had virtually no awareness and no brand image. We featured the NDH number on all our materials, allowing us an even bigger, interactive role within the youth culture fortress.

The creative solution

Working to the brief of communicating facts about drugs from within youth culture, our press ads feature young people in drug-taking situations, with a biology textbook 'cutaway' revealing medical facts. These ads carry detailed information in an easily digestible form.

In radio, scripted ads illustrate health risks, and voxpops have real people talking about their experiences. The end-line 'Know the Score' encapsulates our approach.

Good news

There is evidence from lots of different sources that, since the start of the campaign, instead of the inexorable rise, drug use has declined. Although one can hardly claim that it is the end of the problem, drugs do appear to have receded from their high watermark. The Home Secretary was recently moved to say 'there is evidence that drug use is now stabilising and might even be going down' (*Today*, Radio 4, May 1998).

We will present evidence that shows, beyond reasonable doubt, that the advertising has played the lead role in turning the tide. But first, the evidence that the tide has turned.

Fewer young people are trying drugs

The only long-term trend data available for trial of drugs is for 12 to 15 year olds. These show, after several years of steady growth, two years of downturn (see Figure 2).

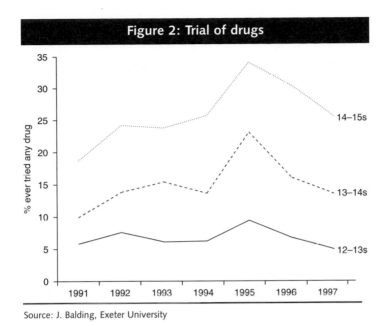

Figure 2: Trial of drugs

Source: J. Balding, Exeter University

And as you'd expect, if fewer people are using drugs, fewer know someone who uses drugs (see Figure 3). This is good news since hearing users' positive feedback often encourages others to experiment. Fewer users means fewer advocates.

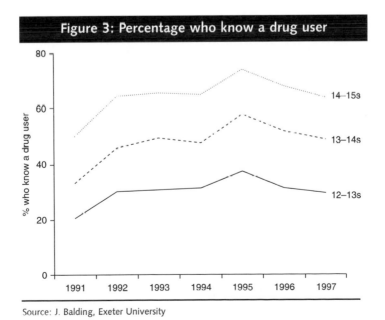

Figure 3: Percentage who know a drug user

Source: J. Balding, Exeter University

Fewer people are planning to use drugs

Looking at a broader age spectrum, NDS found that between 1995 and 1996 the proportions of 11–25s who claim they would definitely or possibly consider using drugs in the future went down by 14%.

More drug users are quitting

At the other end of the drugs life cycle, NDS also found that the proportion of drug users claiming to have given up doubled between 1995 and 1996 (see Figure 4).

And drug users are better able to limit the risks

Our last behavioural objective was to encourage those who continued to use drugs to minimise potential harm. Unfortunately there are no hard data to tell us how many drug users now do so. But the HEA-commissioned qualitative research, almost continuous over the course of the campaign, has shown that many drug users are now better able to reduce the risks they face.

> *All users were aware of harm minimisation messages (especially regarding ecstasy) and felt able to minimise immediate risks.*
>
> CRD, March 1997

So our behavioural objectives had been met. The question is whether it was advertising that was behind this success. There is evidence on a number of fronts that this was indeed the case.

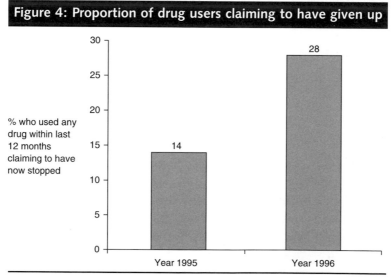

Figure 4: Proportion of drug users claiming to have given up

% who used any drug within last 12 months claiming to have now stopped

Source: NDS

Advertising played the lead role in behavioural changes

Advertising can be shown to have impacted on our audience in ways that strongly suggest it has brought about the reduction in drug use that we have seen.

Advertising was noticed
We know that over our first two bursts prompted press awareness grew to 55% and prompted radio awareness had reached 62%. Two years later *a remarkable 90%* of 15–19s in a test in Anglia recognised our press ads when prompted.

Calls to NDH rise when we advertise
Calls to NDH provide us with clear evidence of a direct link between advertising and behaviour changes. As Figure 5 shows, when we advertise, calls rise steeply; and when we stop, advertising calls decline.

Awareness of risks has risen
Festival Radio reporters interviewed over 600 18–25s over the course of our campaign to collect material for our radio creative work. Respondents were asked what they knew about ecstasy, speed and LSD. Across time, the proportion of people knowing at least one of the health facts we feature has

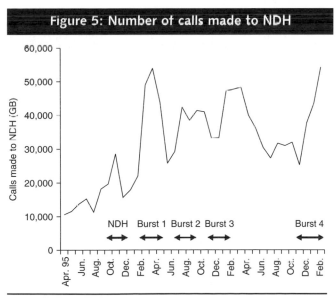

Figure 5: Number of calls made to NDH

Source: Network Scotland (operator of NDH)

grown to double the pre-campaign level. Qualitative research reinforces this finding.

> *Drugs messages are being absorbed and recycled within the culture. Respondents unconsciously parrot wording from press and radio ads – e.g. 'kidney and liver damage', 'drink about a pint an hour'.*
>
> CRD, September 1997

People are less interested in using drugs

Our Anglia test showed a 29% reduction in those who were certain or fairly sure they would use drugs in the future. Taken together, these findings suggest that advertising created attitudinal changes that brought about the reduction in drug use. There is one more set of findings, however, that adds even more weight to this argument, and this is discussed next.

Young people themselves say our advertising has influenced them

A variety of qualitative research projects have found our target audience claiming advertising has affected them. That goes for those who have not yet used drugs:

> *Rejectors and those at risk usually found that the ads reinforced their personal conviction not to take drugs.*
>
> CRD, May 1996

as well as those who are already using:

> *They [the ads] make me think at the end of the day 'Do I need this shit?'*
>
> 18–24 user (Murmur, May 1996)

> *There's a little voice at the back of your head saying 'It's not safe. There's a risk.'*
>
> 18–22 user (DFGW, October 1996)

Our Anglia test found large proportions agreeing that our radio advertising burst made them think twice about drugs or taught them new things (see Figure 6). Young people appreciate the approach we have taken, understand what the campaign is trying to achieve and recognise that we are doing things differently:

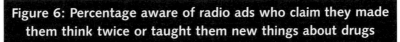

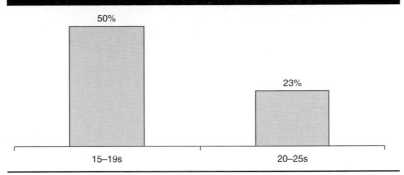

Figure 6: Percentage aware of radio ads who claim they made them think twice or taught them new things about drugs

Base: 285 respondents aware of radio ads
Source: Conquest, May 1998

Whole approach generally well-liked as sympathetic: telling you the facts, not telling you what to do; straightforward and honest, trustworthy, believable, interesting, true to real life. Serious but not preaching and not patronising; looking at the subject from the point of view of young people rather than authorities; encouraging people to find out more.

CRD, January 1996

They're saying be careful of messing with your body ... the dangers of long term damage ... make you aware of the facts.
18–25 (Murmur, May 1996)

This [HEA campaign] was in sharp contrast to their views on drugs education as a whole, which were usually fairly negative. Most associated drugs education with prescriptive messages against drug taking and authority figures with little credibility.

CRD, October 1996

To summarise, evidence strongly suggests that it was advertising that created the attitudinal changes, which led to behavioural shifts.

What else could have created these effects?

There are factors other than advertising that could have impacted on drug use. While we do not claim that none of these has had any effect, we do demonstrate that only advertising could have accounted for the widespread and sudden changes that we see.

Activities linked to drug use

People who go to clubs and who smoke are more likely also to use drugs. If either had declined since 1995, this might account for the change in drug use we have seen. However, clubbing has not changed significantly and teenage smoking is actually rising.

Market forces

There are market forces acting on drug use. However, none of them can account for the decline in drug use we have seen. Prices of drugs have fallen and drugs have become easier to get hold of.

General decline in interest in drugs

This was not suggested by the preceding trends in drug use, which were still rising sharply, not plateauing. Further, it would seem unlikely that we would see a reduction in interest across all ages and for all drugs purely by coincidence.

Overview

Summarising, our campaign is the sole remaining factor that could account for the effects seen among our target audience. We can also show that it has influenced young people in indirect ways, by empowering other people who educate about drugs to do so more effectively.

Beyond the expected

Teachers

Although we did not aim for our materials to be used in classrooms, in fact they were. As a by-product of young people's trust and acceptance of our campaign, teachers themselves have introduced it into their drugs education lessons.

> *The kids brought them [HEA ads] in. I was quite surprised that they were willing to hunt to find them all. Then we stuck them up on the walls and used them in a fact-finding context. It's more effective than discussing and watching videos because when it comes from them it's got to have more of an impact. If it's teacher-directed their response tends to be 'you're just saying that'.*
>
> Bristol secondary school teacher

Drugs educators

There are many professionals working at a local level to tackle the drugs problem. The HEA has had requests for approximately 150,000 copies of our ads by 15,000 organisations. As a result, our campaign has indirectly impacted on young people, by informing those that deal with them on a day-to-day basis.

Counsellors at NDH

NDH counsellors have a very important role within the campaign, giving more detailed and personally tailored information than a press or radio ad ever could. The more information they can get across within a call, the more effective the education. We know that the vast majority of calls are for information, as intended, and not for help in a crisis (see Figure 7).

NDH counsellors say that because young people are better informed about risks, and call to find out more, the quality of the conversation has improved.

> *Older teenagers are becoming more aware of the specific dangers. This makes it a lot easier for us – we can focus in and talk in detail about the long- and short-term risks.*
>
> NDH counsellor

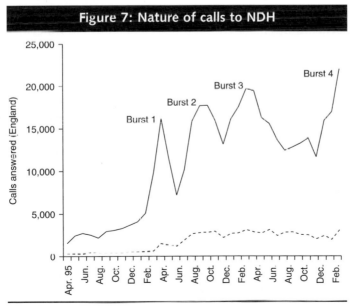

Figure 7: Nature of calls to NDH

Source: Network Scotland

Style press journalists

We demonstrated earlier that by 1995 pro-drug articles were rife in style magazines. This kind of coverage was fuelling demand for drugs. However, we were delighted to find style press editorial covering drugs in an increasingly balanced, or even negative, way over the course of the campaign. Our analysis of *The Face* and *Mixmag*'s content found that by 1997 only 18% of their articles about drugs took a pro-drug stance.

The style press now runs articles about drugs that would have seemed completely at odds with the prevailing climate back in 1995. They can do this now, without adversely affecting their circulation, because young people's attitudes have changed. This is something that advertising has created.

We had achieved our behavioural objectives and beyond. One final question remains and this is addressed next.

Has the campaign been a financial success?

Although this campaign was not intended to generate revenue, we can show that it has been a financial success.

Diverting money from black- to white-market economy

By reducing numbers of young people who use drugs, we calculate that our annual £2.3m adspend has diverted £28m from the criminal fraternity into legal markets such as food, clothing, drink or even savings. This also generates incremental tax revenue.

Reduction in lost working days

By reducing numbers of ecstasy users, our annual £2.3m advertising budget has saved British industry £11m per year in lost working days.

Reduced numbers exposed to potential long-term effects of ecstasy

Scientists believe that ecstasy may lead to serious depression later in life. This has substantial social, health and industry costs. By encouraging young people to quit, the campaign has created potential savings. In order for these to be equivalent to the advertising spend, serious depression would need to be a future outcome experienced by one in 1000 of today's ecstasy users. This seems within the realms of possibility, since 68% of ecstasy users already claim they feel depressed afterwards.

Savings to other drugs education professionals

The HEA received approximately 15,000 requests for sets of our ads from professionals in drug education. If they had not received our materials, they would have had to originate, research and produce materials of their own. If each would otherwise have spent just £200, we saved them a total of £3m.

Summary

We have demonstrated, beyond reasonable doubt, that the HEA campaign played the lead role in turning the tide of drug use. It also empowered several indirect audiences to educate more effectively. Although the campaign was not designed to create revenue, it has been a financial success.

About the Authors

John Bartle co-founded Bartle Bogle Hegarty (BBH) in 1982 and was Joint Chief Executive until the end of 1999. He began his career in 1965 with Cadbury, leaving in 1973 to become a co-founder of the London office of TBWA. Initially Planning Director, he was Joint Managing Director from 1979 until the launch of BBH. He is now involved with a number of organisations in non-executive/advisory capacities. These include the Guardian Media Group, digital media agency i-Level, digital production company Dare and Barnardo's. He is a former President of the IPA, Council member of the UK Advertising Association and President of NABS. He was awarded the CBE in 2003.

Tim Broadbent is Director of BrandCon Ltd, a brand and research consultancy. He is the only person to have twice won the Grand Prix in the IPA Effectiveness Awards, and has been Convenor of Judges of the Awards and Chairman of the IPA Value of Advertising Committee. He was an account planner at BMP, WCRS and Saatchi & Saatchi. Most recently he was the Planning Director of Y&R and then Chief Strategic Officer of the Bates Group EMEA region. He is a Fellow of the IPA.

Will Collin is a partner at Naked Communications. After graduating from Oxford, Will began his career at BMP DDB as a trainee account planner in 1989. There he worked on clients such as H.J. Heinz and Alliance & Leicester, for whom he won an IPA Effectiveness Award in 1992. In 1997 he moved to media specialist PHD as Communications Strategy Director and in 2000 he co-founded Naked Communications with Jon Wilkins and John Harlow. Will is a member of the IPA Strategy Committee and IPA Council, and a module editor for the IPA Excellence Diploma.

Neil Dawson is Executive Planning Director of TBWA\London. He worked for ten years in various research agencies, gaining extensive experience of both qualitative and quantitative methodologies. He joined Euro RSCG London in 1995 and was promoted to Planning Director. He then worked at Miles Calcraft Briginshaw Duffy as Planning Director and Partner before joining TBWA\London in 2001. He is responsible for developing TBWA's proprietary planning tool, Disruption, and also developing the agency's effectiveness culture.

Paul Feldwick is now Strategic Learning Officer at DDB University, following 30 years as an account planner at BMP and DDB. He was Convenor of Judges for the IPA Effectiveness Awards in 1988 and 1990, and won awards himself in 1984 and 1996. His book, *What is Brand Equity, Anyway?* (WARC 2002) deals with questions of advertising effectiveness and brand measurement. He recently graduated with an MSc in Responsibility and Business Practice from the University of Bath.

Niall FitzGerald, KBE became Chairman of Reuters in October 2004. Previously, he was Joint Chairman and CEO of Unilever. His other appointments include: President of the Advertising Association, Chairman of the Conference Board, Co-Chairman of the Transatlantic Business Dialogue and Chairman of the Nelson Mandela Legacy Trust UK. He also serves on the US Business Council, the Foundation Board of the World Economic Forum, the International Advisory Board of the Council on Foreign Relations, and he is a trustee of The Leverhulme Trust.

David Golding is Planning Director at Rainey Kelly Campbell Roalfe/Y&R. He joined Bates UK as a graduate trainee in 1994 and quickly joined the planning department. After three years working on accounts as varied as Spillers dog food and B&Q, David moved to WCRS where in a seven-year stint he worked on Land Rover, BUPA and The National Lottery. He was made Deputy Head of Planning at WCRS in 2002 and moved to Rainey Kelly Campbell Roalfe/Y&R as Head of Planning in 2004. In the meantime David found time to gain an MBA and start a family.

Laurence Green is Planning Partner of Fallon. A graduate of Bristol University, Laurence's formative years in the business were spent primarily at Abbott Mead Vickers and Lowe Howard-Spink. At Lowe he was made Deputy Planning Director and – in addition to planning duties – he ran the Whitbread account, then home to brands and campaigns such as Stella Artois and Heineken. Laurence co-founded Fallon's London office in 1998, and is responsible for the agency's accountability and talent development programmes. He was the author of Fallon's IPA Effectiveness paper for Skoda – awarded Gold in 2002 – and was co-Convenor of the Awards in 2004. He is Convenor of Judges for the 2006 Awards. Laurence sits on the IPA Council and the IPA's Value of Advertising Committee and is a regular contributor to the marketing press.

Guy Murphy is Deputy Chairman of Bartle Bogle Hegarty, the agency he joined in 1991 after being trained in account planning at BMP. At BBH his work on Boddingtons and Murphy's was recognised with Gold awards from the IPA and the Account Planning Group (APG), and he was appointed to the board in 1995. He moved to BBH in Singapore in 1997 to be Head of Planning for the Asia Pacific region. In 2001 he returned to London as Head of Planning for Europe, and was promoted to Deputy Chairman in 2004.

Richard Storey is Planning Director of M&C Saatchi. Graduating from Cambridge, Richard learned his trade at BMP, now DDB London. After ten years he joined the start-up M&C Saatchi. Leading its 'brutal simplicity' approach to planning, he helped it grow into a top five agency with unprecedented speed. Richard has won five IPA Effectiveness awards for clients including British Airways, The Home Office (Police recruitment) and Scottish Amicable. Equally passionate about creativity and effectiveness, Richard has also won five APG Creative Planning awards.

Richard Warren left London School of Economics with a First Class degree in Geography. He has worked in both account management and planning, starting as an account management trainee at Publicis. After a spell at Chiat/Day in 1994 Richard moved to Kirshenbaum Bond & Partners in New York to run the Snapple account. He moved back to London in 1998 as Planning Director of Delaney Fletcher Bozell and in 2000 was part of the management buy-out team that created Delaney Lund Knox Warren. He is now Director of Strategy and works on HBOS, eBay, WHSmith and the AA. Richard has won Golds in both the IPA and APG Awards and is the current Chairman of the IPA Strategy Group.

Malcolm White has been in the advertising business for 18 years, most recently in the roles of Executive Planning Director and Deputy Chairman at Euro RSCG London. Career highlights include the development of the award-winning Umbro strategy at Yellowhammer, winning an IPA Effectiveness Award for Strepsils while at BMP, and guiding The Labour Party back into government in 1997 as Strategy Director for the election campaign, also at BMP. During his time as Planning Director of Partners BDDH, the agency was awarded the Grand Prix in the APG Creative Planning Awards. He is the author of several chapters in IPA publications and has contributed to the *Financial Times*.

IPA dataBANK

Why?

Awareness and use of the IPA effectiveness case database, via the Advertising Works books and/or the WARC.com website, is now almost universal among the planning and research communities within the IPA membership.

However, demand has long existed for a more rigorous search facility, based on a classification of case studies on as many general criteria as possible, to make the database as relevant and accessible as possible. Hence the IPA dataBANK: the new IPA search and select engine for more than 1,000 case studies.

What?

From an original questionnaire developed by the London Business School, the IPA – in association with authors and member agencies – has reclassified individual effectiveness case studies against more than 30 question categories, to provide 10 different fields of analysis.

The dataBANK enables everything from simple multi-field searching (combining fields such as product category, media used and increases in market share) through to complex cross-tabulations of qualitative and quantitative effectiveness measures.

It allows users to search the database for those cases which best address key issues, such as the value of creativity, brand-building versus product-selling, advertising effect and advertising recall, the role of pre-testing and the relative effectiveness of a multi-media approach.

How?

The dataBANK is located in 'The Hub', the knowledge centre of the IPA. Any interested individual from an IPA member agency can make an appointment to visit The Hub, where they will be given access to a PC and training on simple and intermediate interrogation of the system. Expert help and advanced searching are also available from trained IPA staff. This service is currently free of charge to members. E-mail *databank@ipa.co.uk* or contact Louise Rome on 020 7201 8228.

The IPA can also download a portable version of the system and visit member agencies to run one-to-one demonstrations.

A 'light' version of the IPA dataBANK's search capability is available to members only on the IPA website at *www.ipa.co.uk/databank*.

We plan to migrate full search capability to the website as part of the next development stage. Members should click the 'strategy' alert box on the IPA site *www.ipa.co.uk/alertreg.cfm*, if they wish to stay abreast of dataBANK developments.

www.WARC.com

Alternative Route to the Case Studies
The IPA case histories dataBANK can also be accessed through the World Advertising Research Center (WARC). Reached by logging on to www.warc.com, the world's most comprehensive advertising database enables readers to search all the IPA case histories, more than 2000 case histories from similar award schemes around the world, including the Advertising Federation of Australia and the Institute of Communications and Advertising in Canada, plus thousands of 'how to' articles on all areas of communication activity. Sources include the Journal of Advertising Research, Canadian Congress of Advertising, Admap, and the American Association of Advertising Agencies, as well as the IPA.

Index